S0-AXZ-617

ITALY
A geographical introduction

Val d'Aosta

Piedmont

Lombardy

Trentino-
Alto Adige

Veneto

Friuli-
Venezia Giulia

Liguria

Emilia-Romagna

San Marino

Tuscany

Marche

N

0   100 km

Umbria

Latium

Abruzzi

Molise

Campania

Apulia

Basilicata

Sardinia

Calabria

Sicily

ITALY
A geographical introduction

Jacques Bethemont
Professor of Geography
University of Saint-Etienne

and

Jean Pelletier
Professor of Geography
University of Lyons II

Translated by Eleonore Kofman
Lecturer in Geography
Middlesex Polytechnic

Edited by Russell King
Lecturer in Geography
Leicester University

Longman
London and New York

FERNALD LIBRARY
COLBY-SAWYER COLLEGE
NEW LONDON, N.H. 03257

DG
430.2
B4713

Longman Group Limited
Longman House
Burnt Mill, Harlow, Essex, UK

*Published in the United States of America
by Longman Inc., New York*

English translation
© Longman Group Limited 1983

All rights reserved. No part of this publication may be
reproduced, stored in a retrieval system, or transmitted
in any form or by any means, electronic, mechanical,
photocopying, recording, or otherwise, without the
prior permission of the Copyright owner.

First published as *L'Italie: géographie d'un espace en crise (nature, régions,
culture)* by Bordas, Paris in 1979
© Bordas, Paris, 1979
English edition first published in 1983

British Library Cataloguing in Publication Data

Bethemont, Jacques
　　Italy: a geographical introduction.
　　1. Italy
　　1. Title II. Pelletier, Jean
　　III. L'Italie. *English*
　　945.092　　　　DG417

　　ISBN 0-582-30073-8
　　ISBN 0-582-30072-X Pbk

Library of Congress Cataloging in Publication Data

Béthemont, Jacques.
　　Italy: a geographical introduction.

　　Translation of: L'Italie.
　　Bibliography: p.
　　Includes index.
　　1. Italy – Description and travel – 1975-
I. Pelletier, Jean, 1926–　　　II. King, Russell.
III. Title.
DG430.2.B4713　　　945　　81-15661
ISBN 0–582–30073–8　　　AACR2
ISBN 0–582–30072–X (pbk).

93472

Printed in Singapore by
Singapore National Printers Pte Ltd

To Maurice Le Lannou
who awakened in me an interest in the
Mediterranean

Contents

Contents

List of figures

List of tables

List of abbreviations

AGIP	Azienda Generale Petroli Italiani
cif	cost, insurance, freight
CIS	Credito Industriale Sardo
d.w.t.	dead weight tonnage
EAF	Ente Flumendosa
EEC	European Economic Community
EFIM	Ente Participazioni e Finanziamenti Industria Manufatturiera
EGAM	Ente Autonomo di Gestione per le Aziende Minerarie e Metallurgiche
ENEL	Ente Elettrica
ENI	Ente Nazionale Idrocarburi
ERAS	Ente per la Riforma Agraria in Sicilia
ESIT	Ente Sarda per l'Industria Turistica
ETFAS	Ente Sardegna
EUR	Esposizione Universale Roma
FAO	Food and Agriculture Organisation
FEOGA	Common Market Agricultural Fund
fob	free on board
IASM	Istituto per l'Assistenza allo Sviluppo del Mezzogiorno
IRI	Istituto per la Ricostruzione Industriale
IRFIS	Istituto Regionale per il Finanziamento alle Industrie in Sicilia
ISTAT	Istituto Centrale di Statistica
ISVEIMER	Istituto per lo Sviluppo Economico dell'Italia Meridonale
OECD	Organisation for Economic Cooperation and Development
OPEC	Organisation of Petroleum Exporting Countries
SIR	Società Italiana Resine
SME	Società Finanziaria Meridionale

List of abbreviations

STET	Società Finanziaria Telefonica
UNESCO	United Nations Educational, Scientific and Cultural Organisation

A spatial and historical introduction

> The French want to preserve. The Germans want to become.
> The Italians want to recreate.   PAUL VALÉRY

In area and population Italy constitutes an average European country, although among medium-sized powers it is not one of the richest if one compares its *per capita* income (3,500 dollars per annum) with that of other Common Market partners, such as Germany (8,500) or France (7,200). Of course, it is possible to describe it in other terms, both positive and negative, ranging from its industrial competitiveness to the behaviour of its politicians. Equally, one could examine its present situation, either in contrast to the brilliant epochs of its long history when Italy incarnated the values and conscience of the Western world during the periods of the Roman Empire, the Papacy and the Renaissance, or during the Dark Ages when Italy, subjected and reduced to a mere geographical entity, was closed to other nations. Finally, it could be asked if Italy, in the course of this evolution, is the oldest or youngest of European nations.

This issue does not really matter; much more important is to understand the multiplicity of factors which make Italy and Italians, the land and its people, peculiarly influenced by cultural continuity and historical events. Without doubt much has already been said about this, but it remains true, none the less, that Italy is the country where daily events take on grandiose proportions, where everything is a reminder of an old order and where people evoke the crossing of the Rubicon whenever the slightest decision is made. Not to take account of these factors is to misunderstand the spirit of the place and the behaviour of its people. And that is why, in order not to fall into both geographical and historical determinism, it is necessary to provide a brief historical background before moving on to the spatial characteristics.

The weight of the Mediterranean heritage

Without denying or underestimating the considerable differences between North and South, between Milan and Naples, it remains obvious that a common Mediterranean heritage situates the whole of Italy within the Mediterranean culture area.

Landscapes

This cultural heritage is seen notably in the agrarian landscapes which often seem, rightly or wrongly, to be fixed and unchanging. Nothing is more impressive than the *alberatura* frescoes to be found in the Neapolitan hinterland, for example, painted on the walls of the House of Vetii at Pompeii, or the Giotto frescoes in the Assisi countryside or the fresco of the Three Kings. Yet, at the same time, the rigidity of these landscapes reveals a certain incapacity to change, an inability which affects social groups as well as the system of land tenure (Sereni 1962, 1968).

This Mediterranean cultural heritage hangs heavily on many aspects of rural society, such as the relationship between farmers and pastoralists, as Le Lannou (1941) has shown in Sardinia. It might be thought that the intensity of the Sardinian conflict is an exceptional case, but the opposition between groups was similar in many other Italian regions, particularly in the Roman countryside as occurred during the time of the descent of the Sabine shepherds, the storming of Rome by the Gauls or the sacking of the city in 1527 by the Bourbon King Charles III. Although these struggles have now subsided, the basic conflict remains.

Whether these characteristics of a Mediterranean cultural influence are bucolic or terrifying, one is left with the impression of an almost immutable order, not entirely free of determinism. Perhaps this point of view, often held by well-known writers, is not totally without foundation, as long as one includes among the features of the Mediterranean the fundamental fact of the frailty of the human landscapes, such as the reclamation of the plains. This fragility is evident everywhere, as can be seen in the failure of the reclamation undertaken by the House of Este in the Ferrara region during the nineteenth century. But it is especially in the South, for instance in the region of Metaponto, that observers have been struck by this situation: 'A deep solitude surrounds Metaponto, which in Greek times traded with Apulia along the Basento...; from Taranto to Crotone, along 236 kilometres of railway line, not a single village is passed.' Sion's (1934) description of this region goes back nearly fifty years, but Birot said the same thing in a gloomier tone at the outbreak of the Second World War: all that was left of the ancient city was a depleted colonnade in a fever-infested marsh where buffaloes wallowed in the mud in front of the small, bizarre, out-of-the-way station (Birot and Gabert 1964). It is worth mentioning this, for the Metaponto ruins, now restored, are situated between a seaside resort and a reclaimed area of 4,500 hectares. There is something encouraging in this undertaking which seems to be a sign of the times rather than an exception. Nevertheless, there must always be doubt about the permanence of any new construction.

The burden of the past and the apparent difficulty in overcoming the worst aspects of the Mediterranean legacy is unfortunately not restricted to the Italian countryside. Similar traits are easily found in urban landscapes. The most striking and recurrent of these problems is, without doubt, the dilapidated state of many of the old city centres, where the monuments and old buildings exist together with a poor and overcrowded population living in unsalubrious and badly maintained housing. Several successful restoration projects, such as San Lazzaro in Bologna, demonstrate the richness of the urban patrimony and the potential for renovation. Unfortunately, this is the exception. It is more likely that urban centres are developed in a speculative fashion, as in Rome or Milan, or are left to deteriorate, as in Palermo.

The people

It is natural that the Mediterranean cultural heritage, discussed above in rela- tion to landscapes, has its roots in the human groups which have produced it. It is to be expected that this imprint is found in Italian society and its institutions: the family, the Church and the State.

Of all these institutions, the family plays by far the most important role in the Italian mode of socialisation, although the model of the family differs somewhat regionally. For example, the patriarchal family of Central Italy cor- responds to the tight-knit family of the South. Other regional differences relate to the authority of the father and to wedding ceremonies. Yet every- where, relations within the family are more important than outside social con- tacts, and the role and status of women, imposed vehemently in the South, slightly less so in the North, are nevertheless similar throughout the country. For the woman is still denied as an individual in her own right (*la donna non è gente*, the woman is not a person, according to the Sicilian proverb), and only acquires a personality in becoming a wife and mother. From this role follows a whole series of consequences, such as the low level of female par- ticipation in the work-force, 24.5 per cent in 1978.

The corollary of the inferior status of women is the emphasis on marriage and, in fact, since the introduction of divorce in 1972, only 10,000 per year have been granted. It is understandable, then, that the pressure of family institutions provokes violent reactions as is manifested in the liveliness of women's movements.

Ascribing the influence of the Catholic Church to the Mediterranean cultural heritage is open to discussion since the scope of the institution is ecumenical. Rome is the seat of the Catholic Church. Catholicism is more than just a State religion (with the exception of Protestant and Orthodox minorities); it is a fundamental element in daily and family life. The omnipresence of Catholi- cism, including the presence of its symbols in administrative offices, does not seem to pose a problem in a country where in 1976 15 per cent of the electors voted for the Communist Party. At worst, its institutions are mocked, though their right to exist is respected. One should not be astonished at the degree of religious observance, considering, for example, that the role of the priest goes beyond his religious functions and includes that of personal adviser, intermediary and administrative assistant. Possibly more surprising, and yet more Mediterranean, are the cults of saints who bear only a distant relationship to Church dogma. Examples of this are the hysterical procession of St Philomena at Mugnano, the procession of the snakes at Cocullo, Whitsun fêtes at Loreta Aprutino and the entrance into the church of a child dressed in white and mounted on a white bull.

Certain civic and social practices are also related to the Mediterranean legacy. Thus the patron–client relationship leads the Italian in his public and professional life to acquire a protector who will procure him specific benefits. Godfathers are supposed to have the power to obtain pensions, dispensations, even the movement of administrative centres. Of course, the forms that this protectionism takes vary from place to place, from the open paternalism of northern industrialists to the Sicilian godfather, and here and there, advantages procured from membership of the Communist Party. It is not merely in the organisation of the above systems that one encounters this mentality, for the local branch of a political party is an important element of local society and one often belongs to it because of family and local ties. All this happens as if modern social and political life were invested with much older forms of organisation typical of those found in other areas of the Mediterranean. The influence of these traditional ways remains considerable and often explains the local and regional failure or success of agrarian reform and industrialisation. Though irrational, these factors must therefore be taken into account as part of a geographical explanation. At the same time, such traditional influences are certainly less strong in the North than in the South. Should history or geography then be blamed for this situation?

History: a missed opportunity

Old or young Italy? The debate seems to be fairly academic, for Italy acquired its distinctive and apparently permanent features in a very short period between 1859 and 1871. But these features would not have been so strongly imprinted had they not gradually come into being during the major periods that punctuate Italian history.

From Roman Italy to Italian Rome

What is left of the Roman heritage? A legal code and the Church, and, on the landscape, a system of land division, the geometrical layout of the cities, an outline of road systems, and ruins. The memory of the grandeur of Rome lasted through the Dark Ages and the Risorgimento and thereby imposed the choice of Rome as capital despite the difficult problems which this entailed. There also persists a whole set of cumbersome references in official speeches which never fail to exalt the virtues of Romans and the glory that was Rome in contrast to the mediocrity of the present. This myth can have serious consequences, leading, for example, to the conquest of a colonial empire and the rise of Fascism. There is even an architectural style which has survived from the pomp of the Mussolini period. Yet it is true that the healthy moral state of Italians leads them to react against these ridiculous visions of grandeur. In this respect Fellini's *Roma* could be compared with the first Italian films of Caesar's assassination or Augustus' triumphal entry into Rome.

The long period from the invasions to the Renaissance has also left many imprints. The latent duality between North and South became more pronounced in the contrast between the city-states and the patrician and commercial republics of the North and the feudal and theocratic South; between the town hall and the castle dominating the town. This duality did not disappear during the ensuing period of conquest and division. The Spanish and French altered the language here and there, and imposed various architectural and urban styles. Provincial and urban identities became stronger at the same time. Above all, the feeling of impotence in the face of foreign power and Papal conservatism led Italians to react by assuming indifference, lack of public spirit and egoism. Traditions of banditry have their roots in the same reasoning which also spawned Mafia-type counter-societies in reaction to the bad government under the Spanish and others.

The unification of Italy

We shall not dwell here at length on the years between the proclamation of the Italian kingdom and the entry of the King into Rome, years which were more fruitful than glorious and during which Italy had difficulty in fulfilling its destiny. These were decisive years in terms of the succession of economic and social events whose importance was then misunderstood because they were overshadowed by the tumult of political events. Yet, these seemingly unconnected events established the framework within which future developments in Italy took place.

The most striking fact in this context was the artificial nature of the new State, still composed of numerous regions, autonomous in their political, economic and cultural life. These regions had nothing to gain and all to lose if they changed their traditional structures: this was strengthened by the fact that unification had brought most advantage to the House of Savoy which was of foreign origin. The adoption of Tuscan as the only official language rancoured many.

This artificial State was also weak. It was economically weak because of the absence of sufficient capital and infrastructure for a country of this size. But it was possibly the weakness of its administration which was the most serious, for Piedmont alone had the tradition and personnel to provide an effective administrative service. So, if the Piedmontese could supply much of its administrative personnel, it was insufficient for the needs of the country. The incorporation of the existing administrative systems, far from resolving the problem, led to the proliferation of an administration whose complex, Byzantine nature has never been totally sorted out.

These problems of unification were possibly the inevitable faults of the early years, made much more severe by the hostility of the depossessed powers. Thus, until 1871, the former King of Naples formed with impunity armed bands who ravaged his former territories from the safety of the Papal State. The latter also aided in the printing of counterfeit money and refused to recognise the kingdom of Italy until the Lateran Agreement in 1929. The hostility of the Popes was also expressed in the edict of *non expedit* in which the Pope forbade Catholics to participate in the political life of the country. Without necessarily being effective, this attitude served to bring out and reinforce the old tradition of lack of public spirit and antagonism to the State.

It is also true that administrative personnel and politicians did not always know how to respond and show a good example. One need only cite the numerous scandals of which the best known was the participation of Giolitti, architect of the new Italy's liberal economic policy and five times Prime Minister, in a banking collapse. The fact that this well-known figure could take up his career once the affair had blown over explains the lax attitudes which this system seemed to uphold.

The essential problem of the relationship between North and South lies in this situation of weakness, *ad hoc* solutions and political corruption. Nothing in the present state of affairs can be read fatalistically in the nature of things. In 1860 Naples was, with nearly 500,000 inhabitants, the only large city in Italy. Its port activities were more important than Genoa and Venice, and its banking influence was equal to that of Turin. Subsequently, unification was essentially characterised by the confiscation of ecclesiastical property and a general moratorium, particularly significant in the southern provinces. The sale of Church property could have been a unique opportunity for agrarian reform in favour of the peasantry, who formed the majority of the population. They could have been socially and politically integrated. Instead, appropriation benefited the large capitalist landowners and the latifundists, thus leaving no alternative to the peasantry but to emigrate. At the same time the vital accumulation of capital could take place through the export of southern agricultural products, principally wheat, oil and wine. Reinvestment in industry and commerce mainly benefited the North. The establishment of the railway network further aided the penetration of northern manufacturing products into the South. Once this process had begun the South found itself placed in a colonial-type situation, with all that implies in terms of marginalisation and frustration.

Spatial duality: a foregone conclusion or the result of marginalisation?

It is not sufficient to view the duality of Italy just as a cultural feature, accentuated historically. The extent of this duality, its imprint on the landscape, its official recognition since 1950 and the creation of the *Cassa per il Mezzogiorno* ('Fund for the South') indicate a re-evaluation.

There are certainly many Italian geographers who have supported a deterministic theory of development. In its simplest form, this puts the blame on the nature of the physical environment in the South where two difficult sets of physical features dominate: on the one hand, young landforms, mountainous and unstable, combined with a Mediterranean climate beset by torrential rains; on the other hand, the presence of coastal marshes conducive to the spread of malaria. In between these two systems, the unenviable transition is formed by karst deserts and clay landslides. All this is certainly correct, as is the succession of seasons that are too dry, too hot, too cold or too wet.

But it should be noted that all these unfortunate qualities do not apply to all the territory in question, nor do they imply the same consequences at all times and in all places. Similarly, it is apparent that the North and the Centre are not without their own difficult areas, whether it be the hills of Monferrato, the flaking clay soils of Umbria or, lastly, the low-lying flood-hazard lands of the Po Valley. The truth of the matter is that the natural environment is rarely favourable to development which, in order to take place, must overcome this supposedly fatalistic perception.

A more subtle form of determinism, suggested by Gribaudi (1971), puts forward the idea that economic take-off in the North was facilitated and then encouraged by the existence of its own resources (which the South lacked) of hydroelectric power generated in the Alps at the end of the nineteenth century and methane gas available during the period of reconstruction which followed the end of the Second World War. We should appreciate the short span of time which made the Paduan methane gas an advantageous, positive factor of development and the oil of Ragusa and Caltanissetta in Sicily simply a neutral factor. Nevertheless, the advantage acquired by the regions endowed with hydroelectric power needs to be explained. Could one not, however, for example, suggest that, at the same time and within the same technological system, southern ports might have been suitable for coal imports?

The current theory, relating to the advantages enjoyed by coastal regions compared to continental regions, does not seem to hold in Italy. On the contrary, many writers have pointed out the negative and backward characteristics of the southern coastal regions. The expansion of the maritime world as from the fifteenth century precipitated the decline of the Mediterranean, a closed sea, isolated in relation to the major maritime routes. Furthermore, the cultural break between Christian and Muslim worlds brought about a permanent stagnation of the coastal area, especially the coastal fringes of the plains already affected by malaria. There seems to be a sort of inversion in the role attributed to historical factors, so that one might ask what would have been the development of these fringes in a better organised and less fragmented political system. One could also fruitfully compare the dangers arising from seaward invasions by Arabs, Normans and Spanish with continental attacks across the Alps from successive Barbarian, French and Austrian incursions.

The least that can be said is that if there exists a certain spatial determinism, then it has operated for a long time and is present today in a different form. This conclusion, however, is situated in a spatial, historical and cultural context which has led the South to function as a series of weakly connected spaces that are inward-looking and hardly open to the outside world, while the North has become spatially integrated and outward-looking, the latter symbolised by the ports of Genoa and Venice and the Alpine passes.

How, then, does one evaluate the role played by spatial, as compared to other factors, in this slow and complex process of development? Once the falsely deterministic view has been set aside, the problem can then be tackled from the correct perspective, that of macro-economic space. Once again the origin of the current situation can be traced to the decisive years during the foundation of the kingdom. At that time, the Italian diaspora, extending from Constantinople and Alexandria to Marseilles and Tunis, played a crucial role in all sorts of exchanges within the Mediterranean. In what is not at all an obvious paradox, the creation of the Italian State and the development of a Mediterranean policy brought about the disappearance or diminution of these privileged locations just when exchanges with northern and western Europe were growing. This northern polarisation and the stagnation of the Mediterranean have undoubtedly adversely affected the political and economic situation described above, and resulted in the present marginalisation of the Mezzogiorno.

Obviously, Italy's entry into the EEC, with its centre of gravity between the Escaut and Rhine rivers, could not but help to reinforce this peripheral position within the nation space. At least it may be hoped that an advantageous reorientation will result from the enlargement of the Common Market with the inclusion of Iberia and Greece. However, one must concede that these peninsulas will not have much to exchange within the Mediterranean community, while the problems of the Italian South will be swamped within a larger Mediterranean problem, and yet not resolved.

The State and the regions: in search of a compromise

As a late comer, struggling to be accepted and facing a difficult spatial problem, the Italian State also suffered from the drive to unity during the Fascist period. A particular set of events and deep-rooted tendencies forced the establishment of a pluralistic, or more precisely, a regionally organised State in 1947, intermediate between the unitary model of France and Swiss federalism.

Italy's regional structure, laid down in Articles 5 and 115 of the Constitution, was not fully implemented until the passing of the regional statute in June 1971. The length of the delay, the limitations in the 1953 and 1970 legislation and the very incompleteness of the current statute, reveal here, as elsewhere, the fears which regional power engenders, and all that it implies for centrifugal forces and the undermining of central power.

Politically, it is necessary to distinguish between ordinary regions and those with a special status – Val d'Aosta, Trentino-Alto Adige, Friuli-Venezia Giulia, Sicily and Sardinia. These latter regions can enact their own policies, which are different to national ones, principally in the fields of customs, culture and language. The scope of these powers is determined in each region by an individual statute.

Otherwise, the 20 regions (15 ordinary and 5 special statute) constitute entities endowed with political autonomy exercised by Regional Councils, it being understood that the regional power operates within the overall laws laid down by the State, which determines the basic principles, leaving the regions to decide on the way they are applied. At the same time, the region is delegated certain administrative functions by the State. The coordination required for this is carried out by a Government Commission which is responsible for the 'direction of administrative functions of the State and coordination with those under the aegis of the region' (Article 124 of the Constitution).

It is important to note that economic responsibility for planning is divided between Parliament and the regions, the principle being that the distribution of investment between sectors is decided at a national level, while the spatial allocation is basically left to the regions. More generally, decisions concerning urban matters, agriculture and health are left to regional initiative (Art. 117).

The extent of the *modus vivendi* between the State and the regions can be measured by the resources available to both. For example, in 1975, expenditure was divided in the following way – 25,713,000 million lire to the State as against 9,831,000 million to the regions, including regional, provincial and communal budgets. So, although the financial transfer to the regions remains limited, it is, nevertheless, not as constrained as in a unitary state such as France. Bologna is free to give priority within its budget to social services as is Cagliari to support its football team. Of course, such attitudes may be risky and, as the example above shows, regionalisation in itself does not inevitably lead to equality of social services or regional economic potential. At least it can be noted that these budgets reflect fairly well the political, ethical and social decisions of those involved, even going as far as their inequalities.

Invariable tendencies

The first of these tendencies, which is more ancient than its political recognition by Giolitti, is undoubtedly the taste for and the art of compromise, which at present includes the relationship between the State and the regions, as well as the Communist Party's historic compromise as practised, for example, in Naples' regional policies.

The second concerns the frequent occurrence of all sorts of crises – the present institutional crisis with its origins in the anarchistic and Mazzinian tradition; the economic crisis for which there are precedents, such as the crisis that provoked food riots at the end of the last century; and, finally, the moral crisis, another element of the tradition based on clientelism and corruption.

There remains the issue of the Italian miracle which was already present in the profitable failures during the periods of unification and of post-war reconstruction, and which now extends to the increase in national income, the balance of payments surplus, and even the continuation of a national consensus in spite of the present moral crisis.

It is within this complex background, where the tragic mixes with the pathetic, that we need to examine spatial relationships in Italy.

1 The natural environment: harshness and seductive fertility

A largely mountainous relief

The basic element of the environment remains the prominent, sometimes denuded, morphological backbone, which combines hills, small mountains, isolated blocks and mountain chains in a constantly varied landscape. Out of the national area of 300,000 sq. kilometres, plains only cover 70,000, or less than a quarter, hills 125,000 and mountains 100,000.

The sharpness of the relief is due to the interplay of two factors. Firstly, the geological structure contains few elements of a tabular nature (only in Sardinia, Apulia and Mt Gargano) and, is, in fact, formed of two main fold chains, the Apennines and the Alps, and their enclosed plain, the Po. Secondly, the past and present systems of erosion have produced the current equilibrium, bearing in mind that the considerable force of the harsh Mediterranean regime has been accentuated by human action.

Major morphogenic factors

Typically Mediterranean tectonic action

In its position in the centre of the Mediterranean, Italy lies in a zone of extreme tectonic activity characteristic of this part of the Mediterranean and its surrounding land areas. In fact, 90 per cent of Italy is formed by complex fold chains and their outlying areas, such as the Po, while the rest comprises tectonic moles, themselves pushed about but only slightly folded.

Zones of tectonic inactivity

There are three of these zones. Two are situated almost symmetrically in relation to the Apennines: in the west, Sardinia: and in the east, the Adriatic, and its south-western bordering plateaux of Mt Gargano and Apulia. The third zone is the south-east of Sicily.

Tectonically Sardinia is quite distinctive in the Mediterranean and has always been likened to an isolated Hercynian fragment which it indeed resembles in many ways. More than three-fifths of the island is composed of elements of the Primary basement: in the south-west, Iglesiente-Sulcis; in the east mainly granitic zones, mountains and plateaux which extend from Gallura in the north through the Gennargentu massif to Sette Fratelli in the south. This basement, for long resistant to tectonic activity, has preserved only scattered areas of Secondary sedimentary cover and very few more recent sediments. Faults are the basic element of this structure, cutting it deeply into horsts and grabens. These fault lines have created a major tectonic trench – the Campidano – which covers practically the whole of the rest of the island. Elsewhere, especially to the north of the Campidano, thick, soft, lacustrine and marine deposits from the Oligocene and Miocene occur and, since the period of volcanic action, stretching from the Oligocene to the recent Quaternary, acidic and basaltic deposits.

In eastern Sardinia this simple and rigid structure is sharply cut by a major fault which falls abruptly to the great depths of the Tyrrhenian Sea. This is an 'internal' sea in the concavity of the Apennine axis. It is not part of this buffer zone, but is incorporated into the fold chains of which it is a sort of negative face.

The Adriatic is an 'external' sea, an outlying sea between the two fold systems of the Apennines in the south-west and the Dinaric Alps and the mountains of Greece and Albania in the north-east and east. Since it is situated beyond the fold systems it is not very deep. On its south-eastern edge, remnants of a resistant platform protrude and reveal a smooth topography on a rigid structure. This is the Gargano promontory, composed of Cretaceous limestones with striking fault escarpments. This also refers to the long, less elevated Apulian peninsula that is also composed of limestones, Cretaceous in the centre and bordered by Miocenes and Pliocenes, in this totally immobile structure. All of this has acted as a buffer to the north-eastward expansion of the Apennines. Finally, in south-eastern Sicily the Ragusa plateau also forms a rigid block, a fragment of the African shield.

Zones of extreme tectonic activity

These zones, which form the rest of Italy, are divided into two orogenic systems, the Alps and the Apennines, separated by the trench of the Po plain. They are generally due to the meeting of fairly small blocks which have been moved in various ways. It can be said that the major displacements of strata and overthrusting beds truly began in the early Tertiary when the African continent, previously moving in the direction of Europe, started to move westward.

Subduction (subsidence and then lateral displacement) arising from the meeting of blocks was at that time restricted to major direct collisions which, nevertheless, were without much tangential impact. As a result of this changed direction, the contact between Europe and Africa was broken up into a number of small blocks with different displacements and colliding violently with one another. This resulted in the major eastward movement of Sardinia during the Tertiary so that this block formed part of the Apennine orogenesis which was also pushed eastward. The Carnic-Apulian block, the Adriatic and rigid, coastal structures (Gargano, Apulia), which we have just now described, were for long displaced north-eastward, thus explaining the asymmetry and the general curve of the Alpine axis. Thus the Apennines, in terms of the tectonic activity of blocks, is a zone of subduction between the Sardinian block and the Adriatic, and the Alps a similar zone between the Adriatic block and the Hercynian block of central Europe.

The Apennines

This is one of the most complex yet striking fold chains. The work of Italian and French researchers (especially those working in Sicily and Calabria) has now led to a clear understanding of their nature. The Apennines are an excellent example of a chain of double deposition starting from a highly uplifted central section and the working outward of successively folded zones. The system has grown in this way over time. To compensate this outward movement, the interior sections, which previously experienced tectonic action, subsided as the system broadened. This is the normal model of any chain of this type and applies equally to the Alps. The Apennines, however, also display specific features of their own.

Firstly, this chain, which was complete at the beginning, lost during the Miocene its western section which collapsed into the Tyrrhenian Sea. The hinges of this collapse are no longer visible except in the island of Elba and subsidence has even eaten into the eastern section in the Gulf of Genoa. The present Apennine system is thus formed by half of the original structure. All the structures have been displaced north-eastward, thrusting the fringe areas forward practically everywhere along a broad convex curve. On all the transversal sections of this chain two parts can be distinguished. On the internal Tyrrhenian flank the system is fairly ancient, even worn out. Subsidence has dominated since the Pliocene at least (Tuscan plain, Roman Campagna, Campania and the Crati Trench). Owing to faulting, volcanic activity took place and continues today in southern Tuscany, the Lipari Islands (Vulcano and Stromboli) and Vesuvius. (Etna is outside this volcanic system.) On the external, eastern Adriatic flank, movements are more recent and are still in progress. Subsidence and volcanic activity are not so important and the structures are still recognisable and often simpler than in the other zone.

Obviously this rough outline is not uniform throughout the 500 kilometres of the Apennine chain. In the North and in Sicily, more malleable terrains, where marls and clays dominate, have resulted in major horizontal displacements. In the central section limestones dominate, while in the external section and the Abruzzi, there are apparently fairly massive synclines and arch-shaped dislocations. In the internal section, there has occurred considerable subsidence with much volcanic activity, but the type of tectonic activity remains the same.

The Alpine chain

Although only the southern flank belongs to Italy, the extremely wide central and eastern sections of the Alps represent a fairly large region. There was here, it seems, never more than a single section and the structures, though differing slightly, were displaced north, north-west and east. It should be noted that the interior sections, those near the Po plain, have not been affected by subsidence. Thus the tectonic continuity of this chain is much greater than that of the Apennines. However, definite structural variations are visible as one moves from west to east.

The Italian western section is not very wide and corresponds to a major interior nappe of mica schists in the midst of which are peaks composed of green diorites and gabbros, such as Mt Viso and the Gran Paradiso. It is limited in the north by the crystalline peak of Mt Blanc of which Italy possesses the southern face. East from the River Dora Baltea, the orientation of the system changes and roughly becomes east–west due mainly to the presence of new structural zones. A clear broadening out is now perceptible, basically brought about by the southern calcareous Pre-Alps which appear as from Lake Maggiore and reach their maximum width around Lake Garda. From the Dolomites the Alps continue more narrowly and with some slight changes of orientation to the Austrian and Yugoslavian frontiers. This zone is heavily folded, though apparently largely autochthonous. The parallel anticlines and synclines form long lines in the Carnic and Julian Alps at the Austrian frontier. The material is basically Secondary, Triassic and Jurassic.

Behind this region, as far as the Swiss and the Austrian frontiers in the Tyrol, appears the internal zone of this Alpine chain, the nature of which is not unanimously agreed upon by geologists. Without entering fully into this controversy, it can be said that crystalline schists tend to dominate in the Italian section and these are more metamorphosed than the mica schists in the neighbouring areas near the French frontier where there are scattered crystalline peaks, though these are probably in a less autochthonous position than Mt Blanc. These peaks, evidently 'packed' into the nappes, are especially important in the granitic zone of Biella-Orta–Lake Maggiore and then in the large zone of peaks in the Ortles and Adamello.

Towards the interior of the Alpine arc all these zones are cut by subsidences which lead to the tectonic depression of the Po plain. Volcanic elements are associated with these breaks, for example, the Euganean hills in the Verona region.

The Po tectonic trench

The Po plain corresponds to a depression between the Apennines and the Alps, probably caused by the movement of the Apennine chain which drove before it the edge of the block which it overthrust. The strata of the Apennines clearly plunge under the plain, while those of the Alps are cut very obliquely and sharply. This is highly visible in the central and eastern parts of the depression and seems to demonstrate that the driving force is to be sought in the Apennines.

Whatever the reason, the depression is remarkably deep. Surveys carried out by AGIP in prospecting for oil have revealed the presence of recent sediments more than 10,000 metres thick. Since the beginning of the Pliocene it has always been part of a system with a shallow sea, lake or lagoon, and, although the plain is slightly raised today, it is still situated in a zone of clay, sand and pebble deposition. Subsidence continues and sedimentation has not entirely ceased, except in the eastern section where the Monferrato hills, uplifted after the Miocene, form a large raised section. This possibly shows that subsidence is getting weaker in this part of the great Po syncline.

Continuing morphogenesis

In most western European countries, the relief seems to have become fixed due to the present slight rate of erosion and tectonic movements. Italy, together with other Mediterranean countries such as Greece, has the distinction of still having an active morphogenesis.

Neotectonic action

If those researching in morphology and tectonic activity have been able to think that tectonic movements have not been very active since the Pliocene or that their effect was occurring too slowly to be fully discernible, this opinion runs counter to observations in Italy. Nearly everywhere it can be shown that tectonic movements, faults, folds and overthrusts continue at present and at a sufficiently rapid rate to be observed in historic times. Thus the external flank of the Apennines is advancing towards the Po and the Adriatic. Jean Demangeot (1965) has shown that the overthrusting of the Abruzzi, east of the Gran Sasso, occurred after the Wurmian moraines upon which it rests. Hence the subsidence and raising of blocks and trenches in the Tyrrhenian zones persists.

Finally, the existence of neotectonics is verified by seismic activity. Unfortunately, Italy is very greatly affected by earthquakes so that the only regions not much affected by seismic activity are Sardinia and the major part of the Alps. Devastating seismic activity has hit practically half the Apennines, especially the Abruzzi, Calabria, Mt Gargano, south-eastern Sicily and Friuli. Since the beginning of the twentieth century deadly earthquakes, of which only the most serious are mentioned, have struck Messina in 1908 (50,000 dead), Aquila degli Abruzzi in 1909, and, more recently, Friuli in 1976 and the provinces of Avellino and Potenza in 1980.

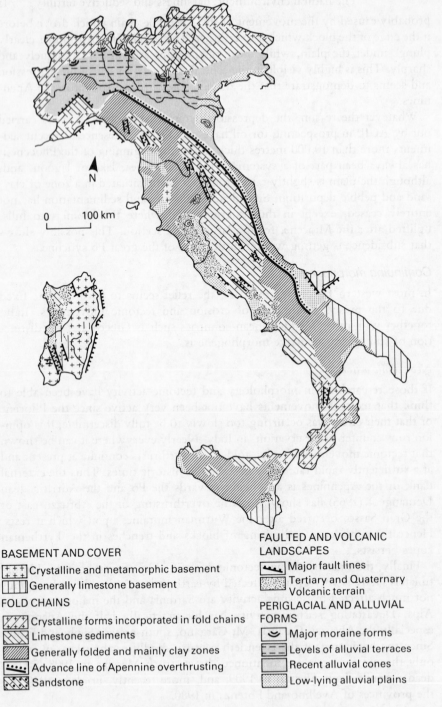

BASEMENT AND COVER

+++	Crystalline and metamorphic basement
	Generally limestone basement

FOLD CHAINS

	Crystalline forms incorporated in fold chains
	Limestone sediments
	Generally folded and mainly clay zones
	Advance line of Apennine overthrusting
	Sandstone

FAULTED AND VOLCANIC LANDSCAPES

	Major fault lines
	Tertiary and Quaternary Volcanic terrain

PERIGLACIAL AND ALLUVIAL FORMS

	Major moraine forms
	Levels of alluvial terraces
	Recent alluvial cones
	Low-lying alluvial plains

Fig. 1.1 A structural morphology of Italy

Complex variations in sea-level

Neotectonic activity has had an effect on variations in sea-level which are caused by retention of glaciers as they are formed and the discharge of water when they melt. Quaternary sea-levels are common along all the coasts, though more so in the south of the peninsula, the Straits of Messina and the Ionian coast of Calabria. The 'raised beaches' have been the object of long-standing controversies because of the difficulty of deciding what is due to movements of the sea and those of the land. Neboit (1975) has neatly shown that one can separate the influences of the two and thus understand the major Calabrian levels whose flat surfaces rise to up to 200 metres above the present sea-level.

The effects of climatic changes

Quaternary climatic changes have affected Italy during the four cold periods, apparently similar to those elsewhere, and interspersed by warmer interglacial periods. The numerous traces of these variations can be grouped under three major headings.

Glacial forms are common in the wettest and highest parts. In the Alps, where there remain 114 sq. kilometres of ice, all the summits are notched by cirques, often isolating sharp peaks (Cervin and Ortles) and deep, U-shaped valleys which alternate between narrow constrictions and enlarged, hollowed-out basins, some of which are very deep. This landscape occurs around the higher parts of Lakes Como and Maggiore. Elsewhere only the peaks are hollowed out by recognisable cirques: above an altitude of 1,400 metres in the northern Apennines and 1,600 metres in the Abruzzi.

The so-called periglacial forms, caused by cold periods associated with the extension of glaciers, are much more widespread, for they are found almost everywhere as calcareous screes at the foot of escarpments, particularly in the central Apennines and in eastern Sardinia.

Lastly, numerous deposits were directly linked with the debris carried by the agents of erosion whose activity changed with the cold. Frontal moraines are common and sometimes very extensive in the Alpine fringe where they form spectacular 'amphitheatres' at Ivrea and Lake Garda. Due to the plentiful material provided by the glaciers and the alternation of freezing and thawing, fluvio-glacial and fluviatile terraces form levels of flat surfaces visible in all the plains, but especially that of the Po where there are four levels ranging from the *ferreto* of the upper moors down to the low terraces bordering the main river course.

Current erosion

Throughout Italy erosion continues in an active and often destructive form. The reasons for this are manifold. Firstly, the nature of the relief itself multiplies the incidence of abrupt changes of levels, with mountain fronts and steep tectonic and structural slopes. Secondly, the Mediterranean climate with its unforgettably torrential downpours (examples to be given later) can set in motion erosion, especially of the linear type, along large and small water-courses. Thirdly, there are large outcrops of soft rocks: Cretaceous black clays in the Apennines, white Pliocene clays almost everywhere, sandy and pebbly material of the Quaternary terraces.

Finally, the fourth, and not the least, is the damaging effect of human actions. Through excessive deforestation and the overgrazing of sheep and goats, man has virtually brought about an artificial balance, an unstable, man-made equilibrium which has already had disastrous consequences. It is clearly seen everywhere, though more so in the southern parts where the vegetation cover and the soils are more fragile.

The consequences of the interplay of these factors is seen in the erosion and deposition that occur. In terms of the first, Italy is the country of gullying in soft rocks: *calanchi* occur everywhere in clays, as can be clearly seen in the small plateau where the old Etruscan town of Volterra is situated. Then there are the various types of large-scale landslides and slow earth movements, known under the general name of *frana* which are very common. The adjective *franate* crops up on road signs everywhere, even on the Autostrada del Sole which is constantly under repair between Florence and Bologna and during the Vietnam War was entitled the Ho Chi Minh trail! Naturally the water-courses, which are frequently overloaded with water and debris, carry an impressive amount of solids and deposit on the plains enormous amounts of alluvial material during the most disastrous floods. It is significant that in Italian *alluvione* means both flood and alluvial deposition. Mountain edges are fringed with alluvial cones, as are coastal deltas such as the Tiber and the Po.

The major morphostructural zones

The combination of tectonic activity and the different forms of erosion upon these systems have created fairly distinctive morphostructural areas.

The Apennine backbone and its Adriatic edge

From Sicily as far as the Ligurian chain, which links the Apennines with the Alps, the entire relief is comprised of the mountainous Apennine backbone (even where the name differs, as in Sicily and Calabria) with its scattered out-liers to the north-east, south-east and east of the orogenic arc.

Northern Apennines

From Genoa to the limit of Tuscany and the Marches the Apennines are marked by the predominance of overthrusting nappes, the general absence of limestones except in the Apuan Alps and a constant contrast between the smooth, uplifted sandstone features, sometimes of a depth of more than 800 metres, and the eroded clay slopes and hills. This is not a very high section of the Apennines for Mt Cimone at 2,140 metres has been heavily eroded. Amont the various features of its 200 kilometres length, one element remains constant – an edge of flattened hills in the marls and Pliocene clays that border the Po plain, a straight edge that initially follows a west–east direction and then north-west–south-east along a major flexure.

In the north-west, in Liguria, the relief is not very high either (Mt Maggiorasca 1,669 m), and has not produced any major flexures in a fairly homogeneous material where the dominant clays envelop green rocks. Westward, the link with the Alps, tectonically very complex, is, in its relief of long ridges with summits of metamorphic rocks, not very different. The seaward limits, resulting everywhere from recent subsidence, have produced steep and not very indented coastlines around the Gulf of Genoa and the Cinque Terre.

In the centre, the chain is more than 100 kilometres wide and arranged in north-west–south-east alignments. Examples of this are the relief carved into the sharp marble crests of the Apuan Alps, the trenches of Garfagnana and Lunigiana, the sandstone ridges culminating in Mt Cimone and the eroded, massive clay hills which reach as far as the edge of the Po plain.

In the south, in Tuscany, zones of subsidence occupy half the area. The plains which they have built up are connected by the river network to the Arno and separate lowish blocks, such as Mt Pisanino. The mountain here is reduced to a line of massive sandstone ridges in Mt Falterona.

The central Apennines

Broadly speaking, these extend from the Marche and Umbria to the northern part of Calabria and Basilicata. This section is characterised by a decrease in overthrusting nappes, the considerable presence of limestones in the topography of the summits and major volcanic activity associated with the spectacular subsidence of the internal section. There are basically two contrasting parts despite the marked differences from the north-west to south-east – the higher, limestone zones of the north-east and the lower south-eastern zone which has experienced more subsidence and volcanic activity.

In the north-east a long, limestone ridge stretches for over 300 kilometres and totally dominates a pedestal of eroded hills that fall away towards the Adriatic. In the northern part of this alignment elongated, Jurassic ridges form the Umbro-Marchesian Apennines; in the centre the massive, anticlinal arches of the Abruzzi rise to 2,910 metres in the Gran Sasso. Intense karst activity has interacted with the process of subsidence to create enclosed depressions of which the best example is the ancient lake of Fucino. In the south, fragmentation of the limestone line increases and this is now cut into major horsts, which are slightly folded, as in the massive limestone block of Maiella, and separated from subsided trenches.

In the south-east fragmentation becomes normal, for firstly in the Colline Metallifere of Tuscany and then in Latium and Campania, rift valleys occupy most of the area. The rocks are diverse: Primary in the north-west, even metamorphic in the flysch in Umbria; limestone coming south from Rome, in Campania and northern Lucania. The nature of these reliefs varies according to the material of which they are composed: massive, not very high, hills in the Metallifere and Chianti blocks; limestone alignments with much karst action where folding is more or less identifiable in Latium and Campania (Mts Aurunci and Ausoni, Sorrento peninsula). A variety of volcanic forms in terms of age and type of eruption are important here: recent, cone-shaped volcanoes (Vesuvius); older craters, some of which are now occupied by lakes (Bolsena and Bracciano); plateaux and domes (Mt Amiata) of consolidated ejected material such as that found in the Roman Campagna between the Eternal City and Civitavecchia; basalt flows from the Alban hills.

The trenches are all recent and probably still subsiding, as evidenced by the present difficulties in the drainage of rivers (Tiber, Liri, Volturno) whose alluvia are not able to infill sufficiently rapidly. Some rift valleys are internal, generally elongated and overlooked by steep, straight sides such as that upon which Monte Cassino monastery sits. The most important trenches are those of Sele-Tanagro, Cassino and Spoleto; others, more extensive and with less well-defined edges, open out on to the sea (Pontine marshes, Campania plains).

The southern Apennines

These form the south-western point of the peninsula (Calabria and part of Basilicata) and, though only covering a small area, are highly distinctive. The nature of the structure is still being debated, but what stands out is the rigid physiognomy imposed by the largely crystalline material. The higher lands are recently raised horsts formed of high plateaux which have a more Hercynian than Apennine appearance due to the wet climate and the presence of large conifer forests. A typical example is the Sila massif (1,928 m), although the Aspromonte (1,995 m) is also largely flattened and terraced. These high plateaux are in total contrast to the low rift valleys and the interior alluvial plains – Crati Trench at Cosenza and, on the coast, the Gioia Tauro plain.

The Adriatic edge of the Apennines

This varies from north-west to south-east in relation to its width and component material. In the Marche, it is narrow, composed mainly of Pliocene material that has been eroded into long parallel ridges by streams descending from the Apennines. South of the Sangro valley, the outlying area widens considerably because the limestone edge of the Apennines moves away to the south-west and new structural elements appear. Basically the regions bordering the Apennines are formed of soft, mainly clay, rocks, heavily eroded, especially in Basilicata and around Macerata; also in this flanking zone are found limestone areas and the ancient Mt Vulture volcano. Other landforms are the depression of the Taviolere plain and the karstic limestone plateau of

Mt Gargano (1,056 m). In Apulia, the relatively high plateaux of the Murge hills (600 m) are flanked by low undulating platforms that gradually fall away to the Adriatic and the Ionian Seas.

Sicily

Although still structurally forming part of the Apennines, the orientation of the mountains in Sicily changes abruptly to east–west as if to close off the curve hemming in the interior areas of the chain, submerged under the Tyrrhenian Sea except for the volcanic Lipari Islands.

In the south of Sicily, the terraced limestone plateaux of Ragusa – the Monti Iblei – are the mirror-images of the Apulian Murge. In the north-west, the Peloritani Mts are a continuation of the Calabrian Aspromonte and have the same crystalline geology. Together with their western extensions into the bare, sedimentary Nebrodi and Madonie ranges, the Peloritani form a backbone which borders the Cefalu coast to the Straits of Messina.

Yet the originality of the island lies in two very different elements: Etna, and the reliefs of western and central Sicily. Etna is an enormous volcano, rising to more than 3,200 metres, and set in a tectonic trench which its own weight helps to hollow out further and of which the Catania plain is a remnant. It is still active, its almost perfect cone often shrouded in the smoke from eruptions. The rest of Sicily displays recurring features which include different sizes of limestone blocks, with karst forms, especially large in the Palermo region, which rise up from the midst of an ocean of hills incised into the soft rocks of the Eocene flysch and Miocene and Pliocene marls and clays. These 'islands' are elements which have been cut off from one or several nappes and were later surrounded by Mio-Pliocene marine intrusions. The strange relief of interior Sicily is a striking mixture of hilltops and undulations incised in clays that have been heavily attacked by all possible forms of erosion, especially *frane*: 'an area of discouraging and irrational adjustment' (Tomasi di Lampedusa 1963). Settlement prefers to cling to the abrupt limestone hilltops.

The Alps

The great arc of the Alps can be simply divided into three basic structural sections – west, centre and east.

The western Alps

These are narrow – only 80 kilometres wide in the parallel section to the upper Po valley – and are, in some ways, a simple slope. The Italian Alps culminate in the south at the French frontier in the crystalline peak of Mt Argentera (3,250 m). To the north they culminate in Mt Blanc, also crystalline, and in the generally less sharp, mica schist reliefs where the metamorphic Gran Paradiso stands out. From these high peaks the relief steadily descends in long ridges eastward where it becomes more rounded and finally peters out in the

Po plain. The Western Alps are incised in uniform material of average resistance and separated by short, though deep, valleys with magnificent glacial landforms.

The central Alps

These stretch from the Biella region and Lake d'Iseo to the Tagliamento basin in Friuli. Despite all the variations in this 250 kilometre section, they remain of considerable width, an average of 100–110 kilometres. There is a system of deep, transverse valleys occupied by lakes or plains, and a west–east orientation of longitudinal bands which contrasts with the higher and sharper peaks of the Alps further north in Switzerland.

The Pre-Alps do not have much structural unity, though they are basically composed of thick Secondary limestones with intensive folding that decreases from west to east. Thus here, north of Vicenza and Verona, there is the karst plateau of Asiago, while in the Lombardian Pre-Alps, to the north of Bergamo and Brescia, the summits not only have steep inclines, but are also slightly higher (more than 2,000 m) and sharper. The steepness of the mountains in this Lombardian zone is accentuated by the depth of the transverse valleys of the Ticino, Adda, Oglio and Mincio. The extensive hollowing-out by ice sheets has created deep parts in lakes (410 m in Lake Como).

The interior Alps begin mainly at Lake Como, for westward the Swiss canton of Ticino drives a wedge into the Italian Alps. The frontier zones are the highest (Bernina 4,049 m), since they form part of the central zone of the Alpine arc. This zone is composed of metamorphic and crystalline rocks and has superb glacial landforms but few very distinctive summits except for the pyramid peaks of the Ortles and Adamello. On the other hand, their eastern part has a wonderful relief of sharp points and arêtes of resistant rock lying in softer, eroded material which has created the spectacular peaks of the Dolomites such as Marmolada and the Tre Cime di Lavaredo.

The major valleys are grooved in these reliefs. This is the case with the Piave and also the Adige whose higher parts are briefly longitudinal (Val Venosta, Val Pusteria) and the Oglio (Val Camonica). Only one river is longitudinal for a considerable length and breadth and that is the high valley of the Adda, the Valtellina.

The eastern Alps

These are characterised by a reduced width of 50 kilometres, by relatively lower summits and especially by passes that facilitate movements of population across the Alps as a result of the notable parallel arrangement of bands of relief. This disposition begins with the Carnic Pre-Alps in the west and the Julian Alps in the east, both of which are much more limestone plateaux than mountains. Behind them the Alps proper only reach 2,800 metres. Practically all this relief is drained by a single river, the Tagliamento, whose main bed is transverse but whose higher reaches and parallel tributaries are oriented from west to east and form the longitudinal valleys of the *canali*.

The Po plain

Stretching from west to east for over 400 kilometres this collection of fairly low levels does not display a uniform landscape. The reasons for this diversity are due to two factors: the deposition of old, and especially recent, infilling material from the Alps and the Apennines; and recent tectonic action. The first factor in general determines the path of the major river, pushed from side to side by the most powerful rivers full of material, which, in theory, are those from the Apennines. The second factor explains the presence of different levels of terraces in those zones without Quaternary tectonic action and, where subsidence is recent, the uniformity of the depositional surface.

Among the subtle variety of landscape in this great basin we may distinguish the following elements: sedimentary and volcanic hills, moraines, terraces, levées and recent alluvial flats. First, the hills. These reveal three basic features. The Miocene and, especially Pliocene, material which forms the bedrock of the Quaternary terrains has sometimes 'risen up' due to recent tectonic movements. These form islands in the middle of flat surfaces. The most extensive of these is in the Monferrato region from Alessandria through Asti, to Turin, and reaching 694 metres at Superga, where it forms a maze of hills infinitely dissected by numerous watercourses.

Volcanic forms have emerged as a result of the neighbouring displacement of the trench and, though rare, they compose the steep reliefs of the Euganean hills to the south-west of Padua and the Berici Mts, south of Vicenza, which are acidic lava flows.

Finally, the glacial moraines from the Alps have created large, complex amphitheatres, breaking into enclosed depressions: kettles containing small lakes (Avigliana, Ivrea), or themselves retaining larger ones in their terminal basins (end of Lake Garda). They fringe the Alpine border, though the largest are at the openings of the main valleys such as Rivoli–Avigliana, Ivrea, Peschiera–Lake Garda.

Layers of terraces, corresponding in theory to the different Quaternary glacial periods, occur in Lombardy north of the Po. From the Alpine edge to the Po there are several levels of plateaux. First there are the *ferreto*, thus called because of their rusty red colour and the ferrous content of the decomposing surface deposits, together with pebbly and malleable heathlands. Then comes a middle zone of terraces enriched by the *fontanili* with water issuing from the higher terraces. Finally there are the lower terraces directly overlooking the present infilled plain of the main bed of the river.

Sloping surfaces of alluvial fans have developed over large areas in zones of recent tectonic activity, as is the case for practically the whole of the plain south of the Po below the Apennines. It is filled by the cones of powerful rivers carrying much alluvia, such as the Taro and Trebbia, although this also occurs in the plains of Veneto.

The plain of recent infilling, though similar, differs in its greater uniformity; it follows the Po for its entire length, forming a large triangle with its apex in Piedmont and its base in the delta. The ancient Quaternary marine gulf has only recently been infilled by the plentiful alluvia transported by the river and its tributaries. The Po flows in complicated meanders and, before the recent containment, frequently changed its course and swept the plain of its deposits. The present bed is raised up between dykes so that the river flows above its plain. At periods of maximum water levels, the danger of disastrous flooding is only too real.

A unique morphological world: Sardinia

Sardinia is a fragment of the basement, as is shown by the rigidity of its coastline which obviously coincides with faults. The main aspect of its interior relief is also distinctive with, in the east, plateaux developed on crystalline, metamorphic and Primary sedimentary rocks. Variety is also added by the shaping of granites, where erosion has cut out crests in Gallura and sculptured the mushroom-shaped *taffoni*; by the deep valleys typified by the Flumendosa; and by examples of overhanging limestone such as the Oliena Mts. In the southwest, the mainly metamorphic basement is highly dissected so that the plateau topography has almost entirely disappeared. It is to be found in the northwest, however, in the sedimentary Miocene terrains of the Sassarese and in ancient (Anglona) and recent (Campeda) volcanoes.

Finally, the Campidano, a major subsidence of the Rhine rift valley type, emphasises the Hercynian aspect in unfolding the uniform horizons of its recent infilled plains which are visible in its eastern section.

The major coastal features

Italy has a very impressive length of coastline, more than 10,000 kilometres. It literally bathes in the sea and more than four-fifths of the towns with more than 10,000 inhabitants are situated less than 100 kilometres from the coast.

The very different types of seas

The Adriatic is not very deep (less than 200 m over four-fifths of its area) and not terribly wide (on average 200 km). It is a large gulf rather than a real sea, especially in the part which most penetrates the continent. The salinity is relatively low in the north-east – 35/000 off Trieste. Surface temperatures vary a great deal depending on the season (from 22 to 9 °C) and the tides can be clearly felt for, still in the zone of Trieste, the tidal range can reach 90 centimetres.

The Tyrrhenian, including the Gulf of Genoa, is quite different. It is quite deep (3,371 m at its deepest) and most of it plunges to more than 500 metres. Surface temperatures vary relatively little: from 25 to 14 °C in its central parts. Tides are slight and barely more than 30 centimetres. The Ionian Sea is similar, though even deeper – the deepest in the Mediterranean (4,901 m), in fact.

On the whole, rough seas are not common and, when they do occur, there is no regularity as happens in the western shores of continents constantly hit by storms at these latitudes in the Atlantic and Pacific. The strong winds, such as the north-easterly *bora* in the Adriatic or the north-westerly *maestrale* in Sardinia, do not blow regularly enough to generate constant and strong sea currents. The displacement of material for the building of coasts reflects this.

Major coastal types

Zones of infilling, low-lying coasts are fairly numerous in the areas bordering plains or low hills. There are three major types. First are the salt or brine lagoons and coastal spits type. Examples here are the *lidi* (plural of *lido*) of the coast between Venice and Trieste, the two ends of Campidano in Sardinia, and the Pontine marshes behind the spit attached to Mt Circeo before it was sealed off by man. A second type is characterised by alluvial plains fringed with coastal dunes and spits but without a definite lagoon. These are the coasts which are excellent for bathing: Massa, Viareggio, the Adriatic Riviera beaches such as Ravenna and Rimini, and the coasts of Apulia. Finally, deltas have developed as a function of the depth of the sea and the extent of fluvial material. The Po delta is the most prominent and is advancing rapidly, especially when it is helped by human action. Those of other major rivers are less marked.

The rocky coastal type, in the process of being eroded, varies according to the component rocks and the degree of tectonic activity. The hilly coast of the Marche from Pesaro to Pescara aligns small cliffs of a few dozen metres in height with sandy indentations at the mouths of the rivers descending from the calcareous Apennines. By contrast, high cliffs occur in limestone or crystalline and resistant metamorphic rocks, or as a result of recent subsidence. This is the coastline of eastern Sardinia from Cala Gonone to Dorgali, the Gulf of Genoa in the Portofino and Porto Venera promontories, the Cinque Terre, Capri and the Amalfi coast south of Salerno, and the tremendous cliffs of Belvedere in Calabria.

The final major coastal type has intermediate gradients, contributed by soil movements and sea-level variations. Here alternate flat surfaces, more or less tipped over, ancient Pliocene and Quaternary beaches, and steep sides produced by erosion and tectonic activity. This coastal type occurs throughout the Calabrian and Apulian coasts, particularly east of the Straits of Messina and north of Reggio di Calabria.

An apparently benign climate

In the popular imagination Italy enjoys a flattering reputation. For northern Europeans it is a land where the orange tree blossoms. Certainly some Italian regions have a pleasant, mild and sunny climate, notably the Riviera, the Gulf of Genoa and Sicily, but these areas are very limited and, furthermore, the exception. In this country dominated by mountains, the climate, even though of Mediterranean type, is harsh, capricious and extreme, not at all a picture corresponding to its reputation for mildness.

Climatic influences

Variations in latitude

Italy's very large variations in latitude have considerable consequences. The northern Alps extend as far as 47 ° N while southern Sicily reaches 37 °, a 10 ° difference that represents a distance of 1,100 kilometres. In other words, northern Italy touches central Europe and Sicily is almost Africa. The influence of this is felt above all on the temperatures which are decidedly higher in the South. This stands out clearly on a map of temperatures standardised to sea-level. For similar altitudes, average annual temperatures are lower by 4 ° in the Po plain than in Sicily.

Airstreams

Situated in the southerly belt of the temperate zone, Italy is traversed by westerly airstreams characteristic of this latitude. In the north this airstream is often blocked in winter by cold air masses, not very dense but slow-moving, due to the enclosed nature of the Po plain. Continental air masses from the north and east bring fog and a dryish cold. It gives the northern part of the country a semi-continental climate with considerable contrast in temperatures brought about by the winter cold and by rainy spells in the intermediate periods towards the beginning and end of summer – May, June and October. On the other hand, summer in the extreme south is typified by the interruption of these wind belts and by the appearance of the tropical high pressures which cover the whole of the Mediterranean basin. Summer dryness is thus accentuated. Elsewhere, summer conditions are principally, though not entirely, Mediterranean; the drought is not so absolute.

Relief

Relief and air masses

The alignment of the mountain chains in the path of the air masses produces an effect on their movements. The most striking example of this orographic effect is in the Gulf of Genoa where a large number of depressions from the west build up and are blocked by the Apennine arc. This draws in northerly and north-easterly airstreams which bring heavier rainfall to the Ligurian mountains. Similar, though less marked, phenomena occur in the northern Adriatic.

Relief and rainfall

It goes without saying that relief influences all aspects of climate; thus temperatures decrease with altitude in Italy as elsewhere, but the rainfall totals are even more affected by topography. Thus the southern slopes, and those close to them, which are not in the path of humid air masses, are much less wet than exposed mountains. All the plains in the Mediterranean zone, whether extensive or small, have low rainfall: the Sardinian Campidano has less than 400 millimetres in its southern part, the Tavoliere less than 500 millimetres. The higher Alps everywhere receive more than 1,500 millimetres: 2,800 millimetres at Mt Rosa, more than 2,000 millimetres in the Apuan Alps and the summits of the central Apennines; the record is held by the mountains of Liguria where the Riviera di Levante gets more than 3,400 millimetres.

Major climatic features

Rainfall

The spatial distribution of rainfall varies in relation to the two major aspects of latitude (it rains or snows less as one moves from north to south) and relief (the lower, sheltered zones are drier). The Alps thus get more than 2,000 millimetres on average, but the interior valleys, like the Val d'Aosta, 1,200 millimetres. The Po plain, relatively protected by mountains, has an average rainfall of 800 millimetres, with higher totals in the areas near the Alps and Apennines. The latter is on the whole fairly rainy; more than 1,000 millimetres in the summit areas, even in the most southerly regions. The lower slopes near the coast do not have much lower rainfall – the Tyrrhenian slopes normally receive more than 800 millimetres and the Adriatic more than 700 millimetres. The only areas in the peninsula which get less than 500 millimetres are the very sheltered parts wedged between the slopes – the Crati Gap, Lake Fucino and the Tavoliere plain.

To find areas with less than 700 millimetres it is necessary to go as far south as Sicily and, even here, most of it gets more; the dry zones are only in the south-east. Even in Sardinia, the 600 millimetre isohyet only appears in the Campidano, protected by the heights of Iglesiente and Sulcis.

Seasonal distribution is more important than quantity because of its influence on human activities, since the effects of evaporation and the availability of moisture for plant growth vary according to the season. Water-levels of the irrigable rivers during the summer depend on the amount of melting snow. The rainfall regime is thus an essential element; Italy, a Mediterranean peninsula rooted in central Europe, has a wide spectrum of them.

The regimes with summer drought are the simplest. They reflect the basic Mediterranean climate where the months of July and August have, from the northern Apennines to Sicily, little rain, though significant variations do exist. Only the very southern areas – the islands and the peninsula south of Campania – are really dry at this time with mean rainfall less than 20 millimetres in both July and August. In Latium, and even more in Tuscany, storms increase this total and, in certain wet years, summer may become the rainiest

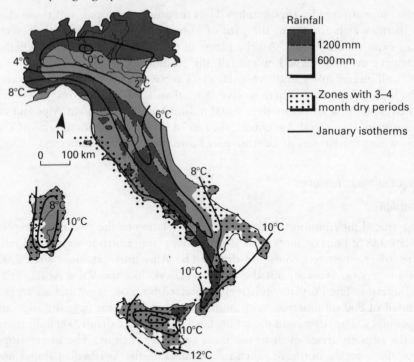

Fig. 1.2   Climatic features: winter temperatures and annual rainfall

season. For example, in 1976, while Palermo remained dry with 2.5 millimetres in July, Florence received 176 millimetres, the monthly maximum for
that year! Northern influences can easily penetrate Mediterranean zones as is
evident in the period of maximum precipitation. In the South winter is clearly
the wettest season; in the northern part of regions falling within the Mediterranean rainfall regime there are two seasonal maxima, that of spring and particularly autumn, for October and November are on average the wettest
months with their torrential, destructive rains.

   The regions which do not suffer from summer drought are those of northern Italy. This does not mean that summer is the wettest period, only that it
does not experience drought. July and August have average rainfalls of 40
millimetres and sometimes more. Only the western regions of the Alps and
northern Piedmont have a truly continental regime with summer maxima.
Everywhere else during this season, the generally torrential and spectacular
rainfalls produce totals that are less than those of one or two 'intermediate'
seasons. The north-eastern part of the Po plain – Lombardy and Veneto – has
an autumn maximum. The southern part, Emilia-Romagna, has double maxima in spring and autumn, the latter being the main one. Finally, Friuli also
displays double maxima, but this time the spring one is the more important.

Winter is nowhere very rainy although it is never really dry; the lack of rainfall is fairly relative and in no way comparable to the Mediterranean aridity. All these 'northern' regimes are, in the last analysis, characterised by a rainfall that is fairly well distributed throughout the year.

Snow and fog are also aspects of precipitation. Snow is relatively frequent in Italy and the whole country can be thought of as having a heavy snow-cover, considering its latitude. In the North snow is abundant; in the South it is largely winter rains and cold, accentuated frequently by high altitudes, that produce the snow-cover. Potenza, which is at no more than 800 metres, had thirteen days of snow in 1975 and eleven in 1976. The peaks above Palermo are normally white for a number of days in winter; it even snows from time to time in the city, as in 1975. The Apennines are mantled with a thick layer of snow down to quite low altitudes; in the northern Apennines above La Spezia, villages at 800 metres are already fully in the mountains and are often cut off in winter.

Fog is much more a speciality of the North, although the marshes in the South are not free of it – the airport at Cagliari has more than fifteen days of fog per year on average. The Po plain, during the period of winter anticyclones when cold airstreams do not disperse, is subject to fogs that often linger for several days. This impedes traffic, especially by air; Milan airport, for example, has more than 110 days of fog each year, Turin and Venice 70 days.

Temperatures

These are of less consequence than rainfall since, with some exceptions, their distribution is relatively uniform.

The 'hot South' does not truly begin until after Rome. As from Latina – Cassino the average January temperatures are higher than 8 °C (except naturally in mountainous areas). Naples has an average of 8.8 °C in this month, Cagliari 9.9 °C and Palermo 10.3 °C. This does not mean that frost is unknown, but that it is exceptional and therefore disastrous for agriculture. The limit of frosts is marked on the ground by the cultivation of citrus trees which are more difficult to grow in the North because of frosts.

Summer is hot, especially in the hills and the interior plains; more than 30 °C in July in the centre of Sicily. July averages are 24.8 °C in Naples, 25.8 °C in Cagliari and 25.7 °C in Palermo, all these places being tempered by their coastal locations. On the other hand, it reaches 30.8 °C at Enna.

The regime of hot summers and cool winters occurs in the northern part of the peninsula – Latium, Marche and Tuscany. Winter temperatures are distinctly lower, particularly inland. Rome has 7.4 °C, but Florence with 5.6 °C has a lower average than the more northerly Marseilles. On the other hand, summers are hot; the July average in Rome is 25.7 °C, identical to that of Palermo.

The 'continental north' has, like the rest of Italy, extremes of temperature and considerable variations. A typical example is the Po plain where Milan has a January average of 1.9 °C and more than 100 days of frost per year, but a July average of 23.9 °C like Naples, with many humid and sultry days. Similarly, Venice has a January average of only 3.8 °C (the edges of the lagoons and certain canals sometimes freeze over). Sunshine and cloud-cover in this country of winter fogs and summer rains is much less than in the South; the brightness, despite some superbly clear days, is less than in the South.

Two different environments are those that are sheltered and around lakes. The rivieras of the Gulf of Genoa benefit from their sheltered position so that temperatures are abnormally mild; winters are extremely clement. Genoa has a January average of 8.4 °C and, above all, frosts are hardly known, thus permitting the cultivation of citrus fruit and flowers. Secondly, the regions close to lakes and the southern slopes of the Alps enjoy a climate in which all temperatures, particularly those in winter, are milder than they should normally be. Averages do not fully reflect this, but the vegetation, which is a better geographical indicator than figures, clearly demonstrates it through the presence of various southern species, such as the olive and citrus tree, around Lake Garda for example.

Winds

These are the final element of a traditional examination of climate. The general characteristics are simple. In addition to the westerly streams characteristic of all the temperate zones, whose effects here are hardly felt on the ground, there are a number of highly specific, local winds felt at ground level.

The hot, dry winds from the south are called *scirocco* in Sicily and Sardinia; these are caused by the path of depressions in the northern Mediterranean and blow mainly in summer.

Cold, dry winds are obviously a northern feature. Of the many winds, two are particularly interesting. The *bora*, a cold, violent, north-westerly wind, sweeps over Friuli and Veneto, causing storms over the Adriatic, while the continental air masses of Central Europe descend towards the Po plain. The latter are cold and dry. The mistral or *maestrale* is the generic name for all these northerly fresh, cold winds, always dry if in the Mediterranean, though the most frequent direction is from the north-east.

The *rain-bearing* winds are those which blow from the sea. In general, they precede the depressions which circulate from west to east. Their names vary from place to place, but they all have the trait of bringing mild temperatures and not being violent or gusty.

Climatic extremes

All the aspects discussed above are expressed in averages. In reality, the situation is altered by deviation from the mean and extremes of climatic conditions.

Irregularity between one year and another is the first of these deviations. It is expressed partly in variations in temperature but mainly in the annual rainfall figures and their seasonal and monthly maxima. Variations from year to year are the rule, the more so as one moves southward. For example, Cagliari received 339 millimetres in 1979, a dry year, but 557 millimetres in 1976, a wet year (the average for 1967–76 was 450 mm). Drought in spring is especially serious for agriculture, since it impedes the normal growth of cereals; only irrigation is able to remedy this rainfall deficiency.

Climatic extremes can become catastrophic if they occur fairly frequently. Over-abundant precipitation can become serious as a result of the obstruction of moisture-laden air masses by the relief. This tends to happen mainly in autumn and the beginning of winter. One has only to remember the disastrous rains of 1964 which caused the level of the Arno to rise and, aided by the lack of flood prevention, seriously damaged Florence.

Extremes of temperature also exist. Heat waves and cold spells occur frequently. The latter, arising from the invasion of cold anti-cyclonic air into Italy from the north-east, can remain for long periods in winter, especially in February when this most commonly occurs. Frost can also affect the entire country, including the extreme south in Sicily and Sardinia, causing considerable damage to vegetation. The severest cold spell in recent years was that of 1956 when frost attacked fig trees in these islands.

Thus climatic variations should be always borne in mind when thinking of a travel brochure picture of a mild Mediterranean climate. In fact, this image masks a harsher, more restrictive reality.

Hydrological systems in Italy

Elements of the hydrological system

There are two basic aspects of relief which have a bearing on hydrology. Firstly, the narrow backbone running down the entire peninsula impedes the formation of large rivers. Only the Tiber manages to reach 400 kilometres. In the North, the very different arrangement of relief enables the Po to reach a length of 652 kilometres and an average volume over eight times that of the Tiber, thus making it one of the principal European rivers. In addition, sharp contrasts in relief give rise to rapid-flowing rivers. Only the lakes and some karst landforms result in a more even river flow, but these examples are again nearly all located in the Po basin.

A river regime in its average and peak flows owes much to climatic influences and, in this respect, Italy has an almost entire range of such regimes from the streams descending from glaciers to the southern *fiumare* which are veritable wadis.

The nature of the bedrock produces two contrasting hydrological systems. The large limestone blocks with karst features, especially those in the central Apennines, result in the formation of notable subterranean water beds that serve to even out the flow. The opposite happens in the clay areas so common in the northern Apennines and Sicily where streams emerge virtually instantaneously wherever there is precipitation and a reasonable gradient.

Major types of hydrological systems

Alpine, northern Apennine and Po plain rivers

The rivers rising in the Alps, that is the tributaries of the left bank of the Po – the Adda, Tessino, and the Adige, Piave and Tagliamento, are fed by melting snow. Thus they have low levels in winter and high levels in summer after the melting of the snow. The Adige (450 km) has an average discharge of 400 cubic metres per second. It is the second river in Italy in terms of both length and discharge. The northern Apennine rivers, especially those which flow to the Po plain, have a regime based on rainfall and melting snow. Winter snow formation means that levels are low and there is high evaporation in summer as well. Fluctuations in regime also differentiate the two types of rivers. Rivers where the flow is balanced by lakes (Tessino by Lake Maggiore, for example) do not usually suffer the enormous fluctuations between high and low levels faced by their Apennine counterparts.

The Po, a river that receives both types of flow, is obviously exceptional in the size of its basin (75,000 sq. km as compared to the Tiber's 17,200, the next largest in this respect), and in its average flow of 1,680 cubic metres per second. Its regime is the result of its location between its Alpine and Apennine tributaries. At Ferrara its flow is almost entirely regular. The low levels in July and December are not very marked in relation to the fairly similar peaks in April and November – a ratio of 7 to 11. However, the peaks resulting from autumn rains can be terrible. In 1952 they reached a discharge of 14,000 cubic metres per second and flooded the whole of the Polesine delta. Works which have controlled the river have unfortunately, by means of dykes, constricted the river and raised its level above the alluvium, thereby literally perching the Po above the plain through which it flows.

Southern rivers

Their regime is dominated by the Mediterranean climate which is drier and, therefore, leads to summer aridity and high evaporation. Firstly, there is the low average flow – the Tiber has an average discharge of 230 cubic metres per second in a catchment basin of 17,200 sq. kilometres compared to the 410 cubic metres of the Ticino which has a basin of only 7,200 sq. kilometres. Secondly, low levels are really very low, except where there are abundant springs.

Furthermore, the rivers are short, and, the further one proceeds south, the more marked the low levels are. The drying-up of river beds is in fact the rule for all the small rivers of the South. This regime is in contrast with rivers that rise in the snow-covered mountains and elsewhere. The former display a regime based on rainfall and snow, similar to those of the southern tributaries of the Po. Those that are not fed by melting snow in spring depend on the seasonal pattern of rainfall and its erratic nature. The levels generally rise in autumn though not necessarily in a very regular pattern. Thus, without major works and barrages, they cannot be relied upon.

The significance of subterranean water sources and lakes

Karst landscapes have given rise to several major reliable springs that were known and praised far back in antiquity (those of Aniene at Tivoli, for example). The Nera, fed by waters from the limestone Apennines, has a virtually constant flow at Terni. Alluvial phreatic water beds also offer potential sources, which are often substantial. They exist in all the major and small alluvial plains and can be tapped by wells. The most important ones are found in gravel and sand soils which form the substratum of the Po plain. We have already mentioned the *fontanili* which have been in use for a long time.

There are many lakes in Italy, especially of glacial and volcanic origins. They are generally deep and provide major sources of fresh water. They also regularise river flows, as in the case of most of the Pre-Alpine lakes.

Major aspects of Italian biogeography

In such a harsh morphological and climatic environment, and in one of the most densely and continously settled countries, with a high level of civilisation, the man-made environment has been profoundly altered and is highly vulnerable.

Endangered soils

The rarity of complete soils

Real soils, according to the scientific definition (that is those in which biological processes are continually taking place and there are distinctive soil horizons above the parent rock), are, in the last analysis, not very common. Erosion of the top layers has gone on for so long now that any such soil which might have existed has disappeared. On the slopes, which after all form two-thirds of the surface of the country, and even on the interfluves in clay rocks, there are no soils strictly speaking, only the rankers most of which are under forest cover. Cultivation even takes place directly on rock surfaces, as long as they are sufficiently friable.

The very different complete soils

In the present climate it appears that the 'climax' soils are the brown soils common in all of western Europe. They occur throughout the peninsula and the hills and lowlands of northern Italy. The only areas where they do not

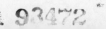

FERNALD LIBRARY
COLBY-SAWYER COLLEGE
NEW LONDON, N.H. 03257

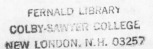

occur are the very low-lying zones, the hottest and most calcareous areas. These brown soils, of an average depth of 30 to 60 centimetres, have weakly developed horizons and are slightly acidic (pH reading of 5.6–6.5). They provide good agricultural soils if protected from erosion.

In other areas, it is the *terra rossa*, the Mediterranean 'red soil', which dominates, and not only in limestone areas. These are clay soils, often compact and of variable depth, especially on limestone, so that major operations to get rid of the stones and break them up have to be carried out if they are to be used agriculturally after clearing. Their origin has been much debated, for it seems that they are partly fossil soils, formed in a hotter and wetter climate.

Finally, there are the black soils, formed under grassland cover in the steppe-like landscape of Apulia and central Sicily. They have qualities similar to the chernozems.

Threatened soils

Almost everywhere soils are threatened by erosion, either because of gullying and slippage or by deposits laid down by peak water-levels which cover the soil with sand and debris. Human action and deforestation have greatly increased the amount of damage. Half the forested area has disappeared in Sicily since the nineteenth century. There have been long-standing attempts to halt erosion by terracing, as in the *fasce* of the Ligurian Riviera and the *ronchi* of the Lombardian hills. In the past thirty years there has been a policy, especially in the South, of reducing the rate of erosion through systematic reafforestation. At the same time, river beds have been regulated. These aims are inevitably long-term. Sometimes, as with the problem of the *frane*, the techniques of control are insufficient or non-existent.

Badly degraded natural vegetation

As in all long-settled countries, the natural vegetation has almost entirely disappeared. Everywhere, except on the high Alpine summits, it has been modified by human actions, crops, herds and deforestation. We need, therefore, to distinguish between the natural evolution of plants and those introduced by man.

Mediterranean vegetation

This type of vegetation is associated with the Mediterranean climate and occurs throughout the peninsula, with several outliers around the Pre-Alpine lakes and, in the north-east of the Po plain, around Padua and in the Euganean mountains. The ubiquitous presence of mountains, however, introduces the major variation of vertical zonation, for the environments differ above the lowlands.

The Mediterranean vegetation of the plains and hills includes species that have both adapted and been degraded. In the few areas which have not been eroded and which have the right soils, the normal vegetation is evergreen holm-oaks with a lower layer consisting of laurel, mastic trees, strawberry trees, small bushes such as the white and Montpellier cistus (*Cistus albus* and *Cistus monspelensis*), grasses, cushions of sweet-smelling plants such as thyme and bulbs such as asphodels. In the thicker bushes there are numerous creepers typified by the perfumed honeysuckle. This vegetation association represents a good example of adaptation to the harsh climatic conditions, especially the summer aridity to which plants have adapted by developing tough, evergreen leaves and aromatic juices which reduce loss of moisture through the stomata. However, few plants combine all these qualities.

Varieties of plants are very great and an increase in moisture or reduction in summer aridity result in an expansion of deciduous oaks, the pubescent oak, with leaves covered in white hairs, being the most common. The cork-oak, diffused partly by man, is also better adapted to wetter areas as well as milder winters and siliceous soils. On the whole, soil differences count for less than degree of degradation. For example, *garrigue* exists on both granite and limestone. Only a few species occur on bedrock – the umbrella pine nearly always grows on coastal sands and heather does well on siliceous soils.

Degraded formations cover substantial areas. The *maquis* (*macchia*) represents the first stage of this process of degradation. The tree cover becomes discontinuous and is replaced by bushes and bushy plants which still make penetration difficult. A good example of this occurs in the vegetation cover of the Monte Circeo National Park south of the Pontine marshes.

The *garrigue* marks a further stage in this process of deterioration, for bare earth appears within the more open pattern of vegetation cover; trees have now disappeared and bushes dominate the thin-spread tufts of grass and sweet-smelling plants. The characteristic species is the kermes oak (*Quercus coccifera*), a bushy oak with prickly leaves.

In the final stage of this degradation bushes have in their turn almost completely disappeared. Three types of vegetation are prominent: cistuses which can withstand the fires lit each year by shepherds; the grassland Mediterranean steppe, scattered with clumps of asphodels, commonly found on the southern limestone plateaux and the uncultivated areas of inland Sicily; and, finally, dwarf palms (*Chamaerops humilis*, called in Arabic *doum*), usually found in the coastal areas of the islands.

Vegetational zones in the mountains

These begin at different altitudes depending on the region: at Abetone in the northern Apennines the beech begins at 1,200 metres; in the Aspromonte it starts 500 metres higher. The general principle, however, remains the same. Apart from the very high summits (central Apennines and especially Etna), high grasslands do not exist, for the typical vegetation type is the beech grove, often magnificent when it is protected. In wetter and cooler zones it occurs together with the pine tree which has been introduced by man. Below this

altitude all the range of transitions based on the general Mediterranean formation exist – forests of pubescent oaks as well as ash, mainly the ash-elm
(*Fraxinus-ulmus*) and chestnut trees on siliceous soils.

Reafforestation, widespread throughout the mountain zone, usually consists
of conifers: Douglas pines in the highest areas; elsewhere, other pines adapted
to poor ecological conditions – black pines and Scots pines (these are, unfortunately, subject to catastrophic fires).

Vegetation of northern Italy

We shall not spend time on the disputed question of the northern limit of
Mediterranean vegetation. Generally, it is sufficient to establish the distribu-
tion of a typical species such as the olive, which basically passes through the
Ligurian Apennines and then to the north of Emilia-Romagna, reaching the
Adriatic between Ravenna and the mouth of the Po.

The Po plain is almost totally cultivated. The natural vegetation was probably deciduous oak forest, although species introduced by man are probably
the most common today: chestnut trees on higher ground, and weeping wil-
lows and the tall, Italian poplars along the drainage and irrigation canals.

The Alps display the complete range of vegetation zones to be expected at
this latitude. The usual succession, with some variations, is the following:

(a)   up to 1,000 metres, oaks and chestnuts;
(b)   from 1,000 to 1,500 metres, beech mixed with oaks;
(c)   from 1,500 to 2,000 metres, conifer forests – Scots pines, larch trees in
      the parts with a drier and more rigorous climate; a zone often interspersed
      with grassland that is frequently due to human action;
(d)   from 2,000 to 2,400 metres, the Alpine zone of bushes: dwarf pines, rho-
      dodendrons, bilberry bushes, heather and grassland with brightly col-
      oured flowers (violets, gentians);
(e)   finally, the zone of rocks and, if high enough, glaciers.

Conclusion

To conclude on the theme of the possibilities offered by the natural environment leaves one open to the twofold accusation of being taken once again for
a determinist and of labouring only the obvious points. It is possible, however,
to list briefly and simply the positive and negative aspects of the natural
environment in Italy.

On a positive note, Italy offers an undeniable variety, almost unique in
Europe, of environments, landscapes and agricultural and tourist potential.
Only France can possibly match it. All types of temperate-latitude ecological
zones can be found here, from the semi-tropical, cotton-growing plains of
south-western Sicily to the Alpine pastures of Valtellina with their cattle-graz-
ing, and including the wine-producing hills of Tuscany and the sugar-beet
plains of Lombardy. This astonishing range of resources is matched by a tour-

ist industry of the first order; in any season those with leisure can find whatever they wish, including both beaches and ski slopes (not to speak of monuments and museums).

On a negative note, the closely related factors of vulnerability and harsh conditions work against the environment. Climatic extremes in terms of temperature and rainfall have certainly generated environmental hazards in the various ways that cause erosion (*frane* and the bursting of stream beds). To this can be added the widespread instability due to earthquakes. This vulnerability is essentially the consequence of the continual encroachment to which the natural environment is subjected; thus almost everywhere, though more markedly in the South, soils and vegetation are under considerable attack. Man has largely contributed to this situation and has only recently begun to do something about it, though even so not everywhere. There are few other countries where the present environment is less in a natural state. Rather, it exhibits the result of an incessant conflict between its potential and the actual, more or less adapted, use of it. This will be the recurrent theme in the chapters that follow.

2 Man and the social environment

Italians are sincere, good people, they unavowedly say what they think; only in spurts are they vacuous; finally, poverty is not ridiculous to them.   STENDHAL

EVOLUTION OF THE POPULATION 1861–1977

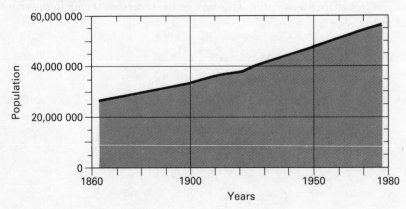

ASPECTS OF THIS EVOLUTION

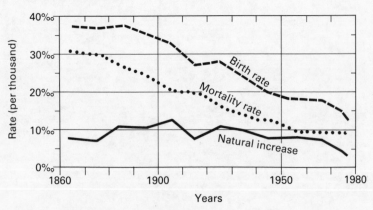

Fig. 2.1   Evolution of the Italian population, 1861–1980

There have always been a great number of inhabitants in the Italy space, richer in denuded hills and marshes than in green slopes and fertile plains. At the end of the eighteenth century there were 18 million Italians, compared to 27 million French in a larger and more fertile territory, only 10 million British and 6 million Prussians.

But thanks in part to their cultural inheritance, this population competed for space with results that were often positive. Towns and the countryside, shaped in the image of an industrious society, frequently supported considerable densities as a result of the implementation of numerous techniques of urbanism and agriculture, which were developed here before being diffused throughout Europe. However, such landscapes had their share of the precariousness and hiatuses common to the Mediterranean world. It is not surprising that harmonious development has been jeopardised and seriously affected by demographic growth, particularly since the second half of the nineteenth century. With 57 million inhabitants in early 1980, the Italian population has more than tripled since the beginning of the nineteenth century, while the French population has not even managed to double itself despite the addition of immigrants. This demographic revolution, which could easily be followed by a shortfall in births, constitutes the most notable feature of modern Italy, one which has influenced the people and transformed their life-styles the most.

The demographic revolution

Italy lived for a long time with an obsession with numbers – sign of vitality but equally of overpopulation – before following the European demographic pattern of the 1960s. In terms of national averages, the present situation is one of balance and harmony, but this picture is sharply contradicted by an analysis of regional data, which reveals such a distortion that one needs to enquire into its causes: is there a basic difference between the North and the Mezzogiorno, or is the whole country suffering some kind of retarded demographic development?

From expansion to normal European demographic patterns

The patterns of national demographic evolution can be followed through a number of indicators:

The main feature is clearly the maintenance of a birth-rate of over 20 per thousand until 1950, accompanied by a mortality rate which had already fallen below that of France by 1930. For several decades the fall in the mortality rate combined with an increase in total population to hide the decline in fertility.

The various indices and statistics which can be calculated also confirm the sudden emergence of the mature demographic stage. This is the case of the average age which rose from 28 years in 1905 to 35 years in 1977; the pro-

Table 2.1 Main parameters of demographic change, 1862–1978

Period	Population ('000)	Rate of fertility (%)	Birth rate (%)	Death-rate (%)	Rate of natural increase (%)	Rate of net emigration (%)	Annual rate of increase (%)
1862–71	27,142	152	33.4	30.3	7.1	− 0.3	6.8
1872–81	28,976	149	36.9	29.6	7.1	− 1.3	6.0
1882–91	30,659	156	37.2	26.9	10.3	− 2.8	7.5
1892–01	32,580	135	34.2	23.7	10.5	− 4.2	6.3
1902–11	34,675	131	32.2	21.3	10.9	− 4.1	6.8
1912–21	37,329	126	27.2	21.8	5.4	− 2.4	3.0
1922–31	38,205	103	27.5	16.3	11.3	− 2.3	9.0
1932–41	41,765	91	23.0	13.9	9.1	− 0.6	8.5
1942–51	44,861	78	20.1	12.8	7.3	− 1.4	5.9
1952–61	48,500	71	18.0	9.6	8.4	− 2.7	5.7
1962–71	52,158	68	18.2	9.8	8.4	− 0.9	7.5
1978	56,601	51	13.2	9.6	3.6	+ 0.5	4.1

Table 2.2   Age distribution in 1861 and 1978

Year	Age groups (years)					
	0–20 ('000)	%	21–64 ('000)	%	over 65 ('000)	%
1861	9,573	44.3	11,383	51.6	908	4.1
1978	18,324	32.4	31,119	55.0	7,256	12.6

portion of old people per 100 young has risen during this same period from 30 to 74; and the differential mortality rate for men and women has increased the percentage of women from 48.9 to 51.1. Yet, the most significant index is the changing age distribution of the population.

Among the changes correlated with this evolution is the decline in the percentage of active population which now only accounts for 35.5 per cent of the population as against 48 per cent in 1911. At the same time, the distribution of the active population between the three major sectors has had a similar evolution, though slightly behind that of industrial Europe. Agriculture, which represented 58 per cent of the active population in 1871, still had 17.6 per cent in 1977, while industry increased from 22 to 38.2 per cent and the tertiary sector from 20 to 46.2 per cent.

Despite these changes, a more balanced situation has not been achieved. Italians have experienced difficulties in adapting from a density of 90 inhabitants per sq. kilometre at the time of the foundation of the kingdom to 188 at present. The latter figure means that the cultivated land surface now supports two people per hectare. Progress in agriculture and the economy have only very recently partially mitigated the tension which had expressed itself for a long time in poverty, unemployment and social conflicts, set in turn within a context of colonial expansion and Fascism.

From international to interregional migration

Poverty and various crises have, nevertheless, been alleviated by emigration. This is an old tradition. The Italian diaspora in the Mediterranean included, during the middle of the nineteenth century, 10,000 people in Tunisia, almost as many in Egypt, and not less than 20,000 in Marseilles alone. But, between 1861 and 1975, altogether 29 million people emigrated. The intensity of this phenomenon was matched by the unusual feature of return migration which has been evaluated at 20 million (only roughly measured before 1921). If one takes into account 9 million permanent migrants and their descendants, a potential population of 71 million would result instead of the 57 million of today. This, therefore, is the importance of migration in the demography of the country.

Besides, the flow and rhythm of migration have been far from regular and constant. Until 1880 the average number of departures was around 120,000 persons per annum; it increased rapidly to 872,000 emigrants in 1913. The flow was then interrupted by the First and Second World wars and continued to decrease from 390,000 persons in 1923 to 30,000 in 1939. It shot to 300,000 in 1948 and fell back to 85,000 in 1978. The novel feature now is that for several years the number of returnees has exceeded the departures (90,000 in 1978). Now, as in the past, it is the southern regions, especially Sicily and Calabria, which provide the largest number of emigrants.

Another remarkable aspect of Italian migration is the diversity of receiving countries. A list drawn up since 1876 underlines the overall dominance of European countries which have taken 55 per cent of those recorded. However, a more detailed breakdown by country shows that it is the United States which heads the list with 5.7 million migrants, followed by France with 4.8 million and Switzerland with 3.9 million. All this occurred with considerable variations from one period to another, depending on employment possibilities and diplomatic relations.

For internal migrants, moving out of the local area yet still within their own country, conditions have been and remain very difficult. For a long time this movement has replaced international migration, although it also has to do with a long-standing tradition which has gathered pace since the second half of the nineteenth century. Usually these movements are short distance, from the highest and poorest lands towards the long-deserted coastal strips and small towns and, from there, normally within a generation, towards the big cities. This movement, which has emptied vast areas of the Apennines such as the hills of Liguria and the interior of Sicily, is similar to that of most countries. What is more unusual is another migration that settled large concentrations of landless farmers, many from Veneto and Romagna, on reclaimed lands encountered around the edge of the Po delta, in the Maccarese and on the Agro Pontino (Pontine marshes).

At present, the most significant movement, the amplitude of which is difficult to measure, is the dual pull of southerners to Latium and to the richest provinces of the north-west, principally Milan and Turin. These two cities also exert a considerable attraction on the poorest northern provinces – Cuneo, for example, is losing out to Turin and Sondrio to Milan. An analysis of movements for 1972–76 (Fig. 2.2) reveals nothing surprising in the recent migration towards Tuscany and Friuli. Furthermore, Trentino-Alto Adige's negative balance demonstrates that the Alps are not able to retain a population which is still prolific.

Finally, it should be noted that, as with international migration, interregional migration is also now tending to decrease; it now involves on average less than 1 million per year, as against 2 million in the 1960s. The diminished pressure is related to factors such as demographic evolution and the regional policy for the Mezzogiorno, but this is a hypothesis which needs to be tested.

Taking account of the number of return migrants and their demographic characteristics, it would seem that this human chain, which conveys people from the Sicilian countryside to the factories of Turin and Milan, ought to produce a relatively homogeneous demographic structure throughout the country. Yet the analysis of regional data reveals that this is far from being the situation.

Regions of demographic disequilibrium

The size and duration of internal migration pose a dual problem of assessment and prediction of future trends. Should these massive transfers be considered as the beginning of a demographic decline in the most affected regions, or seen as a remedy for relative or absolute overpopulation? It is worth asking this question in so far as several Italian demographers have analysed the situation in terms of overpopulation and have suggested an index of overpopulation, which is especially high in Calabria, northern Apulia, Sicily and the Po delta.

In reality, the results obtained do not appear very convincing, as demonstrated by the successive variations in the definition of indices used. It seems that the interpretation of the data is tenuous, even at the simplest level of densities and population variations. In effect, the latter takes on a different meaning, depending on whether a short- or a medium-term perspective is adopted. Thus, for the period 1951–77, one notes, in contrast to the high growth of Latium, Lombardy and Piedmont, a negative balance in four regions of high emigration – Basilicata, Abruzzi, Molise and Umbria. These results are both logical, and yet worrying, to the extent that they point to the beginning of a permanent decline similar to that of the southern Alps and the Massif Central in France. Yet, on the other hand, a short-term analysis of data for the most recent period (1975–77) indicates a positive net migration in all regions. Should this be attributed to economic uncertainty or to the regional development policy for the Mezzogiorno which has begun to bear fruit? The ambiguity still prevails.

Measurement of migration on a regional scale must not, however, obscure the complexity of the processes which have depopulated the mountains, especially the Apennines. Since 1951 mountain communes have lost on average 30 per cent of their inhabitants and, in some cases, 50 per cent. After all, was not the net increase in the province of Genoa achieved at the expense of the northern Apennines, which have lost 150,000 inhabitants in the past 20 years? The same situation applies further south where Christ would now indeed stop at Eboli because there are no more people or things beyond Campania. On the other hand, all the communes on the plain, especially the medium-sized settlements on the coast, have benefited from the exodus in the areas higher up.

This explains why changes in density are not as great as one might think. During the years from 1951 to 1977, when there was an increase of 9.5 million

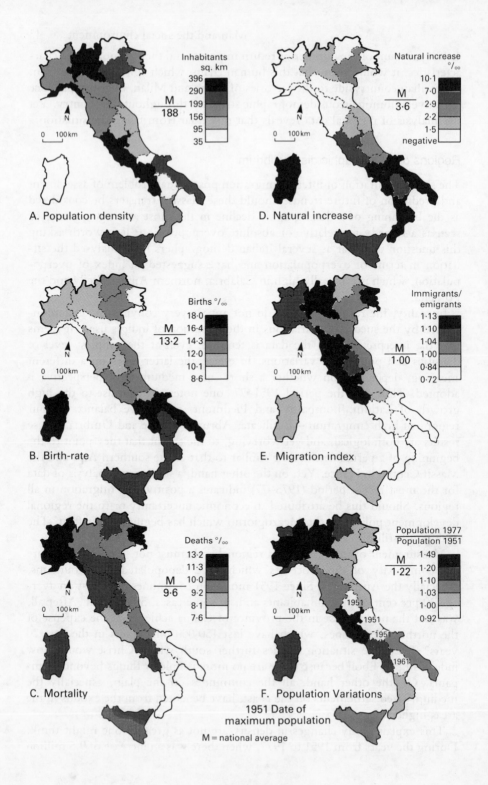

A. Population density

Inhabitants
sq. km

	396
	290
	199
M	156
188	95
	35

0   100 km

D. Natural increase

Natural increase
°/∞

	10·1
	7·0
M	2·9
3·6	2·2
	1·5
	negative

0   100 km

B. Birth-rate

Births °/∞

	18·0
	16·4
	14·3
M	12·0
13·2	10·1
	8·6

0   100 km

E. Migration index

Immigrants/
emigrants

	1·13
	1·10
	1·04
M	1·00
1·00	0·84
	0·72

0   100 km

C. Mortality

Deaths °/∞

	13·2
	11·3
	10·0
M	9·2
9·6	8·1
	7·6

0   100 km

F. Population Variations

Population 1977
Population 1951

	1·49
	1·20
M	1·10
1·22	1·03
	1·00
	0·92

0   100 km

1951 Date of
maximum population

M = national average

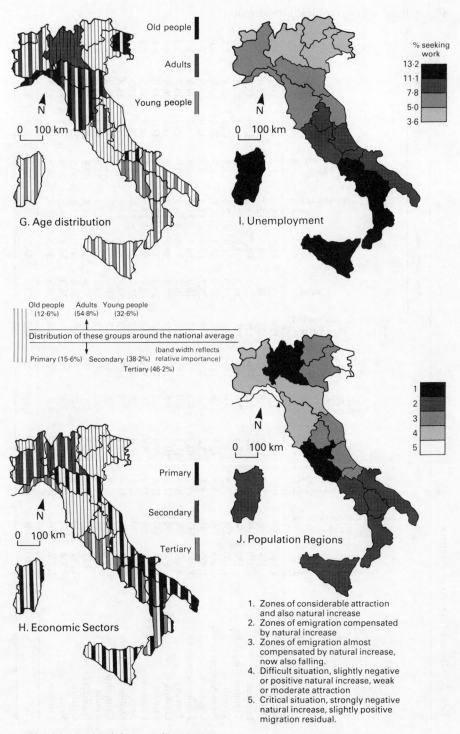

G. Age distribution

Old people
Adults
Young people

0   100 km

I. Unemployment

% seeking
work
13·2
11·1
7·8
5·0
3·6

0   100 km

Old people   Adults   Young people
(12·6%)   (54·8%)   (32·6%)

Distribution of these groups around the national average

(band width reflects
relative importance)

Primary (15·6%)   Secondary (38·2%)
Tertiary (46·2%)

J. Population Regions

0   100 km

1
2
3
4
5

Primary

Secondary

Tertiary

H. Economic Sectors

0   100 km

1. Zones of considerable attraction
   and also natural increase
2. Zones of emigration compensated
   by natural increase
3. Zones of emigration almost
   compensated by natural increase,
   now also falling.
4. Difficult situation, slightly negative
   or positive natural increase, weak
   or moderate attraction
5. Critical situation, strongly negative
   natural increase, slightly positive
   migration residual.

Fig. 2.2   Regional demographic patterns

Table 2.3   Regional demographic patterns

	Population (1977)	Density per sq. km (1977)	Birth-rate (%o, 1977)	Mortality rate (%o, 1977)	Natural increase (%o, 1977)	Internal migration index (%o, 1974-76)	Variation in population (%o, 1951-77)	Age structure (%)			Active population (%)			
								Young (0-20 years)	Adults (21-64 years)	Old (over 65 years)	Primary sector	Secondary sector	Tertiary sector	Those seeking work
Piedmont	4,540	179	10,8	11,8	-1,0	107	129	27,7	57,3	15	11,2	50,6	38,2	5,8
Val d'Aosta	114	35	9,5	11,3	-1,8	107	121	28,5	58,8	12,7	13,1	36,9	50,0	4,1
Lombardy	8,910	374	11,9	9,7	2,2	110	136	24,3	62,5	13,2	4,6	53,9	41,5	4,3
Trentino–Alto Adige	372	64	12,6	10,0	2,6	97	121	34,3	53,5	12,2	16,3	31,4	52,3	3,6
Veneto	4,320	235	12,3	9,7	2,6	105	110	33,0	55,0	12,0	12,8	43,8	43,4	4,8
Friuli-Venezia Giulia	1,245	159	9,9	12,7	-2,8	110	102	27,0	56,5	16,5	8,5	38,5	53,0	5,0
Liguria	1,859	343	8,6	13,2	-4,6	106	119	25,2	57,6	17,2	8,0	32,0	60,0	7,7
Emilia-Romagna	3,936	179	9,7	10,9	-1,2	101	101	26,9	58,3	14,8	16,8	38,7	44,5	5,2
Tuscany	3,587	156	10,1	11,1	-1,0	113	113	26,7	57,3	16,0	10,0	43,3	46,7	5,5
Umbria	802	95	11,5	10,0	1,5	107	99	27,5	58,3	14,2	15,0	38,5	46,5	8,8
Marche	1.104	145	12,0	9,8	2,2	100	103	29,3	57,2	13,5	20,0	41,0	39,0	5,1
Latium	4.997	290	13,2	8,4	4,8	114	149	33,0	56,2	18,0	10,5	26,0	63,5	10,0
Abruzzi	1.227	114	12,3	9,4	2,9	96	92	31,7	54,4	13,8	24,0	28,7	47,3	9,1
Molise	331	75	11,7	9,2	2,5	94	92	32,1	53,4	14,5	43,2	22,0	34,8	7,8
Campania	5,380	396	18,0	8,2	9,8	83	123	40,0	50,5	9,5	24,3	27,5	48,2	10,1
Apulia	3,855	199	17,8	7,7	10,1	82	119	39,1	50,7	10,2	33,0	25,0	42,0	8,1
Basilicata	619	62	14,3	7,8	6,5	75	99	37,5	50,7	11,8	39,5	26,5	34,0	10,4
Calabria	3,057	136	15,8	7,6	8,2	72	100	38,6	50,0	11,4	30,5	25,5	40,0	13,2
Sicily	4,936	192	15,8	8,8	7,0	84	110	36,5	51,7	11,8	26,0	26,5	47,7	10,5
Sardinia	1,572	66	16,4	8,1	8,3	95	124	38,8	50,5	10,7	19,3	28,2	52,5	11,7
Italy	56,601	188	13,2	9,6	3,6	100	122	32,6	54,8	12,6	15,6	38,2	46,2	7,1

Table 2.4 Variation in regional population densities, 1951–78

	1951			1978	
Regions	Density	Index	Regions	Density	Index
Campania	320	202	Campania	399	210
Liguria	290	183	Lombardy	374	198
Lombardy	275	174	Liguria	342	182
Veneto	213	135	Latium	293	154
Latium	194	123	Veneto	236	125
Sicily	175	111	Apulia	201	105
Apulia	166	105	Sicily	193	102
Emilia-Romagna	160	101	Piedmont	179	95
Friuli-V.G.	156	99	Emilia-Romagna	179	95
Marche	141	89	Friuli-V.G.	159	84
Tuscany	137	86	Tuscany	156	83
Calabria	135	85	Marche	145	77
Piedmont	134	84	Calabria	137	72
Abruzzi-Molise	111	75	Abruzzi	114	60
Umbria	95	64	Umbria	95	50
Basilicata	63	40	Molise	75	39
Trentino-A.A.	54	34	Sardinia	66	35
Sardinia	53	33	Trentino-A.A.	64	34
Aosta	32	20	Basilicata	62	33
Italy	158	100	Aosta	35	19
			Italy	189	100

inhabitants and an increase in density from 158 to 188 persons per sq. kilometre, the variations, in decreasing order, are as in Table 2.4.

It will be noticed that changes in order are relatively slight, except for Basilicata and Piedmont. It is the changes in the index compared to the national
average of 100 which best measure the variations in the share of each region
in the national total.

The most important factor contributing to this stability would seem to be
natural increase, greater in the South than in the North, but which is itself
part of the basic decline in the birth-rate. There is, nevertheless, nothing that
links the sudden fall in the birth-rate in certain northern regions over 1951–77
and the more even, steady drop further south. If the rate in Campania has
dropped from 24.6 to 18.0 per thousand, a figure which several years ago
would have been undreamt of, and if that of Calabria has plummeted from
27.9 to 15.8 per thousand, these figures do not, however, jeopardise future
development to the same extent as do the seemingly slight variations from 10
to 8.6 per thousand in Liguria and 14.7 to 9.7 per thousand in Friuli. These
changes are further accentuated by the movement of mortality rates in the
Mezzogiorno in the opposite direction (from 10.2 to 7.6 per thousand in Calabria) to those of the ageing northern provinces (from 10.7 to 13.2 per thousand in Liguria). The overall effect of these opposing movements is quite
striking, since six of the northern provinces now have natural decrease, while
some, notably Piedmont, are poles of attraction for migrants from the Mez-

zogiorno. The most drastic situation is without any doubt that of the city-province of Trieste, where there is both net immigration and a fall in total population. On the other hand, southern provinces often have rates of natural increase almost as high as in the past (Campania from 14.5 to 9.8 per thousand during 1951–77), with the only sizeable declines corresponding to the mountain regions of Abruzzi and Molise (from 10 to 2.9 per 1,000).

It remains unknown whether this balance between a South, as a reservoir of people, and a North, where they finally end their days and which depends on this transfer of population, can be anything other than precarious. Two remarks must be made on this issue. The first relates to the high proportion of young people remaining in southern regions, a proportion which attains almost 40 per cent in Campania. And yet, even with this transfer of young people, certain northern provinces do not manage to raise their proportion to 30 per cent; while the percentage of old people reaches almost French proportions in Friuli and Liguria (17%). Rome is like a city of retired folk, comparable in some ways to Nice or Miami. In relation to the age structure, the distinctiveness of Lombardy, where the proportion of adults reaches 62.5 per cent, should be noted. These statistics lead one to believe that the South will undoubtedly be able to continue, at least for some time, its role as a provider of migrants, although this does not mean that these transfers of population will be sufficient to prevent a serious problem of ageing in other regions, particularly Friuli, Liguria and Emilia-Romagna.

The second comment pertains to the socio-economic composition of the active population (Fig. 2.2). There are proportionally ten times more farmers in Molise than in Lombardy, although the value of agricultural production, based on the productivity of farmers, is very much lower. More generally, the importance of the primary sector in relation to the secondary, and the insignificance of the latter south of a line from the Marche to Umbria, lead one to suspect that the Mezzogiorno will remain for a long time incapable of retaining its population increase. The human exodus will not cease until an economic crisis reduces in a drastic way the pull of the richer and demographically devitalised provinces of northern Italy. In the meantime demand for employment continues in the whole of central and southern Italy.

A classification of population regions

Only when diverse demographic variables are synthesised at a regional level does their full significance become clear. The first type of region (Fig. 2.2) corresponds to Lombardy and Latium. Both regions are characterised by their demographic pull and rapid expansion. Latium has a natural dynamism not found in Lombardy, but where however, thanks to a surplus of young adults, natural increase remains at an almost balanced level.

A second group includes the southern regions of Campania, Apulia, Basilicata, Calabria, Sicily and Sardinia. Of course, all these regions have their distinctive characteristics, especially Sardinia with its sparse population and slow growth, but they all share certain traits with their negative migratory balances compensated by a considerable natural increase. The question to be asked is whether these continuing and substantial losses are to be interpreted as the move to a new equilibrium or as the beginning of the end. The case of Basilicata is fairly inconclusive on this issue.

The situation is less ambiguous for the regions of Marche, Abruzzi and Molise whose still continuing natural increase is mitigated by the amount of emigration. A similar imbalance is found in the regions of the north-east, Veneto and Trentino-Alto Adige. Veneto, in particular, has long supplied the rest of the Po plain with farmers to such an extent that its equilibrium is permanently endangered.

Conversely, five other regions, Val d'Aosta, Piedmont, Emilia-Romagna, Tuscany and Umbria, enjoy a moderately positive surplus where a steady influx of migrants is enough to make good the shortfall in natural increase. Even here, nuances must be recognised, especially in the case of Piedmont, where the province of Turin displays similar characteristics to those of Lombardy, while Cuneo and Asti have completely negative indices. This is also the problem of the so-called central regions of Tuscany, Umbria and Emilia-Romagna, which seem to be the most disturbing because of their signs of a rapidly ageing population.

Nevertheless, they still have a long way to go before reaching the dire situation of the 'graveyard' provinces of Friuli and Liguria where even the flow of relatively numerous immigrants does not manage to cover up the disastrously low natural increase. As a tangible sign of this decline, the growth rate of even the large cities is either very slow (Genoa) or negligible (Trieste). It is in these two regions that the demographic crisis symptomatic of modern Italy is most acutely felt, for it is not occurring in an isolated and poorly endowed region, but in a coastal one with ports and one which figures high on the list of those with an active economy.

All in all, what a strange picture of a country beset, on the one hand, by demographic vitality without an adequate economic base and, on the other hand, sapped by a crisis in the birth-rate, whose proportions are often more severe than in other similarly rich countries! Clearly, this disequilibrium is corrected nationally by the migrations, but is this a satisfactory solution? Quite apart from the possibility of a demographic 'drying up' which could strike the areas of emigration, one would do well to mention the uprootedness which many southerners experience. Their fate is that of all migrant workers: frequent uncertainty of employment; housing problems which put the slums of Turin in the same league as the *bassi* of Naples; the problem of children who are educated in the streets; the problem of women unable to cope with a social organisation that remains foreign to them; the problem of men, peasants or day labourers, resignedly accepting the discipline of the work place. And all of them, foreigners in their own country, recognisable by their height, skin colouring and accents. The rate of crime rises in the large cities of the North with the arrival of southerners who are disliked but indispensable. It is not easy to see how this marginalisation, not to speak of the segregation, could lessen in the foreseeable future.

Not everything is gloomy in this picture: remittances to the southern provinces ought to be mentioned; the retired and their pensions; and the new houses which are being constructed everywhere in otherwise unrewarding rural regions.

Ill-adapted life-styles

Towns and villages are places of production and spatial organisation, as well as landscapes and life-styles, and must be examined as such, that is, as the outcome of successive compromises between society and the physical environment in which it is situated. It goes without saying that the clear-cut distinction between town and country is only one of convenience, particularly in a country where the countryside reflects more the shortcomings and impetus of the city in the past and the present than physical constraints.

The countryside: towards the end of the *bel paesaggio*

Certainly physical constraints have largely fashioned Italian landscapes, but this theme has been so often discussed that we need not dwell upon it, especially as Sereni (1962) has shown the relativity of these constraints in terms of the spatial organisation of societies, which are mostly urban, and whose past activities still perpetuate the maintenance of obsolete systems.

Relative influence of physical constraints

Problems of planning in Italy, particularly land settlement, revolve around three key elements – climate, slope and marshes – whose influence is not separate, but complexly interrelated, due to their frequent juxtaposition.

A dual problem of irrigation and drainage arises in the marshes, and more specifically concerns the difficulty of controlling the flow of water in the low-lying plains at the foot of steep slopes where the streams fan out. Without appropriate schemes these *maremme* are malaria infested and unfit to be used as wet pastures or as wheatfields, whatever their natural fertility. But these improvements require capital, labour and technology. Above all, it needs an equitable division between pastoralists and peasants and a constant vigilance against external encroachment, which usually signals the return to a marshy state. It goes without saying that such improvements, including a developed collective organisation, are beyond the capability of groups of farmers. They imply the means and ability to organise effectively on a large scale – something which is only within the power of urban-based society.

Urban impetus and stagnation

The problem of slopes is apparently less complex in that its treatment – terracing – is widespread. Terracing demands more work than capital and techniques. Even so, it seems that such improvements historically have gone together in the Italian countryside with the cultivation of commercial crops, mainly vines and olives. And this development is indissociably related to urban centres as providers of capital and markets.

More generally, the relief is commonly divided into small basins, or mountains and plains separated by benches. Such a pattern posed the problem of an equitable allocation between those raising sheep and the cereal farmers. Often, the more mobile and better-organised shepherd was able to impose his demands for grazing land – pasture, even cereals, but not trees. One realises immediately the role that cities like Florence could play in this situation in their demand for wheat and wool. It was they who imposed an often complex organisation on the agricultural landscape of central Italy, in spite of problems deriving from the physical environment and the Mediterranean climate. In certain Italian landscapes, such as those of Umbria, of Naples, and of many other regions with long-standing urban traditions, everything attests to the power of cities and their organisation.

Apart from the imprint of the Romans, still visible in the divisions derived from their land survey, one can give credit to the relationship between town and country for the shaping of classical landscapes in Lombardy and Umbria, the latter illustrated by Lorezetti's fresco, *Good Government*, an inventory as meticulous as that which inspired the well-ordered landscape of the sixteenth century. The characteristics of a harmonious equilibrium between town and country clearly showed through, particularly the free and safe movement along good roads between the town and its surrounding concentric circles: first watered gardens and vines, then cultivated fields, open fields and further out, a sort of frontier where castles and large properties replaced the dispersed buildings of share-croppers belonging to the urban bourgeoisie. The Lombardy plain had known a still more advanced development from the twelfth to fifteenth centuries with the division between dry uplands and lowlands which were drained, irrigated and divided into enormous farms with interior courtyards (*corte*), the model of which was to be diffused as far as Emilia and Veneto.

Different, yet equally productive landscapes, are to be found more or less around large Italian cities, including Naples which was equipped in the Middle Ages with the first good road system, providing the city with supplies from a largely irrigated hinterland (*agro*), divided into numerous little plots where fields were combined with gardens. In the eighteenth century a wider network of roads linked the foremost Mediterranean city to areas which supplied it with wheat (Apulia) and wool and meat (the Abruzzi).

Finally, we mention those landscapes, constructed not at a city or regional level, but at a progressively enlarged and national dimension. These are the zones of land reclamation, which in our age reveal the continuation of a beneficent osmosis between town and country.

Continuity in time but hardly continuity in space. In the light of these spatial developments, it is necessary to evaluate the role of the southern regions, where a feudal system of poorly cultivated, large properties, based on a cycle of wheat and sheep, continued or was strengthened until the beginning of agrarian reform. Thus Calabria and the uplands of Basilicata regressed under the feudal rule of the Sanserverino, Carafa and others. The same system occurred in a good part of Sicily where the latifundia buts on to the urban gardens of Catania and Palermo. In Sardinia, it was not the latifundia but the shepherds who enforced lengthy fallow periods, the absence of trees and a reduction in cereal cultivation.

Discontinuity exists in space as well as time. Italy has seen periods of prosperity and stability succeed each other, under Greek colonisation, the Roman Empire, and in the early stages of the Renaissance. These periods of stability, varying in time and space, essentially defined the *bel paessaggio* but they never lasted, either for political reasons (invasions, decline of the city-state), or economic ones (notably the decline beginning with the shifting of trade from the Mediterranean to the Atlantic, and, three centuries later, the opening up of the internal market to agricultural imports in the 1880s). Without fear of contradiction, we can say that for many Italian regions the present period corresponds to one of these crises of rural society, manifested in the landscape.

Outdated systems

If, indeed, there are regions which have adapted to modern forms of agricultural production, mainly those in the Po plain and certain regions of specialised production such as the vineyards of Apulia, signs of maladjustment and decay spread yearly to new areas. The main reason for functional maladjustment is certainly the growth in population between the establishment of the nation and the end of the Second World War, a period during which smallholdings and share-cropping were divided, while arable land was extended beyond reasonable limits in the central mountainous zone down the length of the Apennines. Too fragmented and unrewarding, many holdings were later abandoned due to the lure of urban areas, especially after the Second World War.

Some attempts at change have only resulted in accelerating the pace of decline. Efforts to mechanise agriculture on poor soils in areas of rugged relief – for example, the *calanchi* of the northern Apennines and the *bolge* of Teramo – have produced erosion and clay landslides (*frane*).

It is not only marginal lands which have not been able to keep up with changes in agricultural techniques and methods. Even prosperous regions have begun to show signs of maladjustment and permanent decline. This is the case of a good part of Emilia where land is cultivated under the system of *coltura promiscua*, that is, arrangement on the same plot of arable crops, rows of vines and lines of trees. The land is difficult to work with tractors, but is well adapted to the Mediterranean climate both ecologically (reduction of sunshine reaching the soil) and economically (increase of harvests and corresponding reduction of disastrous seasons for the same plot). One must, therefore, be resigned to destroying the *filari* by pulling out rows of trees and vines, yet, at the same time, the overall structural equilibrium of farms, that are only just average, is at stake.

The same signs of decline are present in coastal areas and with vineyards on the slopes which can no longer maintain their terraced plots with anything less than highly profitable products (vineyards producing quality wine, flowers), needing more labour and commercialisation than mechanisation. But, even here, attempts at modernisation, such as ploughing with winches on terraces that have been levelled, rapidly turn out to be disastrous.

Even towns, which had previously created rich landscape and residential zones at their periphery, now frequently destroy these products in their present stage of expansion. Urbanisation, following a period of social fallow, has particularly affected the area around Milan with its magnificent irrigated fields. Even more so, in the area surrounding Naples, urban growth has disrupted the irrigation system leading to the replacement of the lovely gardens described by Sion (1934) with non-irrigated agriculture which here is totally out of place.

An inventory

This term is the right one, for inventories are necessary in cases of death and before liquidation of stock. Although over-simplifying, it allows one to distinguish the main landscapes cartographically and geographically (Fig. 2.3). In any case, whether these landscapes have adjusted, have shown a capacity to do so, or are in the process of disappearing, they remain Mediterranean in their ever-present diversity and their fragmentation into small areas.

Alpine and mountainous landscapes

These are typified by an altitudinal progression of vegetation and agricultural zones, and especially in the Alps, the presence of a zone of chestnut trees, multiplication of settlements and the concentration of agricultural activity in valleys and basins. Intensity of pastoral activity depends on the quality and extent of common lands. One can distinguish an Alpine system, where valleys and high mountain pastures play a central part, and an Apennine system, where basins under agriculture are more important and the transition to the Umbrian type of landscape (see below) is often imperceptible.

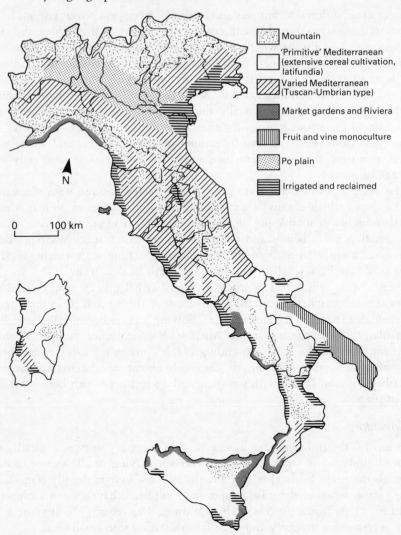

Mountain

'Primitive' Mediterranean
(extensive cereal cultivation,
latifundia)

Varied Mediterranean
(Tuscan-Umbrian type)

Market gardens and Riviera

Fruit and vine monoculture

Po plain

Irrigated and reclaimed

N

0   100 km

Fig. 2.3 Agrarian landscapes

Original Mediterranean landscapes

These exist where a rotation of fallow land and wheat is combined with sheep-
raising in the same area, although the two are not always undertaken by the
same group – a situation which explains the continuing conflicts described by
Le Lannou (1941) in Sardinia. Most of these extensively cultivated zones,
especially in Sicily and Basilicata, have been abandoned to such an extent that
even the pastoralists are now leaving the most difficult areas. Nevertheless,
it is possible to distinguish sub-types of landscapes: the Sardinian type with

its enclosed plots of land (*tancas*) and a spatial domination by pastoralists who often only tolerate an unstable cereal cultivation; and the Basilicatan type with large latifundist landlords who were at the root of the deforestation of pastoral lands in the eighteenth century and the maintenance of landless peasants and smallholders in vast, purely agricultural agro-towns.

Umbrian and Tuscan types of Mediterranean landscape

These are characterised by a more or less dispersed settlement pattern, division of the land into numerous small properties, with several large modern estates in zones which are isolated or were reclaimed a long time ago (Fucino, Val di Chiana). Even here, there are numerous sub-types, which vary according to settlement pattern, importance of trees in the property, and so on. In the south of the plains of Emilia-Romagna, the flatness of the land and the quality of the agriculture mean that a landscape of the *coltura promiscua* type forms a successful transition with the Po valley agriculture.

Riviera and Mediterranean gardens

These are like the Spanish *huerta* and are characterised by their small size, intensive production and highly commercialised marketing. Originally the two types were more differentiated: Riviera gardens were coastal and terraced; Mediterranean gardens were oriented to urban markets, town and *orto* creating a remarkably successful symbiosis in Naples, Palermo, Catania, etc. Now these differences are becoming less marked as the connection between town and *orto* lessens; the same type of crops (citrus, flowers) are found in both areas; hothouses and irrigation are spreading. The most typical landscapes, those of the Ligurian Riviera, Amalfi coast, Naples and Sicily, constitute enviable, but unstable, successes. Urban expansion, restricted space and steep slopes must be compensated by the value of the produce, good marketing and the incorporation of technical advances. What then is the future of these landscapes?

Monocultural landscapes

These are relatively rare in Italy where extreme specialisation is not always a guarantee of success. Among regions of monoculture, Apulia is the most striking in its extent and juxtaposition of several specialised areas – vineyards, table grapes, olives. Olives are also found in large areas of Calabria, while vineyards are found in Tuscany (Chianti), Piedmont (Asti) and Sicily (Marsala). Perhaps one could add to these specialised areas the orchards between Ferrara and Verona, which in many ways resemble the agricultural regime of the Po valley.

The Po river landscapes

Far from forming a homogeneous whole, the agrarian landscapes of the Po plain are of very different types: ricefields in Lomellina, irrigated fields (*mar-*

cite) in Lombardy, orchards in the Basso Veronese, and a complex rotation system, based mainly on corn and sugar-beet, in Emilia. Nor is there any greater uniformity in terms of agrarian structures, for medium-sized holdings exist side by side with large *aziende* with capital invested by industry. But these numerous regions and types of holdings do share some traits, namely those related to water management, degree of contact with towns, high level of mechanisation and the use of large quantities of fertiliser. In short, these well-ordered landscapes, of a rational, even industrial, appearance, present a singular contrast with those seen elsewhere in Italy.

Irrigated areas

Although spatially dispersed, these landscapes have in common flat land, scattered settlement and ubiquitous water channels. They cover 3.5 million hectares. Here again the uniformity of the landscape should not blind us to the diversity of systems, for this type includes large capitalist enterprises and the major part of the lands developed under the agrarian reforms. Each of these types is having problems with rationalisation and spatial rigidity of land use; a far cry from the diversity of the Umbrian landscapes. Nevertheless, these irrigated areas come closest to a present-day example of the *bel paesaggio*.

The cities: a crisis of growth or of society as a whole?

The population at the end of 1977 included more than 30 million, 53.5 per cent of the total population, living in settlements with more than 20,000 inhabitants. This striking percentage is quite usual in the present era in which national values give priority to urban life through large meetings, be they sporting or social – as in the ritual of the *passeggiata*. This tendency towards spatial concentration, extending even to farmers, poses formidable problems for the increase in numbers – the proportion of inhabitants in settlements with over 20,000 was only 35 per cent in 1936. Furthermore, suburban municipalities were then still rare due to the large size of the central municipalities, so the increase in the urban population from before the war, taking into account the growth of dormitory towns, is 18 million rather than the 13 million suggested by the statistics. What urban tradition could withstand such an influx? There is nothing astonishing if the problem of growth is coupled with one of acculturation. The complexity of the resulting situation is further aggravated by an urban planning problem that is specifically Italian: the need to administer a very rich architectural heritage, whose integration into a modern urban life-style often seems difficult and sometimes impossible.

The vitality of cities

Despite migration, the growth of Italian settlement has remained fairly close to an inherited pattern, related to age-old political divisions which favour the maintenance of the ancient small capitals, still at a high order in the urban hierarchy. Corresponding to this is the fact that the difference in population size between the capital and the major provincial cities is less than that in most European countries. Rome does not have a population double that of Milan, while Paris is seven and a half times that of the next city, Lyons. Another unique feature of the urban system is that one cannot establish a clear correlation, as in France, between degree of urbanisation, industrialisation and economic activity. The population of towns with more than 20,000 inhabitants represents 61 per cent of the total in the islands, 59 per cent in the South and 65 per cent in the Centre (which includes Latium); it is only 48 per cent in the North, which contains most of the productive capacity of the country.

There is also the same tendency towards a fairly similar degree of population increase in towns of over 50,000 inhabitants during the period 1961–77 (Fig. 2.4). First of all, it can be noted that among the 12 provincial capitals of less than 50,000 people, 4 are situated in the Alps, 5 in the Apennines and 3 in the islands. The same widespread pattern from north to south holds true for those towns which are stagnating or only growing slowly; if one includes in this list all the Sicilian towns, with the exception of Syracuse, one equally finds a good number in central Italy between Ancona and La Spezia, including Florence and Lucca, and also towns in the North, some of which are medium-sized, such as Ferrara and Cremona, others of major importance, such as Genoa and, above all, Trieste, whose population is stagnating without the slightest expansion into the non-existent suburbs. Finally, the distribution of the most rapidly growing towns displays the same dispersion from Trento to Taranto, including many towns in central Italy, of which the most remarkable is definitely Latina, until recently situated too far from Rome to be incorporated into an outlying suburb.

In this list, the three largest cities occupy a special position to the extent that only Rome gives the impression of an unusual dynamism with a growth rate of 32 per cent in sixteen years. This anomaly is because the city boundary embraces suburban municipalities. On the other hand, Naples, Milan, Turin, and to a lesser degree, Venice and Bologna, which have less extensive municipal limits, remain stable or appear to lose part of their population. This is explained by the traditional urban centres recording losses, whereas the increases for the outer conurbations are ignored because these districts do not lie within municipal limits as in most other countries. The explanation can be applied to Venice whose conurbation really grew from 400,000 to almost 500,000 inhabitants, but where the flight from the historic centre (now less than 60,000) leaves the impression of stagnation described above.

Are there no other major differences among Italian cities? On the whole, no. From this one concludes that if the Mezzogiorno is tending to depopulate slowly, the towns, with the clear exception of some Sicilian ones, are not following this trend and constitute poles of attraction for migrants from the surrounding countryside. But it could well be that this situation is only temporary, a transitional period in a cycle of long-term decline.

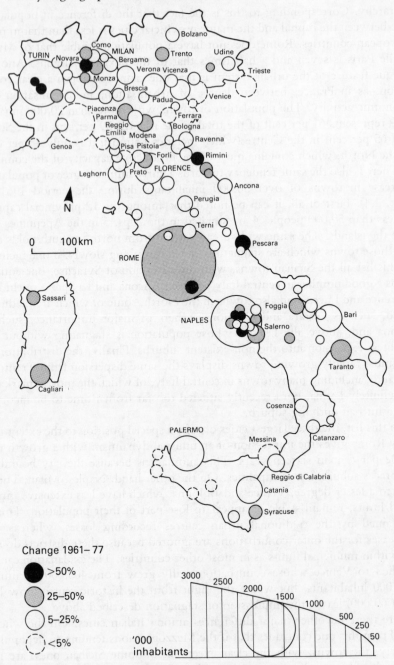

Fig. 2.4 Size and growth of towns of more than 50,000 inhabitants

The essential difference, beyond an analysis in terms of function and hierarchy, does not lie here, but rather in the urban system. The towns of the Po plain tend to form a sort of megalopolis or, at least, a zone of high densities extending between Turin, Ravenna and Treviso. Another urban network, less dense and dynamic, but perfectly coherent, occurs around Florence. Nothing similar appears further south, where Rome, Taranto, Bari and Syracuse rise up, without any transition, from a strikingly lifeless countryside. Only Naples reproduces some semblance of the northern network, though in a less dense system. This overall difference is not negated by the example of Naples; it reveals the two urban systems dividing Italy. The boundary between them coincides approximately with the previously mentioned distinction between countrysides that have enjoyed the benefits of urban influence and those that have suffered from urban shortcomings and stagnation. Thus it is a question of a cultural boundary, yet also one between a dominating and a dominated system.

The problem of a heritage

Italy has the rare and difficult privilege of possessing an urban archaeological heritage covering all regions and historical epochs. An inventory of urban Italy should have two aims: firstly to show that the typology of Italian cities is much greater and more complex than the tourist thinks, for one needs to include new towns, ranging from Trieste, begun in 1719 by the Austrians, to Latina, founded in 1932 and showing in a small area the basic features of Fascist architecture; secondly, to emphasise the varying fortunes undergone by nearly all cities, and instancing first that of Rome, the Eternal City, which has known an almost total eclipse and whose future is not at all certain. In this list must be included Venice, in the process of disintegrating, Trieste, which has lost its hinterland, Turin and Florence, once capitals of Italy, and Palermo, one of the greatest cities during the time of the Crusades.

All the same, several themes stand out in this set of archaeological and urban facts. One of them again contrasts, from a cultural perspective, the towns of northern Italy, which assign importance to civic architecture, with the feudal cities of the Mezzogiorno, where the buildings of interest are divided between the cathedral and the feudal monuments – the fortified castle and the prince's palace. Florentine and Neapolitan urbanism can also be profitably compared. All these cities have in common certain architectural features such as arcade-lined streets.

Apart from the cultural aspects, three types of cities can be contrasted in terms of the problems resulting from historic centres. The first type corresponds to small cities rich in a prestigious past, but which have lost all dynamism, such as Assisi and Urbino. These cities face not so much problems of adaptation, but that of conservation and use of an archaeological heritage. The second type, fairly uncommon in Italy, where urban and historic centres have coincided with surprising persistence, corresponds to cities with modern areas which are clearly distinct from the historic centre. The most notable of these is Venice, whose population has progressively moved to firm ground where places of work have been established and the cost of living is cheaper, leaving the noble city, now more and more deserted, to tourists and hoteliers. Thirdly, there remains the vast majority of living cities with extensive and complex historic centres that have to adapt for better (prestige and tourism) or for worse (traffic, health, high densities, deterioration).

Sometimes councillors propose rather original architectural solutions for these traditional problems. In Genoa the gardens of the former palace have been incorporated into the public land in the Via Garibaldi, giving a surprising freshness to the ancient core of this congested city. In Bologna as well, the current municipality is trying, within its limited budget, to prevent the abandonment of the centre which results from the replacement of residences by offices and by land speculation in which the rich replace the less wealthy groups of artisans and workers. The area of San Lazzaro demonstrates rather well the fruitful results of this gamble, which involves the scrupulous renovation of the architectural heritage, while guaranteeing the original inhabitants their accommodation.

The realisation of the historic value of the centre revealed in these projects is, however, tardy. The history of the centre of Italian cities since the Risorgimento is concerned with sacrifices rather than with praise. The transfer of the capital to Florence, and then to Rome, served principally as pretexts to carry through Hausmann-type developments, a model which was subsequently widely diffused. The long arteries, everywhere lined by the residences of the bourgeoisie, where the Via Garibaldi crosses the Via Mazzini before emerging at the Corso Vittorio-Emmanuele, are the results of this development. These schemes, carried out for aesthetic purposes and sanitation, have often destroyed old quarters of considerable archaeological interest and have produced an almost unimaginable speculation in land and buildings. However, one cannot totally condemn all these schemes; the creation of the Rettifilio in Naples, a long artery that opened up the worst *bassi* or working-class quarters, occurred as a result of a sanitation scheme considered inevitable after the cholera epidemic which swept through the city in 1885. The only problem is to know why those thrown out were not rehoused instead of contributing to the creation of the excessively high densities which have plagued the city ever since.

This mixture of aestheticism, functional urbanism and various forms of speculation is again encountered in the urban planning of the Mussolini period which profoundly modified many Italian cities in the inter-war years and, even later, during the post-war reconstruction. It was an aestheticism that emphasised an architectural style which combined in a somewhat static way long façades and what are termed Roman arches, and alternated stately materials, such as marble and cut stone, with brick. It was a period of urbanism in which many historic centres were renovated, especially Rome, where the Forum was given a clear perspective and integrated into the urban landscape. A number of roads were driven through – the Corso Vittorio-Emmanuele II and then, after the Second World War, the Via della Consiliazione: projects that were part of the baroque heritage and less highly considered than those of the Roman heritage. Finally, speculation occurred not only for profit motives but also for political ends, as witnessed by the expulsion of the reputedly unruly inner-urban populace and its dumping in Rome, Turin and Milan at the out-lying periphery where the monotonous architecture did not always ensure the hygienic conditions and comforts promised to those who were shifted. Thus the ex-urban *borgate* of Rome lose nothing in comparison to the slums of London or those which previously existed in Paris.

Despite the diversity of each case and the ideas associated with each period, one cannot fail to be struck by the contrast between the variety of urban landscapes of the periods until the baroque and the subsequent uniformity of architectural styles adopted from one end of the peninsula to the other from the time of the formation of the new State. The same, more or less successful imitation of the Grand Gallery in Milan, is to be found in Turin, Rome and Naples, and identical streets bear identical names everywhere. The same uniformity recurs in official statues, as in the squares constructed during the Mussolini period. It appears, then, that for a century now Italian urbanism has rigorously copied stereotypes with a fidelity rarely encountered elsewhere: possibly a logical solution to the extent that it expresses visually a long sought after political unity that has been difficult to achieve. Yet it is also a regrettable course of action in the uniform façades that it has plastered, not only over many central areas, but also over the whole urban expansion, itself too architecturally boring and of mediocre quality to be capable of facilitating the process of assimilation, which could have eased the problems of massive urbanisation facing Italy. Can this possibly be interpreted as one of the elements of the current urban crisis?

The current urban crisis

That the concept of crisis in contemporary urbanism needs to be added to the stock of new ideas, no one will dispute. But the feeling that this crisis is more acutely felt in Italy than in other countries is an accepted fact, as shown by the audience of Italian radicalism, by the action of the Red Brigade, or even simply the increase in criminality. How is it that Italians, after having imagined visually the nature of the ideal city, have come to experience the tragic megalopolis?

Undoubtedly, this feeling of decay owes much to the continuing, if not worsening, poverty of southern cities. A child born at present in Naples has a 7 per cent chance of not reaching the age of 1, a 1 in 5 chance of remaining illiterate and little more than a 1 in 2 chance of not finding work at the age of 20. There is hardly any future for these children of the *bassi* other than to enter into crime or prostitution. Houses still collapse after each rainfall and the last cholera epidemic broke out as recently as 1973. The picture that could be painted of Palermo or many other large cities, including the industrial city of Taranto, would not be very different.

All this is too well known, and dare one say it, too commonplace to stir anyone, least of all northern Italians. On the other hand, what is novel is the spread of these social problems to the whole of Italy, leading in reality to the 'southernisation' of the large northern cities, as highlighted by Novelli, the mayor of Turin. In a 1977 interview he said: 'this city, having become a southern city, has acquired a southern mentality based on clientelistic relationships and revolving around the two poles of the church and the town-hall tower. This mentality has an incredible influence on patterns of behaviour'. Of course, this is the mixing so much wished for by the architects of the Risorgimento, though they did not foresee it in this debased form, where the northern regions have lost both their spirit and identity.

The wretched departure of southerners northward would not be the sole reason for this state of affairs; blame must be equally apportioned to the chaotic mode of urban expansion. Since 1942 this expansion has been covered by planning regulations which, in theory, must be observed. But, in practice, legislation was only passed much later, for example in 1964 in Rome and in 1972 in Naples, thus leaving sufficient time for property speculators to operate. Subsequently, certain pieces of legislation were implemented in an attempt to put some order into the particularly anarchic development in the years of the 'Italian miracle'. This applied notably to Law 167 (1962) which allowed municipal authorities to push through compulsory purchase orders for the construction of council housing. Unfortunately, the Constitutional Court virtually negated the spirit and impact of the Law by fixing prices of the expropriated land in line with market prices. This explains why, of the 5,000 hectares defined in 1964 as expropriable in Rome, only 30 hectares were acquired by the city for the construction of council housing. Other legislation which could have been effective has suffered the same fate, particularly Law 765 (1967) with which it was planned to levy a value added tax on land outside the urban boundary that was to become building land. All that was needed to find a way around the law, was to institute a moratorium during which time a sufficient volume of precautionary transactions were made to keep property developers in business for many years.

These are only some of the examples to which one can add 'the putting in order' on the eve of municipal elections and many other skilful moves in which collusion was less overt. These practices have in all instances produced a widening gap between the development of choice sites (Pausilippo in Naples and Monte Mario in Rome) on the one hand, and the spread of vast peripheral estates where the mediocre quality of the housing is far from being made up for by the provision of educational, social and hospital services. Even so, this is the lesser of evils compared to the proliferation of *borghetti* and other shanty towns where the poorest migrants crowd in, while waiting to acquire the urban status which would give them work and housing. In the end, after long years of patient waiting, this results in violent rejection and contestation of a social system, judged to be antiquated and unfair. A system that is ill-adapted to the problems of our time.

3 Economic transformation and disequilibrium

The 'Italian miracle', now only a memory of a bygone era during which national income doubled in the space of twelve years between 1951 and 1963, is no longer spoken about. This performance (in fact equalled by many other countries) was the more remarkable in that it followed a long period of average performance during which there were numerous changes in economic policy. The national income, starting from a fairly modest level, had doubled between 1861 and 1916, a period of 55 years; subsequently, it had taken 38 years to double again between 1916 and 1954.

The years of the economic miracle, though a break with the period of average performance, could be said to coincide with a propitious economic climate. Italy certainly knew how to get the best out of the years after the Second World War by taking advantage of the opportunities offered by the Marshall Plan and European integration. But, in the framework of these institutions, it benefited, in comparison with its Common Market partners, from a good labour supply. It had a plentiful and cheap labour force whose employment, at least in the industrial sector, permitted an accumulation of capital which was at the root of the profound transformation of the economic system.

This phase of rapid development now seems past, if only because of the integration of the Italian economy into a wider system, now in a state of crisis whose severity goes beyond simple changes in economic conditions. It is worth remembering that the main impetus of this past development has slowed down since salary increases are greater in Italy than in the majority of European countries (an index of 179 (a base of 100 in 1975) in 1978 as against 145 in France, 119 in West Germany, etc). Despite this evolution, the ups and downs of the economy and the breakdown of government, the Italian economy is managing fairly well. From a base index of 100 in 1975, its index of industrial production reached 113 in 1978, a level comparable to that of West Germany and France and much higher than that of the Netherlands and Great Britain.

However, this impression needs to be modified in the light of several other criteria of performance such as GNP which was valued at 193,000 million dollars as against 469,000 million in West Germany and 376,000 million in France. This figure places Italy sixth in the list of OECD countries, though with a *per capita* income of 3,500 dollars it can be seen to be in a fairly average position.

Inadequate natural resources

If the view that wealth resides only in manpower is correct, then Italy is well provided. Otherwise, it lacks resources, a fact that has held back its economic development. On the other hand, there are few other countries which have managed so well to extract the best from the natural resources they possess.

Problems of renewable resources

As in all Mediterranean countries, Italy faces a problem of soil conservation. The parent soil is basically composed of rendzinas and lithosoils in the Alps, of fluvial alluvia interspersed with large areas of hydromorphic soils in the Po valley plain and along the lower slopes of hillsides, brown Mediterranean soils in the greater part of the peninsula, and *terra rossa* in eastern Apulia which, as we have seen, are of mediocre quality and vulnerable. This potential has been very unequally preserved: *coltura promiscua*, terracing and drainage improvements have developed certain soils to the maximum, depending on investment by farmers and the interest of urban centres. But the application of these methods has, especially in Apennine regions, encountered two obstacles, those of slope and lithology (scaly clays and zones of landslips). Overgrazing, transhumance and excessive extension of cultivation at the time of demographic growth have caused the deterioration of fragile soils and consequent rampant erosion.

Soil deterioration and expansion of uncultivated areas are also at the root of the recent increase in woodland which now covers 6.3 million hectares compared to 5 million at the beginning of the century. The value and potential use of this cover, now extending to 20 per cent of the territory, is still uneven. Timber stands in the Alps are rarely matched in the rest of peninsula, with the exception of certain considerable ones in Tuscany and Sila. Usually the scale of production in the southern regions does not go beyond clearing and thinning out and the artisanal manufacture of charcoal.

The last aspect of this evaluation of renewable natural resources is the availability of water, which is distributed unevenly from north to south in the peninsula in the same way as soils and forests. Theoretically, the basic equation relating to water potential on a national level is fairly encouraging, that is: precipitation (999 mm/year) – evaporation (480 mm/year) – flow (519 mm/year). This is equivalent to a coefficient of discharge of 0.52 and an average availability of 16.3 litres per second per sq. kilometre, or a potential of 2,770 cubic metres per inhabitant per year, an amount clearly greater than that of other Mediterranean peninsulas.

Examined in terms of macroregions, this figure, however, highlights basic inequalities (Table 3.1)

Clearly, regional inequalities are accentuated by the more favourable river regimes in the North (higher summer rates of flow) than in the South, where there is a marked shortfall between the period of maximum flow in winter and maximum demand in summer. Of course, a considerable amount is stored (7,720 hm³ stored in 444 reservoirs), but the coefficient of water stored (34%) is almost the same in the Alps as in the islands.

Taking into account this index of storage and the need to maintain a minimum flow, the resources of each region are distributed as shown in Table 3.2. At first glance, this supply seems roughly to satisfy the different sources of demand which have been approximately assessed for 1980 in Table 3.3.

Naturally, these average calculations only take partial account of the needs during peak periods which are very important in the agricultural sector. The very serious problem, above all for the Mezzogiorno, is to know whether the current and projected provision will be able to satisfy future agricultural demand.

Mineral resources – more varied than abundant

There is nothing more impressive than the list of extractive industries – iron in the island of Elba and the Val di Cogne, bauxite in Apulia, antimony in Sardinia, manganese in Piedmont, mercury in Monte Amiata in Tuscany, lead and zinc in the region of Iglesias, asbestos in Piedmont and Val Malengo, sulphur in Sicily, rock and sea salt, etc. Unfortunately, many of these deposits, having had an acknowledged importance during the pre-industrial period as well as more recently, as was the case with sulphur, no longer have much economic significance. This is especially true for iron deposits, which barely provide 478,000 tons of metal, and sulphur whose production has fallen to 600,000 tons. After some limited exports, the quantity of manganese is not enough for national demands. As for bauxite, despite a production of 35,000 tons per annum, its significance is declining yearly. The only minerals of some consequence are zinc (170,000 tons), pyrites (860,000 tons), salt, asbestos and, above all, mercury, of which Italy is the second largest producer in the world (300,000 tons).

Seriously deficient energy resources

A list of fossil-based resources is easily made. For a long time these were limited to lignite in Sulcis and peat in Tuscany, with a small anthracite deposit at La Thuile: together these yield an annual production of 1.8 million tons.

Table 3.1   Surface water resources

Zone	'000 million cubic metres	%
North	81.8	52.8
Centre	30.1	19.4
South	31.1	20.7
Sicily	4.9	3.2
Sardinia	6.1	3.9
National	154.0	100.0

Table 3.2   Consumption of surface water resources (in '000 million m³)

Zone	Domestic and industrial	Agricultural consumption
North	32.4	26.9
Centre	2.8	2.9
South	14.1	5.7
Sicily	0.6	0.6
Sardinia	1.6	2.0
National	51.5	38.1

Table 3.3   Evaluation of water requirements by sectors and regions ('000 million m³)

	Domestic	Industrial	Agricultural
North	2.7–3.7	3.4–4	22.5
Centre	1.2–1.6	0.8–1.0	2.1
South, Islands	2.2–2.9	0.8–1.0	7.6
Total	6–8	5–6	32.2

Fossil fuels increased after the Second World War when oilfields were discovered, but these, distributed in the Po plain (Cortemaggiore), Abruzzi (asphalt of Alanno),Calabria and Sicily (Ragusa, Gela), hardly produce 1 million tons of hydrocarbons. On the other hand, the production of natural gas from these same deposits reaches almost 14,000 million cubic metres.

For some time the deficiency of fossil fuels has been balanced by the development of hydroelectric power, mainly concentrated in the Alps. At present, there is a capacity of 15,500 MW with an average annual production of 52 TWh. Despite the considerable amount, the proportion of hydroelectric power in total energy resources has been declining. In 1957 it attained the remarkable proportion of 75 per cent (32 TWh out of the national electricity production of 42 TWh). In 1977 it accounted for no more than a third of a total consumption of 166 TWh (Table 3.4).

In all likelihood, the proportion of geothermal energy produced at the Larderello and Castelnuovo power stations, will not increase significantly. Hydroelectric projects will by 1987 provide no more than an extra 10 thousand million kWh. The development of nuclear energy (in dispute since 1963, when

Table 3.4   Sources of electricity generation, 1977

Type of energy	Production (million Wh)	%
HEP	52,800	31.7
Thermal	108,000	64.8
Geothermal	2,500	1.5
Nuclear	3,334	2.0
TOTAL	166,700	100.0

Trino, Latina, Garigliano and, above all, Tavazanno stations provided 3.5 TWh) depends on political decisions about a plan for 12 nuclear power stations with a total capacity of 11,000 MW.

This outline of the energy picture shows that the foreseeable demand in years to come will only be satisfied by traditional thermal power stations. Yet these stations run on oil for which Italy has great difficulty in paying. In 1973 imports of crude oil reached 132 million tons bought for 2,150 thousand million lire, or an eighth of all imports; in 1977 these imports were reduced to 103 million tons, but cost 10,300 thousand million lire, which represented a quarter of all imports. Dependence on imported energy reached 83 per cent in 1975, and it is predicted to reach 90 per cent in 1985, with imports of petrol expected to make up the difference in demand. This impasse seems inescapable and serious, the more so as Italy's economic development has, for a number of years, been associated with a policy of freely available oil supplies and the creation of an important petrochemical industry.

It could well be that this phase of economic expansion, based on cheap oil supplies and free world trade, is now in question.

Unequally developed economic structures

The young Italian State, which could have started off with a clean slate, attempted paradoxically to preserve the archaic structures which it inherited. Subsequently, these structures evolved in line with liberal doctrines. But, on the whole, Italy's productive apparatus has juxtaposed new and obsolete elements. This combination created such distortions that the liberal State had to intervene early on in a number of fields, though with variable success. As a result, one still has today the impression of a spatially incoherent economic mosaic.

Agrarian structures: large-scale reforms and small changes

The combination of irrationality and confusion emerges strongly from an examination of agrarian structures. Considering that three agrarian reforms took place between the Baccarini Law (1882) and the series of laws in 1950,

Table 3.5 Evolution of agrarian structures between 1933 and 1975

| Size of holdings | No. | 1933 | | 1975 | | |
		Area	%	No.	Area	% Area
0.5– 5 ha	2,387,000	4,937,000	15.0	1,588,000	3,698,000	16.5
5.0– 10 ha	492,000	3,482,000	13.2	418,297	2,990,000	13.3
10.0– 50 ha	361,000	6,724,000	25.6	325,000	6,365,000	28.3
50.0–100 ha	26,000	1,782,000	6.7	29,051	2,105,000	9.3
>100 ha	21,000	9,127,000	34.7	19,502	7,175,000	32.0
	4,197,000	26,251,000		2,379,502	22,400,000	

including the major piece of legislation on land improvements (*bonifica*) in 1933, it is surprising that land structures have remained so stable (Table 3.5).

The 1933 statistics clearly revealed the tensions which could exist between minifundists and latifundists. On the one hand were 3,790,000 small farmers with holdings of less than 0.5 hectares scattered over one-third of the agricultural land; on the other hand, 47,000 owners held 41 per cent of the land. Between these two extremes, the group of medium-sized farmers, which gave the French peasantry, for example, its influence and character, was literally squeezed out. Nor do these statistics tell anything of the mass of salaried agricultural labourers (3.5 million *braccianti*), few of whom were assured a steady income.

Having said that, one is astonished to find that half a century later large properties have maintained their position and the very small ones increased. A more detailed regional analysis clarifies certain apparent anomalies (see Fig. 3.3. Table 3.9). Many of the large properties in the Alps simply consist of pasture land, while the statistics do not bring out the economic significance of the smallholdings perched on south-facing slopes. Conversely, a good number of holdings in Liguria and Campania can be economically viable with less than 10 hectares. There then remains the considerable mass of very large and very small properties which, in contrast to the Lombardian *fattorie* and Ligurian *orti*, have not much economic *raison d'être*. ISTAT's report which accompanied the last agricultural census in 1970 admitted simply that 97 per cent of properties covering 72 per cent of the agricultural land are not adapted to the present conditions of production and marketing.

With so much obviously still to do, why has so much discussion been devoted to agrarian reform? When the three Land Reform Laws (no. 230 Sila, 841 Stralcio, R. 104 Sicily) were passed in 1950, the legislators and those involved in the operation of reclamation had a good precedent upon which to base their reforms: the Fascist colonisation schemes. An evaluation of the Mussolinian reforms underlined the two major defects of the works undertaken during the 1930s: firstly, the reclaimed lands had been divided into plots of 0.5–1.5 hectares, a size patently incapable of forming viable holdings; secondly, opting for cereal production did not yield sufficient income to pay off debts entered into by the community.

In relation to this last point, a policy was quickly formulated thanks to the action of the *Cassa per il Mezzogiorno*:

1. Reclamation of marshy lands which were systematically provided with irrigation and then oriented mainly towards the production of specialised crops such as sugar beet and fruit trees.

2. The development of the *latifondo* areas with the aim of bringing about a more equitable distribution of land through the acquisition of property by landless peasants.

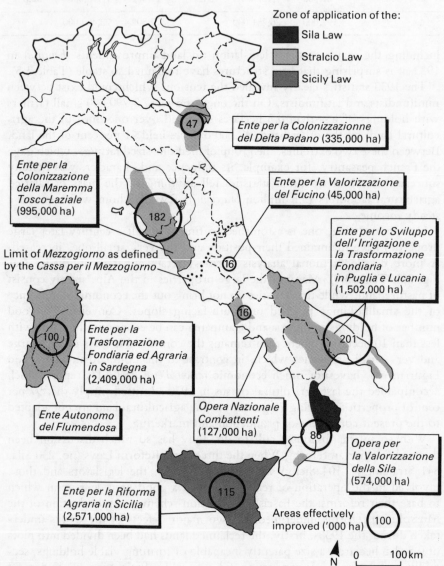

Zone of application of the:

Sila Law

Stralcio Law

Sicily Law

47

Ente per la Colonizzazionne
del Delta Padano (335,000 ha)

Ente per la
Colonizzazione
della Maremma
Tosco-Laziale
(995,000 ha)

Ente per la Valorizzazione
del Fucino (45,000 ha)

182

16

Ente per lo Sviluppo
dell' Irrigazione e
la Trasformazione
Fondiaria
in Puglia e Lucania
(1,502,000 ha)

Limit of *Mezzogiorno* as defined
by the *Cassa per il Mezzogiorno*

16

100

Ente per la
Trasformazione
Fondiaria ed Agraria
in Sardegna
(2,409,000 ha)

201

Ente Autonomo
del Flumendosa

Opera Nazionale
Combattenti
(127,000 ha)

86

Opera per
la Valorizzazione
della Sila
(574,000 ha)

Ente per la Riforma
Agraria in Sicilia
(2,571,000 ha)

115

Areas effectively
improved ('000 ha)   100

N   0   100km

Fig. 3.1 Agrarian reform

3. The development of depopulated mountainous areas through reafforestation and replenishment of the soil as well as changes in the pastoral economy.

This policy has been implemented over a vast area of 8.5 million hectares, 28 per cent of the national territory, and is distributed between the *comprensori di riforma* (Fig. 3.1) in the following way:

(a) 335,000 hectares in the Po delta (Ente per la Colonizzazione del Delta Padano);

(b) 995,000 hectares in the Maremma (Ente Maremma Tosco-Laziale);

(c) 45,000 hectares in the Fucino plain (Ente Fucino) already improved in the nineteenth century through the private initiative of Prince Torlonia;

(d) 127,000 hectares in the Campanian plains of Volturno, Garigliano and Sele (Opera Nazionale Combattenti);

(e) 1,502,000 hectares in Apulia, Lucania and Molise (Ente Apulia-Lucania);

(f) 574,000 hectares in the Calabrian Sila (Opera Valorizzazione Sila);

(g) 2,571,000 hectares in Sicily (Ente Riforma Agraria in Sicilia);

(h) 2,409,000 hectares in Sardinia, split between Ente Sardegna or ETFAS, with Ente Flumendosa (EAF) operating in the Campidano.

However, despite extremely vociferous demands for land, marked by occupation of property and the formation of spontaneous peasant groups, the majority of the reform areas were not systematically redistributed and developed; only those properties producing a taxable income of over 30,000 lire were affected. Even so, their owners could keep 300 hectares if efficiently cultivated, while another regulation exempted from all expropriation those lands which were sufficiently well run to be classified as model farms (what, however, constitutes a model farm?). In any case, the operations of the reform agencies were limited by their financial resources and the need to indemnify the landowners, so that practically all land purchases have ceased since 1960. The total amount of land involved is not much: 767,000 hectares have been acquired and 113,000 properties set up for an investment of 637,500 million lire, that is, at a cost of 800,000 lire per hectare or 5.6 million lire per property. King's (1973) evaluation of the reform is rather harsh. Yet it is difficult to deny that Italy lost a unique opportunity after the end of the Second World War to reorganise her landholdings.

A nebulous industrial structure

In industry the same immobile structures do not recur as in the agricultural sector. Nevertheless, once this undeniable dynamism is accepted, a uniquely constant mixture of archaic and anarchistic traditions, which some large private and state enterprises have attempted to restructure, characterise most sectors. Which of these two tendencies will prevail – lively chaos or a system more in keeping with international norms of business enterprise – is a long-debated problem with no definite answer.

The 1971 census reveals a remarkably large number of firms in relation to the numbers employed: 605,500 firms and 5,373,000 employees in manufacturing industries, to which one must add 4,300 firms and 65,000 employees in extractive industries and 130,000 firms with almost 1 million workers in the construction industry. This dispersed pattern does not contain a high proportion of large enterprises. In the manufacturing sector, 324 firms employ more than 1,000 workers with a total work-force of 1,300,000 as against 1,200,000 in those firms employing less than 10 workers, and 1,500,000 for firms with 10 to 100 workers. Even more surprising is the fact that the number of workers in small and medium-sized firms is expanding more rapidly than those in larger firms: from 1951 to 1975, the largest firms (those with more than 1,000 workers) increased their work-force by more than 400,000, in contrast to the 1 million growth of firms employing fewer than 100. In terms of employment, there exists an undeniable dynamism of the small firm in contrast to a sclerosis among large companies.

The Italian industrial system expanded during the years of the economic miracle when firms settled on the periphery of towns and near motorways and gas pipelines. Located for the most part towards the edges of the Milan–Turin–Genoa industrial triangle, in the direction of Cuneo, Pordenone and Bologna, these firms, initially medium-seized, experienced a rapid growth aided by the availability of a plentiful, semi-rural work-force, and by access to the maintenance, sales service and research expertise of the neighbouring metropolitan areas. The favourable economic climate provided the rest and, within a few years, Italian production of household appliances, furniture, textile machines, etc. rose to prominence on the European market, even at times beating German competitors whose ability to adapt and innovate was less great.

In contrast to the expansion of medium-sized firms, large international firms are very few and are rarely to be found among the leaders as classified by the specialised press. This small group has, however, some striking features. The twenty-five largest firms employ just 10 per cent of the industrial work-force but account for 50 per cent of industrial production. A sectoral analysis (Table 3.6) shows some surprising gaps in aeronautics, mechanical engineering and glass and, on the other hand, some noteworthy successes in cars (Fiat), large-scale semi-public works (IRI), rubber (Pirelli), chemicals (Montedison), hydrocarbons (ENI), steel (Italsider) and textiles (TGF). These variations, and the fact that there is only one real leading firm in most sectors, indicates an industrial structure which has not been fully developed and which has entered too late into a virtually saturated international market. Furthermore, most big firms are at least partially under state control.

Although less important in terms of capital than Montedison, Fiat is rightly considered the most typical of the privately owned Italian firms. A study of its evolution will illustrate some of the basic characteristics of Italian firms and

Table 3.6   Large Italian companies in 1978 (after the *Nouvel Économiste* list of European companies, 1978)

Company	Value (million francs)	No. of employees	Rank in Europe	Branch
Ferrero	2,624,588	5,813	42	Food
Buitoni Perugina	1,717,026	9,545	68	Food
Fiat (Fiat group)	21,590,046	341,693	7	Cars
Alfa Romeo (Finmeccanica IRI)	5,569,927	44,712	16	Cars
Lancia (Fiat group)	2,434,066	10,420	24	Cars
Acritalia (Finmeccanica IRI)	6,269,78	4,480	12	Aeronautical
Italstat (IRI)	4,187,712	23,000	12	Public works
Condotti e acqua (IRI)	1,888,977	10,406	45	Public works
Pirelli (Dunlop-Pirelli)	3,901,327	6,400	5	Tyres
Montedison	29,567,952	51,543	6	Chemicals
Snia Viscosa	4,820,365	34,016	20	Chemicals
IRI Services	77,102,541	524,000	1	Services
Mondadori	1,135,185	5,392	15	Publishing
Olivetti	7,375,777	66,073	10	Electrical
Fiat Meccanica (Fiat group)	71,477,428	—	1	Mechanical
ENI	63,064,788	103,349	3	Oil
Agip (ENI)	28,992,609	8,141	5	Oil
Italsider (IRI)	12,370,654	53,524	8	Metallurgy
Alitalia (IRI)	5,165,746	18,477	32	Transport
Standa	4,197,776	19,000	69	Commerce
IRI group	77,102,541		4	
Fiat group	71,477,498		5	
ENI group	69,064,788			

their economic role. It is worth noting the complex strategies of these firms in their attempts both to integrate and diversify. The presence of Ferriere Fiat in the group indicates an attempt at vertical integration. This firm directly makes 900,000 tons of steel and processes almost 3 million. Another example is the takeover of Magnetti Marelli which makes spark plugs for all Italian cars. In diversifying through horizontal integration, they have extended production to heavy vehicles (Iveco), fork-lift trucks (OM), diesel motors for boats, railway engines, airplane parts (airframes, jet engines), tractors, machine tools and even nuclear material (SIGEW group). This policy of diversification will no doubt be called upon to play a vital role in the coming years in the eventuality of any collapse in the Italian automobile market, of which 92 per cent is held by Fiat. Since 1974 the firm has begun to bolster its truck and construction vehicles division as well as engaging in a research programme on new forms of energy. In 1980 the automobile sector represented no more than a third of the group's business. Oddly enough, though fundamentally rational, the tendency towards greater concentration is balanced by a programme of sub-contracting for various parts such as batteries and horns.

Finally, as with other large firms, Fiat has been asked to play an active part in the regional development of the Mezzogiorno. For a long time the firm chose to expand where it had started (Turin: Mirafiori, Rivalta, Stura; six plants in all), then in the Piedmont region (steel production at Avigliana, Carmagnola, Cuneo), and lastly, in the Po Valley (trolleybuses at Novara, trucks in Milan, tractors in Modena). Following on from this, the search for workers led it to Florence and Marina di Pisa, prior to the special legislation which directed its investment to the Mezzogiorno where 25,000 jobs were created in various plants in Naples (trucks), Termoli, Cassino, Bari, Lecce, Sulmona and even Termini Imerese in Sicily. A plant is under construction at Grottaminarda near Avezzano. There is no need to mention the international expansion of the firm in Spain, Chile, Argentina, etc.

Finally, it might be worth mentioning that Fiat, among large Italian firms integrated into the market economy, possesses the very rare feature of being almost entirely in the hands of national capital, apart from the recent injection of petrodollars.

IRI (*Istituto per la Ricostruzione Industriale*) is only the largest of the *Enti di gestione pubblica* whose original charter occupies a special place in the Italian economy. Among the *enti* there are ENI (*Ente Nazionale Idrocarburi*), EGAM (mines and metallurgy), EFIM (industries in difficulty) etc. Also called *enti* are services such as electricity, the Post Office and the railways, which are in fact nationalised industries with a different statute.

ENI was originally (1945) a simple company set up to dispose of the assets of AGIP founded during the Fascist period. Under Enrico Mattei, who died accidentally in 1962, it became first an oil distribution company, then one with drilling interests and which also constructed the gas pipelines, and finally, an international operation both in drilling and importing. The development of the Italian petrochemical industry is due to ENI.

IRI, also the result of state acquisition, has a different programme and way of doing things. The group began in 1933 following a rescue operation put forward by Mussolini to save firms in difficulty from bankruptcy and to prevent the ensuing unemployment. With this in mind, the State acquired majority shares in these firms, and IRI was given the role of an investment trust, a role which it has kept ever since. More specifically, this is to set up firms, regroup others and control them through participation in shareholding. IRI also intervenes as an instrument of state policy in key sectors (steel), industries in difficulty (shipbuilding) or underdeveloped regions, basically the Mezzogiorno.

Within this framework, IRI has developed a whole series of activities grouped into 10 sectors: the most important are –
(a) steel: Finsider group (195,000 million lire) controls the largest Italian steel firm (Italsider) as well as other steel works, tubes and cement works;
(b) mechanical sector: Finmeccanica group (306,000 million lire), 86,000 employees, produces engines, electrical material, electrical components, nuclear material, cars (Alfa Romeo, Alfasud);

(c) shipbuilding: Fincantieri group with eight shipbuilding yards and nine repair yards;

(d) telecommunications: STET group (280,000 million lire) makes electrical equipment, computers and cables;

(e) maritime sector: Finmare which includes eight shipping companies, the two main ones being Lloyd Triestino and Italia di Navigazione;

(f) infrastructure and construction: Italstat group builds in Italy and throughout the world roads, airports, aqueducts and sanitation systems.

Among the less important sectors, SME is responsible for investments in the Mezzogiorno. Finally, the banking sector includes the Banca Commerciale Italiana, Banco di Roma and Banco di Santo Spirito.

Given the size of IRI, and the fact that it could be considered the largest investment and service company in Europe, one may question whether the Italian State controls it or vice versa.

A disquieting expansion of services

More than in other countries, the structures and activities of the service sector are difficult to evaluate fully. It is not that this is a minor sector for, with 6.7 million people employed in the service sector, it represents a third of the working population and is the only one to expand at an annual rate of 2 per cent in the past few years. Nor does it constitute a small sector, for it contributes 41 per cent of the gross national product. Even more than the industrial sector, it appears as a sector which is hard to measure and evaluate clearly.

This irritating aspect is due partly to an incredible fragmentation, for the commercial sector includes no less than 1,179,000 firms with 2.7 million employees; firms with less than 10 employees account for 99 per cent of the total number and 80 per cent of employment.

In order to understand the rationale of this system one has only to observe the purchasing habits of Italians. Hypermarkets and other large complexes are unknown; department stores with several branches are only found in large cities and these are the exception. Only the medium-sized suburban shops which form the Standa chain have succeeded in breaking into a significant number of northern towns. Otherwise, everyone uses the services of the small shop.

Indeed, the patterns established in the retailing sector also affect a whole range of other types of commercial behaviour. Italians know their insurance agent personally and would reprimand him for belonging to a group; with the smallest deposit they will get to know their bank manager personally. For better or for worse, there exists a style of human relations, which is not well understood in other countries, but to which people here are deeply attached.

What about the efficiency of this system? Certainly the turnover in relation to the numbers employed is low in a large number of commercial establishments of this type. Equally it is certain that tax evasion seems often to be elevated into a principle which allows a lower price to be passed on to the customers. But this apparently advantageous arrangement on this simplest of levels is not always to be highly recommended in other spheres!

The transport system: a basic component of economic development

The nature of Italian topography means that the problem of infrastructure has been difficult to solve. Unstable landforms and broken topography have brought about a proliferation of bends, slopes and tunnels on railway lines; road links were appalling for a long time; long stretches of coast were without port facilities, and those that existed, were situated in rocky bays cut off from their hinterland or suffered from silting up (Ostia). The length of the peninsula has not facilitated the creation of major nodal junctions.

Due to these problems the railway network has, for a long time, played an essential political and economic role, even though it has not been able to cope fully with the demands of increasing trade. Its density gradually decreases from Lombardy (8 km per 100 km^2) to Sardinia (5 km per 100 km^2). Of a total of 20,000 kilometres of track there are 12,000 kilometres of double track, of which 9,500 are electrified. There are also 2,000 kilometres of narrow-gauge track. If one adds that improvements have been rare in the past few decades, apart from the laying of double track on the main Naples–Reggio line, then the present decline, evidenced by the drop in freight traffic from 59 million tons in 1958 to 50 million in 1977, is understandable.

This virtual stagnation, together with the concentration of traffic on several main routes, can be seen in relation to the construction of the motorway network, begun in 1951 when several stretches (Turin–Milan–Brescia), totalling 480 kilometres, were already in use. By 1979 this network, including urban peripheral routes, had a total distance of 5,800 kilometres. The network was constructed using many tunnels and viaducts made of prefabricated materials and standardised size. Motorways often reduce the distance between two points in comparison to the railway and make competition all the more to be feared, especially since these roads follow the more rational route. The principal routes are organised around a double axis which runs through the Po plain in the north linking Turin–Milan–Venice–Trieste and in the south Turin–Bologna–Rimini; this dual axis serves as the basic route in an interlinked chain which reaches the main Alpine passes and the port of Genoa; it is bisected by a broad Southern axis which goes from the Brenner Pass to the South, passing through Verona, Bologna, Florence, Rome, Naples, Reggio and on to Sicily.

On a national scale this network has obviously profoundly altered the economic life of the country; either directly in competition with the railways in its ability to offer door-to-door delivery and in attracting a number of industrial plants; or indirectly by encouraging the fantastic growth of the Italian car industry. The effects on the provision of infrastructure still need to questioned. The motorways in the North often have three lanes and are congested, but their construction came after the development of the industrial system which they helped to decentralise. On the other hand, empty southern motorways outside the tourist season reveal the weakness of the regional economy.

Finally, in surveying internal transport, one might note the insignificance of fluvial transport which is limited to the mouths of rivers and the principal axis of the Po.

Air traffic forms only a small part of this picture, for it has increased relatively slowly compared to other European countries – 2 million passengers in 1961, 9 million in 1971 and 11.7 million in 1978. The southern extension of the peninsula explains the relative importance of internal traffic (47 per cent of the total traffic).

More significant in this survey of the transport system is the port network which is highly original. The first notable feature is the volume of total cargo which reached the high figure of 350 million tons in 1976 after peaking at 375 million tons in 1973. Equally remarkable is the gross capacity of the national fleet at 11 million d.w.t. of which 45 per cent is in tankers. This fleet is mainly owned by the State through IRI, although it also includes several large private groups such as Flotta Lauro, Costa Armatori and Magliveras.

Naturally in a peninsula with islands, coastal shipping is important in the national transport system. The proportion of traffic with the mainland (83% of total traffic at Cagliari and 31% at Porto Torres) is not at all unexpected, nor is the function of redistribution which now occurs at Brindisi (63%). Specific characteristics of places also explain the significance of passenger traffic which, after a regular increase, now attains 25 million passengers per year with an overwhelming proportion (23 million) of internal traffic. (Table 3.7, Fig. 3.2).

Although coastal shipping offers an element of stability, Italian ports handle a greater proportion of incoming traffic (269 million tons) than outgoing (84 million tons). Even so, this ratio is better than in other countries when one takes into account the lack of raw materials in Italy and the deficit in agricultural and food provision. The relatively small proportion of imports of coal, minerals and agricultural produce is surprising compared to the proportion of hydrocarbons which comprise 68 per cent of imports.

Themes and problems of a feeble economy

Taking the Gross Domestic Product as an index, the Italian economy is that of a developed country where the primary sector continually decreases in favour of other activities. This decrease, however, is not accompanied by a proportional gain in productivity. Farmers are still numerous, while their contribution to the Gross Domestic Product has declined relatively. On the other hand, the service and administrative sector has increased to a level which is perhaps excessive in relation to the industrial sector. The overall pattern indicates an unequal dynamism and vulnerability. Despite this, the balance of payments is positive (Table 3.8).

Table 3.7 Main components of Italian port traffic

Port	Inward								Outward			
	Total traffic ('000 t)	Coastal shipping (%)	Total ('000 t)	Oil (%)	Coal (%)	Agricultural products (%)	Minerals (%)	Metallurgical products (%)	Total ('000 t)	Oil (%)	Chemical fertilisers (%)	Mechanical, cars (%)
Savona	15,000	13.0	12,800	20.5	9.6	8.4			2,200	30.8	18.5	43.5
Genoa	48,500	15.6	44,500	75.5	3.1	3.5	6.3	5.3	4,000			60.0
La Spezia	13,000	23.8	10,000	71.2		15.4			3,000	70.5		33.0
Leghorn	10,700	18.6	8,300	62.0		12.6			2,400			
Piombino	5,000	40.0	5,700	65.5					1,000			
Civitavecchia	6,800	78.0	5,700	72.0					1,100			
Fiumicino	4,600	28.2	3,600	100.0								
Bagnoli	4,500	11.1	4,100	10.0	26.2		67.0		400			
Naples	10,400	22.1	8,300	72.9		14.0		3.5	2,100	57.0	12.1	20.4
Taranto	28,200	19.6	21,200	20.0	24.0		54.0		7,000			62.5
Brindisi	4,100	63.4	3,300	84.0					800			
Bari	1,800	30.5	1,500	85.8					300			
Ancona	1,300	0.0	1,300	80.0					80			
Falconara	3,300	24.2	2,500	100.0					800			
Ravenna	12,600	23.0	10,300	49.7		9.2			2,300	49.0		
Venice	23,500	37.8	21,000	60.5	3.2	4.0	4.1	5.0	2,500	32.4	20.5	17.3
Trieste	35,300	6.5	33,000	85.0					2,300	39.1		26.0
Milazzo	12,900	39.5	7,200	100.0					5,700	57.9		
Augusta	32,000	20.3	19,300	99.5					13,000		15.5	
Syracuse	10,900	21.2	8,100	77.5					2,800			
Porto-Foxi	17,200	27.3	9,600	100.0					7,600			
Cagliari	3,000	83.3	1,600	10.0					1,400			
Porto-Torres	7,100	31.0	4,500	15.0					2,600			
Total (including various ports)	353,000	29.7	269,000	68.5	3.7	6.2	7.4	2.3	84,000	54.7	9.6	13.9

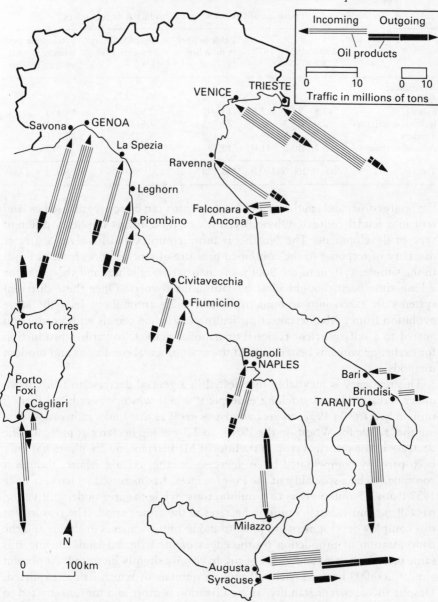

Fig. 3.2   Italian port traffic

Similarities and differences in the agricultural sector

A survey of agricultural systems

The aim here is not to discuss again the differences between northern agriculture, corresponding to urban markets and financed by capital belonging to

Table 3.8 Evolution and composition of Gross Domestic Product at market prices

	1907	% 1957	1977	Value in '000 million lire, 1977	No. of workers by sector 1977 ('000)	Production per worker in each sector ('000 lire)
Agriculture, forestry, fishing	43.8	17.9	7.5	13,097	2,950	4,430
Industrial activities	22.0	36.3	41.9	73,285	7,544	9,714
Tertiary	28.1	35.5	39.6	69,449	6,722.2	10,331
Administration	6.1	10.3	11.0	19,297	2,833.8	6,815
Total	100.0	100.0	100.0	175,128	20,050.0	8,734

the bourgeoisie, and southern agriculture, which can be conceptualised as land rent in a feudal context. Obviously, each of these forms implies a different type of development. The North's is more complex and involves a greater diversity of response to the combined pressure of rent and provision of food. In the simpler system of the South, the association of wheat and sheep has for a long time been thought ideal by latifundist owners. Once these different systems are taken into account, there still exists throughout Italy the same evolution from a Mediterranean agriculture, based on cereals with production geared to a self-sufficient regional or national market, towards a production for exchange which is better adapted to environmental conditions and modern methods.

This tendency is inevitably manifested in a general decrease in fields sown under cereals. The most telling example is wheat which was reduced from 5 million hectares in 1957, an area almost as great as that under cultivation during the 'Battle for Wheat' in the 1930s, to 2.7 million hectares at present. The decrease in the principal crop in traditional Mediterranean agriculture has only been partially compensated by an increase in other cereals. Maize, though it continues to be a speciality of the Po provinces, has increased its harvest since 1957 from 2.5 million tons to 6 million tons, while the area under cultivation has fallen from 1.2 to 0.9 million hectares in the same period. The reasons for this complex development are to be found in improvements in strains and the concentration of production on the edges of the irrigated land. During this same period, the area and yields of rice have only slightly increased. At present almost 200,000 hectares yield 10 million quintals of which half is exported. Despite this apparent stability, rice cultivation is more and more restricted to the compact, low-lying land and has been totally modernised. Seedlings are planted directly in beds, weeding is no longer done and the harvest is mechanised. Of all the cereals, only barley, introduced from the north and used for the brewing of beer and feeding of cattle, has really increased (600,000 quintals from 300,000 hectares).

At first sight the same impression is gained about the evolution of the other traditional component of Mediterranean agriculture, sheep. The total reached 15 million head in the inter-war period, then decreased to 12 million in the 1950s and is now only just over 8 million, including goats. Grazing is confined to the Apennines and the Mezzogiorno where numbers have remained almost static, especially the numbers in Sardinia which retains almost 3 million head of sheep. Yet, during this same period, the rate of lambing has become more rapid, particularly in Tuscany and the Abruzzi, while the amount of milk has risen from 3 to 5 million quintals per annum.

The same type of evolution is found again in the last and most characteristic feature of Mediterranean agriculture, the olive tree. Its area has declined from 150,000 to 100,000 hectares, but the yield of an average harvest has increased from 20 to 30 million hectolitres per year.

Finally, there remains the question of wine. Italy, with an estimated production of around 65 to 70 million hectolitres per year, is becoming the major world producer and equal to France. In fact, it is rather difficult to follow the development of vineyards because the reduction in vineyards under *coltura promiscua* is more than balanced by an increase in specialised vineyards. The carefully maintained lack of distinction between wine and table grapes further adds an element of imprecision. Yet the quantity produced from the average wine harvest has increased by over 20 million hectolitres since the beginning of the Common Market. There has been an expansion in all types of wines. Ordinary wines are produced everywhere, and for the most part, consumed locally. Blended wines with a high alcoholic content are bought by France. Finally, there are quality wines whose promotion has not always succeeded in reviving the declining economies of regions such as Asti.

The development of wine production thus illustrates the trends in a Mediterranean agriculture which has been modernised and is now oriented towards the export of specific crops. This new orientation has particularly benefited producers of fruit and vegetables throughout Italy. All in all, this very diversified production now attains 250 million quintals, after reaching a peak of 260 million quintals in 1970. Leaving aside potatoes, this quantity forms almost half that harvested in the EEC. In 1978 it also represented 27 per cent of the value of Italian agricultural production and was the main agricultural export earner (1,250,000 million lire). It would thus seem that Italy has taken advantage of European integration to stress and refine the Mediterranean aspects of its agriculture.

An indication of the evolution of the area under grass is given less by the varying breakdown into temporary grazing, fodder crops, meadows and pastures, than by a doubling of production, expressed in units of fodder, during the past 15 years, to 21.6 million units. By international standards, this is a relatively modest figure, basically brought about by production in Emilia and Lombardy, and, to a lesser extent, in Piedmont, Veneto and Latium. An increase in livestock has not followed the same trend, for, if the number of

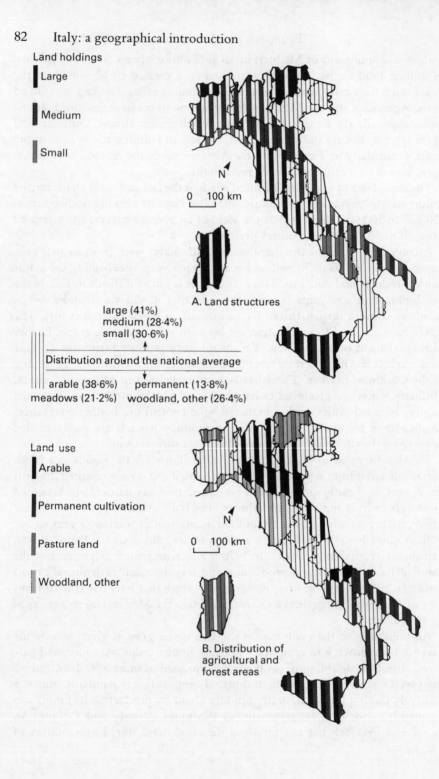

Land holdings
Large
Medium
Small

N

0   100 km

A. Land structures

large (41%)
medium (28·4%)
small (30·6%)

Distribution around the national average

arable (38·6%)   permanent (13·8%)
meadows (21·2%)   woodland, other (26·4%)

Land use

Arable
Permanent cultivation
Pasture land
Woodland, other

N

0   100 km

B. Distribution of
agricultural and
forest areas

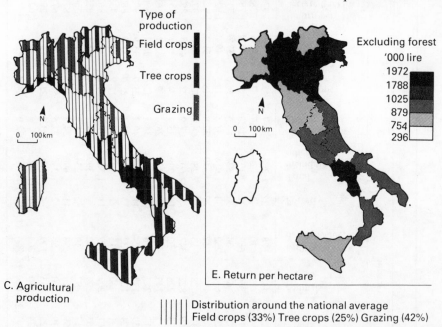

Type of
production

Field crops

Tree crops

Grazing

C. Agricultural
production

Excluding forest

'000 lire

1972
1788
1025
879
754
296

E. Return per hectare

||||| Distribution around the national average
||||| Field crops (33%) Tree crops (25%) Grazing (42%)

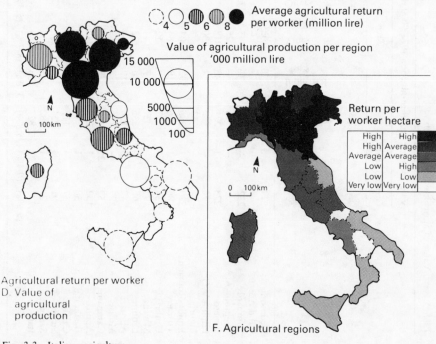

Average agricultural return
per worker (million lire)
4 5 6 8

Value of agricultural production per region
'000 million lire

15 000
10 000
5000
1000
100

Agricultural return per worker
D. Value of
   agricultural
   production

Return per
worker hectare

High	High
High	Average
Average	Average
Low	High
Low	Low
Very low	Very low

F. Agricultural regions

Fig. 3.3   Italian agriculture

Table 3.9(a) Value of agricultural production

Value of agricultural production 1977 ('000 million lire)

	Ground crops				Tree			Grazing		Forestry	Total including other	Ground crops (%)	Tree crops (%)	Animal (%)	Return per hectare ('000 lire) excluding forests
	Cereals	Leguminous	Vegetables	Industrial crops	Vines	Olives	Citrus	Animals	Milk & dairy products						
Piedmont	214	5	140	8	102	–	79	443	178	22	1,263	31.4	15.1	51.9	971
Val d'Aosta	–	–	1	–	–	–	1	12	10	1	28	7.7	7.2	82.6	285
Lombardy	232	–	113	16	45	1.7	17	864	687	46	2,193	18.3	3.6	75.8	1,788
Trentino-A.A.	–	–	16	–	25	2	124	64	54	32	327	6.3	46.3	37.6	717
Veneto	273	1	271	45	218	2	124	611	252	11	1,916	31.6	18.5	49.2	1,925
Friuli – V.G.	76	–	30	1	30	–	9	99	67	7	349	32.8	13.7	51.4	1,122
Liguria	–	–	53	–	7	21	12	28	13	4	280	66.9	17.0	16.7	1,972
Emilia-Romagna	229	1	286	192	204	1	369	822	347	5	2,607	27.9	22.4	49.3	1,897
Tuscany	86	1	116	18	84	39	25	226	52	16	799	35.7	24.1	38.1	754
Umbria	34	–	17	20	12	11	–	145	13	5	280	26.4	9.3	62.1	662
Marche	97	–	27	7	44	7	17	227	16	2	542	36.5	13.6	49.3	896
Latium	65	4	235	10	122	49	39	173	124	11	972	40.3	25.0	33.9	992
Abruzzi	42	3	136	19	64	40	24	125	32	3	522	40.3	25.0	33.9	883
Molise	29	–	16	3	9	10	1	30	15	1	123	40.3	17.9	40.3	433
Campania	57	38	469	75	68	57	301	207	109	11	1,523	47.8	28.2	23.2	1,862
Apulia	132	1	297	74	242	378	63	90	62	–	1,399	38.2	49.4	12.3	855
Basilicata	50	1	44	10	10	15	17	57	19	2	234	45.9	18.7	34.4	354
Calabria	37	4	117	7	25	214	99	116	38	11	690	24.7	49.5	24.2	879
Sicily	91	4	254	1	188	77	419	170	58	2	1,340	27.5	51.8	20.4	671
Sardinia	21	1	82	5	50	25	23	153	109	4	501	23.2	21.1	54.6	296
Italy	1,773 (9.9%)	72 (0.4%)	2,827 (15.8%)	535 (3.0%)	1,558 (8.7%)	955 (5.3%)	1,774 (9.9%)	4,670 (26.0%)	2,263 (12.6%)	201 (1.1%)	17,900 (100%)	32.0	24.7	42.1	1,025

Table 3.9(b) Regional distribution of size of holdings and type of agricultural production

	Size of holding by area (%)					Agricultural & forest area (%)				
	1–5 ha	5–10 ha	10–50 ha	50–100 ha	100 ha	Total ('000 ha)	Arable	Permanent Cultivation	Pastures	Wood & others
Piedmont	16.5	17.8	31.5	5.9	27.3	2,256	36.0	8.4	26.8	28.2
Val d'Aosta	7.6	7.6	12.7	5.1	67.8	216	1.4	0.9	54.9	42.8
Lombardy	11.3	10.0	33.3	13.1	32.3	1,935	49.3	2.8	21.9	26.0
Trentino–A.A.	12.5	6.0	19.5	6.8	60.6	1,153	2.4	4.7	36.2	56.7
Veneto	23.0	16.9	28.9	6.0	24.1	1,535	46.0	11.8	15.2	27.0
Friuli–V.G.	18.6	15.2	23.3	3.9	39.0	640	36.4	5.5	15.5	42.6
Liguria	22.9	20.9	29.3	2.5	21.3	489	8.6	16.0	18.9	56.5
Emilia–Romagna	11.1	17.7	47.2	8.5	15.0	1,984	56.8	11.4	7.4	24.4
Tuscany	8.8	9.1	26.3	10.5	44.6	2,126	32.5	14.8	10.7	42.0
Umbria	8.8	10.5	32.2	9.0	40.4	784	40.5	9.3	12.8	37.4
Marche	13.6	18.5	38.6	8.5	41.2	1,554	37.3	16.2	19.4	26.9
Latium	19.4	11.8	19.4	6.3	20.3	909	57.7	4.7	10.7	27.0
Abruzzi	20.9	14.6	14.8	1.3	47.4	1,008	33.1	8.5	26.6	31.8
Molise	19.9	12.1	31.3	4.5	21.8	415	55.3	6.5	14.4	23.8
Campania	32.6	16.0	19.5	3.6	24.0	1,235	40.3	19.9	15.0	24.8
Apulia	30.0	14.4	30.4	11.4	20.1	1,801	44.0	37.6	11.9	6.5
Basilicata	12.6	14.0	28.8	10.3	33.5	934	48.7	7.0	23.5	20.5
Calabria	21.0	12.6	21.6	8.1	34.4	1,397	28.7	24.7	16.0	30.6
Sicily	24.2	16.6	30.5	9.4	17.0	2,383	51.8	25.1	14.6	8.5
Sardinia	4.7	4.7	24.6	19.4	46.2	2,264	17.2	6.8	59.3	16.7
Italy	15.9	13.3	28.4	9.0	32.0	27,028 (100.0)	9,306 (34.5%)	2,698 (11%)	5,176 (19.1%)	9,574 (35.4%)

pigs has tripled in 20 years to 8 million, the number of cattle has remained stable at 8.5 million head. However, cattle production has concentrated more and more in the provinces mentioned above as well as in the Alps. New breeds (Friesian and Holstein) have replaced traditional ones with the exception of Friulian and Camina. As a result of these changes, the production of meat has risen from 5,000 to 8,000 million quintals in 20 years, and that of milk from 50 to 95 million.

Improvement in agricultural technology, often quite spectacular in the Lombardy landscape, with its mechanised cow sheds, silos and factories producing foodstuffs, is still insufficient to meet the increase in consumption, which is another aspect of the Europeanisation of the country. In addition to the 8.3 million quintals of meat produced in 1977, 5,150,000 quintals of beef alone were imported. To this must be added 5 million tons of maize for the feeding of livestock.

As for fishing, the amount caught is as misleading as the livestock statistics. A fleet of 21,600 boats, employing 120,000 fishermen, supplies just 360,000 tons or three-quarters of a rather modest national consumption (7 kg per person per annum).

A deceiving picture

By reducing its production of cereals and developing that of Mediterranean products, Italy has made a pact to renounce the old dream of self-sufficiency in food, which always resulted in lack of it, and to enter a cycle of exchange in which shortfalls in production are compensated by the quality and specialisation of production to a large degree destined for northern European markets.

The opening up the European markets has proved after some years to be disappointing to the extent that imports of cereals, meat and milk products have not been adequately balanced by exports of wine, fruits and vegetables; in 1977 3,017,000 million lire of exports at fob prices were paired with 6,698,000 million lire of imports at cif prices. The immediate situation is less worrying than the future, when the Common Market will be enlarged to include Spain, Portugal and Greece, whose costs of production are lower and whose productive structures sometimes better. Some envisage in the long run a recession in the most productive sector (fruit and vegetables) without any foreseeable replacement in other areas. Although there exists a Green Plan for the improvement of productivity, restructuring of farms and adaptation of supply to national and international demand, the budget at the disposal of the Ministry of Agriculture seems insufficient (750,000 million lire per year for 1977–79). Equally, much is expected of the Common Market's agricultural fund (FEOGA), but it appears there is some decline in the efficient use of these funds as one moves southward. Once more, the regional question is encountered.

Manufacturing industry

Problems in the location of industry: traditions, policies, results

The usual factors evoked in the geographical analysis of industrial location, such as primary materials and historical factors, are not very relevant in the Italian context. At the most, one can acknowledge their relative importance in the textile industry with its traditional area of production in Lombardy, the Piedmontese Alps, Tuscany and around Naples. But then the differential development, which arose from fairly similar initial cores and eventually favoured northern Italy, has to be explained. Similarly, how does one explain the fact that, beginning with two groups of armament factories at Terni and Brescia, the former remains isolated, while the latter has given rise to a considerable, and unexpected, diversification.

In the above two examples, as in all those one could cite, the answer is the same. In northern Italy there exists an urban and manufacturing tradition, which is somewhat weaker in central Italy, and unknown south of Florence. Once again, one finds a contrast between the *rentiers* of the South and the entrepreneurs of the North.

The regional composition of the active population (see Table 2.3) brings out the fairly regular decrease in the proportion of those employed in the secondary sector from north to south. Only Piedmont and Lombardy exceed 50 per cent, although they are closely followed by Veneto, Friuli and Emilia-Romagna. Around this cluster, a proportion of 30–40 per cent occurs in Liguria, Marche, Tuscany and Umbria. Further south, and even in Latium, the proportion in the secondary sector reaches at most 28 per cent in Sardinia, falling as low as 22 per cent in Molise. Another aspect of the analysis is the regional distribution of the industrial work-force in terms of the national total which is 36.8 per cent for Lombardy and Piedmont, and 54.6 per cent for the larger area including Veneto and Emilia-Romagna. The concentration of half the industrial work-force in 29 per cent of the national territory speaks for itself, but one should not forget that a region like Apulia, which began with no industry in 1950, now has 4.1 per cent of Italy's industrial workers.

An analysis of industrial production by regions (Fig. 3.4) is even more amazing. Piedmont and Lombardy's share of the total national industrial production of 54,458,000 million lire is 40.9 per cent, and that of the first four regions is 58 per cent. It is as if all the investments in the South were for the advantage of the North. Indeed, there are, on the one hand, basic industries which require considerable capital for each job created; on the other hand, there are a variety of industries whose creation and development are more profitable, the less costly they are. In fact, northern industries, such as mechanical engineering, require proportionately more manpower than the southern-type industries, such as steel and petrochemicals, which were supposed to resolve the problem of unemployment.

Table 3.10 Distribution and evolution of employment by branches, 1961–71

Industrial branches	No. 1971 ('000)	‰ Branch	Variation 1961–71
Extractive	71	13.6	– 30
Food, tobacco	400	61,5	– 5.7
Textiles	541	83,2	– 8.4
Clothing	416	64.0	– 22.2
Shoes, leather	228	35.0	+ 3.6
Wood, furniture	396	60.9	+ 4.2
Metallurgy	245	37.6	– 5.8
Mechanical engineering	1,569	241.2	+ 40.0
Motor cars and other vehicles	336	64.6	+ 46.0
Non-ferrous metals	330	58.9	+ 6.4
Chemicals, petrochemicals	271	41.6	+ 17.8
Rubber	84	15.0	+ 61.1
Cellulose	47	8.3	+ 39.1
Paper	94	16.7	+ 12.1
Reproduction, publishing	139	24.8	+ 26.3
Photographic	23	4.1	+ 12.3
Plastics	101	18.0	+ 129.5
Others	75	13.3	+ 27.1
Construction	997	178.0	+ 12.0
Water, gas, electricity	155	27.6	+ 38.0
	6,524	1,000.0	16.5

A production adapted to the market

In order to comprehend the dynamism of Italian industry, it is necessary to refer to two sets of slightly different statistics. Firstly, there is the 1971 industrial census which enables one to measure for that period the significance of, and changes within, each branch and, secondly, there are national accounts, which give for each sector the value added, from which it is possible to calculate the productivity per worker. Understanding these tables, however, is not a simple exercise. Changes in the work-force would suggest a classification of industries into four groups according to whether they have declined (textiles, foodstuffs, metallurgy), stagnated (leather, shoes), modestly increased (non-ferrous metals, construction, paper, chemicals, clothes, reprographic industries) or rapidly increased (mechanical engineering, vehicles, rubber and plastics). In fact, the decrease in workers, indicated by metallurgy, belies an improvement in productivity in this branch, corresponding to a rationalisation and large increases in productivity per worker. The same applies to the decrease in employment in foodstuffs in which extremely rapid concentration will soon put Italy on an equal footing with her Common Market partners in this sector. Finally, the decrease in textiles should be explained by the fact that part of the production has now moved into the chemical sector (synthetic fibres), and

Fig. 3.4   Regional industrial production

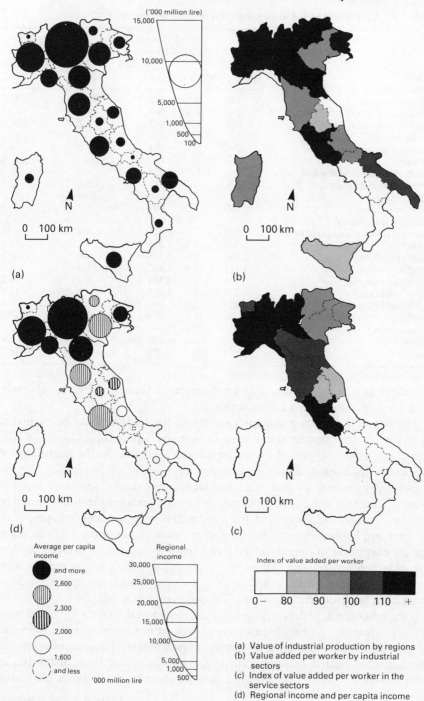

('000 million lire)
15,000
10,000
5,000
1,000
500
100

0 100 km

N

(a)

(b)

0 100 km

N

(d)

0 100 km

N

(c)

0 100 km

N

Average per capita
income

and more
2,600
2,300
2,000
1,600
and less

Regional
income
30,000
25,000
20,000
15,000
10,000
5,000
1,000
500

'000 million lire

Index of value added per worker

0 –   80   90   100   110   +

(a) Value of industrial production by regions
(b) Value added per worker by industrial
     sectors
(c) Index of value added per worker in the
     service sectors
(d) Regional income and per capita income

Table 3.11 Value added by industrial branch and productivity per job, 1977

Branch	Nos. ('000)	%	Value added ('000 million lire)	%	Value added per worker ('000 million lire)
Energy products	187	2.8	8,866	12.1	47.0
Minerals and metals	288	4.4	3,087	4.2	10.7
Minerals and metal-based products	373	5.7	3,833	5.2	10.2
Chemical and pharmaceutical products	297	4.5	4,174	5.7	14.0
Metals (excluding mechanical)	401	6.1	3,424	4.6	8.5
Agricultural and industrial machinery	371	5.7	4,527	6.2	12.2
Office machinery, instruments, optical	80	1.2	879	1.2	10.9
Electrical material and supplies	388	5.9	3,616	4.9	9.3
Transport	366	5.6	4,215	5.7	11.5
Food and tobacco	383	5.8	6,348	8.6	16.5
Textiles, clothes, leather	1,113	17.0	8,452	11.5	7.6
Wood and furniture	343	5.2	3,155	4.3	9.2
Paper, publishing	238	3.6	2,655	3.6	11.1
Rubber and plastics	200	3.0	1,890	2.5	9.4
Diverse	65	1.0	859	1.2	13.2
Construction	1,437	22.0	13,305	18.1	9.2
Total	6,534	100.0	73,285	100.0	11.2

that there is also an attempt at rationalisation, as witnessed by the relatively high level of value added in this sector.

The degree to which production structures have adapted can be evaluated in a particularly simple and telling fashion by using the example of the numerous industries linked to the metallurgical sector. At the beginning of rapid industrialisation, Italian steel production was one of the smallest. It progressively increased so that steel production eventually surpassed that of France. This was not due to a planned expansion programme but occurred in response to demand emanating from industries with forward linkages, such as sheet and laminated metal for the construction of a commercial fleet, pipes for the expansion of the oil industry and large-scale building projects, orders for rods and girders, etc. However, with rising orders in the steel sector, overproduction occurred and this, in turn, contributed to exports, such as marketing the production from the Taranto plant to the Middle East oilfields. On the other hand, orders arising from the mechanical sector were based both on large quantites of simple products as well as not inconsiderable tonnages of products with a diversity of specific requirements. These conditions and the lack of inherited tradition explain the basic characteristics of the Italian steel industry. These include large, new plants, situated at ports and using

Fig. 3.5   Italian industry

PETROLEUM

Volpiano
Rho
Marghera
Sannarazo
Trieste
Genoa
Ravenna
Leghorn
Falconara

Fossacesia

Porto Torres
Naples
Taranto

Sarroch   N

0   100km

Milazzo

Licata
Augusta
Priolo

● ● Refineries
○ Refineries under construction
— Pipeline

STEEL AND ALUMINIUM

Aosta
Marghera
Novi
Milan
Cornigliano

Piombino
Terni

Bagnoli
Taranto

0   100km   N

● Steelworks
▲ Alumina, aluminium

MECHANICAL ENGINEERING

Turin
Bolzano
Milan
Udine
Verona
Modena
Trieste
Genoa
Bologna
Pisa
Florence

Rome

Naples
Bari
Matera

N

0   100km

░ Zone of maximum concentration
● Centre of manufacturing, research and decision making
● Industrial regional centre
· Isolated centre

TEXTILES

Biella
Como
Bergamo
Turin
Valdagno
Prato
Pontedera

Naples

N

0   100km   Palermo

Traditional textile centres
▥ Cotton   ▨ Wool
▢ Silk   ▦ Hemp, linen
· Principal centres

imported materials where continuous production processes are important (Bagnoli, Cornigliano, Taranto), as well as specialised plants using imported scrap metal which is then turned into high-quality steel. These latter are located either in other ports (Pescara, La Spezia), in expanded and rebuilt centres (Piombino, Aosta, Terni), in centres in the Turin area (Novi Ligure, Susa, Avigliana) or in the Milan area (Sesto San Giovanni, Dalmine).

Similarly, the use made of steel in the forward linkage industries is impressive both in its quantity, as in the car industry where production rose from 120,000 cars in 1951 to 1.5 million in 1977, and in the extraordinary variety, which extends from giant turbines, precision instruments, drilling rigs to coffee grinders. An extreme specialisation and an unquestionable sense of design and aesthetic taste mean that these articles export successfully the more they are mass-produced. It is, nevertheless, worth noting that there are some singular omissions from the list of Italian industrial products, particularly those using the latest technology. Examples here are electronics, nuclear industries, aeronautics and those that are usually associated with, or under the cover of, foreign patents. Of course, it is preferable to make profits with coffee grinders than lose money with unsaleable aeroplanes but, at the same time, Italy cannot claim to figure among the leading industrial nations.

As for traditional industries, we shall now mention the major trends in the textile industry. In the regions where this industry was traditionally located, there has been either horizontal integration (Bassetti, Marzotto), or vertical integration between spinning, weaving and printing, on the one hand, and sales networks and exports, on the other. The machinery has also been modernised so that fewer spindles now produce a larger amount of cloth.

Among the newly developed branches of industry, the chemicals sector deserves our attention because of its size and type of expansion. Although almost non-existent before the Second World War, this sector was established through the policy of developing oil production which supplied the basis of a new fertiliser industry, polymers and urea. This new development has given rise to two types of industrial enterprises, one situated at ports and refineries in the Mezzogiorno, at Venice-Marghera and Trieste, the other in the traditional centres of Lombardy, and Piedmont, with several extensions in Emilia and Friuli.

Some hurdles still to overcome

Italian industry, which was still in its early stages of development at the end of the Second World War, now possesses, despite some gaps, an international dimension, which has been encouraged by a highly effective export policy. Barely had this young industrial system reached a peak, however, than it was threatened by a crisis. Two statistics illustrate this threat. Firstly, the index of industrial production, after hitting a peak of 130 in the first quarter of 1977 (base 100 in 1970), became stuck at 125 during the whole of 1978; secondly, the average rate of activity of firms did not exceed 70 per cent of their production capacity.

Other worrying factors add to the gloomy economic situation. New competitors appear on international markets, exploiting the same traditional advantages previously held by Italy – commercial aggression and a cheap labour force. Can a Korean or Malaysian miracle after the Italian one not be envisaged, and at the expense of the Italian miracle?

Tourism

Italy has the good fortune to possess many highly attractive tourist locations visited by large numbers of people, with variations depending on fashion and seasons. Very schematically, there are various types of tourist centre. Firstly, there are towns with a cultural heritage or which are places of pilgrimage, such as Rome, Assisi or Padua. Next there are coastal regions with several marked concentrations: the Gulf of Leghorn between San Remo and Viareggio, the Costa Smeralda in Sardinia, the Adriatic Coast between Cervia and Pesaro and the area of lidos between Sabbiadoro and Venice. There are also mountain, ski and Alpine resorts which are situated between Piedmont (Sestrières, Cournayeur) and the Dolomites (Cortina d'Ampezzo), passing through the Tyrol and Trentino (Madonna di Campiglio, Merano), as well as the more southerly resorts in the Apennines around Gran Sasso. Finally, there are thermal spas which are found throughout Italy with several popular ones such as Salsomaggiore and Montecatini. It is interesting to note that the range of sites is at present being extended with the development of new coastal areas. Some of these are located as close as possible to Alpine routes (Lido Ferrarese), whereas others openly woo the sunseekers (Calabria and the coast of southern Sicily).

For a long time attention was paid to the number of tourists from abroad and their prodigious increase, evidenced by the increased inflow of foreign currency from 1951 (270,000 million lire) to 1971 (2,000,000 million lire) and 1978 (5,500,000 million lire). In 1977, almost 15 million foreign tourists spent 81 million nights (average of 5.5 per tourist). Germans were the dominant group (4 million), followed a long way behind by Americans (1.8 million, among whom there were many Italian Americans), then the French (1.6 million), Swiss (700,000), Belgians, etc. Once again, it was astonishingly Lombardy which received the greatest number of visitors (4.8 million). Obviously, the region constitutes an almost inevitable stop on the way south for tourists coming from northern Europe, but one must also add the attractiveness of lake, mountain and artistic sites, to say nothing of commercial visits, on a greater scale than in the rest of the country. After Lombardy come Tuscany and Rome, which both receive 4 million visitors, then Trentino, Campania (2 million), etc. Despite progress made in air and road transport, the Mezzogiorno remains handicapped by its distance and its poorer facilities. Out of a hotel capacity of 1.1 million beds distributed between 21,000 hotels, northern Italy's share is 750,000 beds, while the islands only offer 71,000. One should not therefore overvalue the amount of income derived from tourism in the southern regions.

The novel element in tourism is not so much the predictable increase in foreign tourists but the beginning and development of two types of Italian tourism. The first is international, taking an estimated 1,000,000 million lire out of the country in 1978 (which still leaves a surplus of 4,500,000 million lire from tourist receipts); the second is internal, accounting for a total of 505 million nights in 1978, with an annual increase estimated at 6 per cent.

Qualitative and quantitative aspects of the tertiary sector

The proportion employed in the tertiary sector does not vary greatly from one region to another (see Table 2.3) in relation to the national average of 46.2 per cent. However, if certain variations from the average seem logical, like the figure of 60 per cent in Liguria, a percentage to be expected in a region with port and tourist activities, then one is naturally surprised by the 47 per cent in Abruzzi and 52 per cent in Sicily, while Piedmont only just reaches 50 per cent and Lombardy 54 per cent. It seems that in the Mezzogiorno the numbers employed are only excessive in relation to the amount of work done. An analysis of the value added by province confirms both the degree and nature of this overemployment. Services constitute 61 per cent of the regional product in Liguria, but more than 50 per cent in Campania, Calabria, Sicily and Sardinia, and only 41 per cent in Lombardy. It is not in the least surprising that the value added per worker in this sector falls to 6.6. million lire in Lombardy, 5.1 million in Sicily, 4.3 in Campania and as low as 3.9 million in Calabria (Fig. 3.4c).

The figures given above clarify certain Italian problems, notably the increasing number of provinces (Enna, Oristano, Isernia) and regions (Molise). The creation of these administrative units has generated additional employment, especially lower-level jobs, provided more clients for local commerce and encouraged the creation of regional bodies such as chambers of commerce, etc. For a relatively poor region the presence of administrative personnel in a town can become a vital issue, and this explains the violent riots between the inhabitants of Cantanzaro and Reggio di Calabria over the choice of regional capital for Calabria.

These statistics also lead us to contrast two types of tertiary sector: the one high level, associated with industry, banks and, above all, large-scale commercial activities, well represented in the North, but fairly weak in the Mezzogiorno; the other of a lower level, linked to the proliferation of very small-scale commercial activities, parasitic middlemen, sellers of smuggled cigarettes, and particularly well implanted in the Mezzogiorno. In describing this contrast one should not forget to mention the theory of dual circuits in the tertiary sector developed in Milton Santos' work on underdevelopment (Santos 1979). Does the Third World already begin south of Rome?

Conclusion

Throughout this analysis, the same themes recur. One is dynamism, manifested in the quantity and quality of production, in the development of original management methods, and with perceptible changes in the landscape. Yet we also have inertia in production structures and in economic behaviour, and a spatial inequality which predictably emerges as soon as any measure is not applied uniformly. These opposing tendencies lead one, in summing up, to ask two questions, one about the value of a policy of economic development expressed in terms of the overall balance of trade, and the other about the real significance of regional inequalities.

Relationship of production and exchange

The table below (Table 3.12) of agricultural and industrial production allows us to classify the evolution, or to be more accurate, the origin of the new Italian economy.

One should refrain, nevertheless, from constructing, on the basis of these statistics, a simple and uniform trend from one year to the next. Due to its export orientation, the level of Italian production has proved to be closely influenced by the state of the international economy, so that good and bad years follow on from one another, even during periods of favourable economic growth. Hence it was that 1960 was considered at that time to be catastrophic or that 1967 was supposed already to herald the end of the economic miracle. In 1978, as in 1977, industrial production only increased by 1.1 per cent of the Gross Industrial Product which now stands at 173,000,000 million lire. Similarly household demand has clearly taken a downturn, because its rate of increase declined from 5.5 per cent per year for the period 1965–70 to 1.4 per cent per annum for the period 1974–78. Production is thus barely maintained by foreign exchange which now accounts for 19.4 per cent of the Gross Industrial Product in imports and 24.5 per cent in exports (18% and 17% in 1970).

The slow-down in demand and production has not hit all sectors. Employment in industry has remained stable, while that in the service sector increased by 128,000 in 1978, thus making up for the loss of 70,000 jobs in agriculture and, particularly, 14,000 in the construction industry which is highly sensitive to economic conditions and influenced by contraction in demand from households. Unemployment is now estimated at 2 million (including 700,000 young people in search of their first job), which equals an unemployment rate of 7.2

Table 3.12 Evolution of main agricultural and industrial products, 1951–77

Agriculture	1951	1965	1977
Wheat ('000 tons)	6,960	9,759	6,328
Rice ('000 tons)	750	508	730
Maize ('000 tons)	2,748	3,369	6,450
Sugar beet ('000 tons)	5,960	9,078	11,557
Wine ('000s)	49,760	68,206	64,072
Olive oil ('000s hectolitres)	3,712	4,200	5,300
Fresh fruit ('000s hectolitres)	11,100	21,200	26,500
Cattle ('000 head)	8,395	9,429	8,568
Sheep ('000 head)	12,400	9,100	8,700
Pigs ('000 head)	3,512	5,176	9,420
Milk ('000 quintals)	61,600	82,400	96,085
Butter ('000 quintals)	508	640	718
Cheese ('000 quintals)	3,422	4,471	5,548
Fish ('000 quintals)	2,132	3,300	2,509

Industry			
Oil ('000 tons)	17	2,209	1,082
Methane gas ('000 million m^3)	966	7,800	13,700
Electricity (million kWh)	29,220	82,968	159,840
of which HEP (million kWh)	24,968	36,250	53,000
Iron ('000 tons)	952	5,489	11,480
Steel ('000 tons)	3,062	12,680	23,313
Aluminium ('000 tons)	49	123	260
Motor cars ('000)	118	1,103	1,452
Heavy vehicles ('000)	20	71	143
Shipbuilding ('000 d.w.t.)	123	458	605
Cotton thread ('000 tons)	191	156	154
Cotton fabric woven ('000 tons)	123	120	103
Wool ('000 tons)	576	550	480
Artificial fibres ('000 tons)	65	85	62
Synthetic fibres ('000 tons)	15	45	127
Sulphuric acid ('000 tons)	2,340	3,500	2,700
Nitrate fertiliser ('000 tons)	538	2,730	3,400

per cent. This has resulted in a greater burden on the social services, already inflated by 5 million retired and a large number of industrially disabled.

Let us be clear at the outset that the balance of payments recorded a surplus in 1978 for services and foreign trade. This should be emphasised since the surplus has succeeded a series of deficit balances resulting from the rise in oil prices since 1973. In 1976 the balance of payments deficit stood at 2,800 million dollars and in 1977 2,200 million dollars, before being converted to a surplus of 5,506 million dollars in 1978. In 1977 the deficit was slightly less through a negative trade balance despite a lower repayment of the external debt. The figures for 1977, a fairly representative year, are given below together with those for 1969, the two showing the structural evolution of commercial activities in Italy in recent years.

The 1977 trade balance reveals a relatively modest imbalance with a 94 per

Table 3.13   Foreign trade by type of product, 1969 and 1977

Imports, cif ('000 million lire)	1969	%	1977	%
Food, drink, tobacco	1,486	19.0	6,698	16.0
Crude oil	972	12.5	8,615	20.5
Metals and minerals	1,074	13.8	4,711	11.2
Textiles and raw materials	595	7.6	2,484	5.9
Wood and wood products	291	3.8	1,281	3.0
Automobiles and parts	306	3.9	2,586	6.1
Other mechanical products	1,353	17.3	5,713	13.6
Chemicals	739	9.5	4,649	11.1
Paper products	179	2.3	643	1.5
Other	797	10.3	4,578	11.0
Total	7,792	100.0	41,958	100.0

Exports, fob ('000 million lire)				
Food, drink, tobacco	653	8.9	3,017	7.6
Metals and minerals	421	5.7	3,283	8.3
Textiles and raw materials	929	12.7	3,463	8.7
Clothing and shoes	567	7.7	3,055	7.6
Automobiles and parts	634	8.6	3,682	9.3
Other means of transport	265	3.6	1,329	3.3
Other mechanical products	1,994	27.2	10,325	26.0
Chemicals	902	12.3	5,203	13.1
Other	965	13.2	6,374	16.1
Total	7,330	100.0	39,736	100.0

cent rate of coverage. An examination of past figures shows that this rate was, on average, 72 per cent between 1951 and 1960, 88 per cent between 1961 and 1970 and, lastly, 93 per cent between 1971 and 1975. There is therefore a continual and regular improvement.

The relationship between the various elements of the balance of payments remains constant with a marked dominance of raw materials in imports and finished products in exports. In the past few years there has arisen a sale of semi-finished steel products (tubes, girders). The size of the oil bill varies according to the amount of imports which, though slightly less than before, still reach 100 million tons.

The geographical distribution of exports similarly reveals an undeniable consistency of trade flows (Table 3.14). The Common Market is in first place, but sales of finished products and equipment to OPEC and Third World countries are on the increase. Indeed, whenever there are pipelines to be installed, large barrages and airports to be built in the world, Italy makes its presence felt in three ways – supply of materials, machinery and technology. Clearly Italy has discovered an opening which it plugs. Sometimes, however, this causes difficulty, as proved by its accounting problems with post-revolution Iran.

Table 3.14 Geographical pattern of foreign trade (millions US dollars)

	Imports cif				Exports fob			
	1969	%	1977	%	1969	%	1977	%
World	1,037		3,963		977		3,753	
EEC	453	*43.0*	1,706	*43*	461	*47.1*	1,747	*46.5*
West Germany	195	*18.8*	665	*16.8*	192	*19.6*	697	*18.5*
Belgium, Luxemburg	837	*3.5*	132	*3.3*	38	*3.8*	133	*3.5*
France	129	*12.0*	551	*13.9*	141	*14.4*	536	*14.2*
Netherlands	41	*4*	164	*4.1*	43	*4.4*	142	*3.7*
UK	42	*4*	146	*3.6*	35	*3.5*	198	*5.2*
USA	118	*11.0*	274	*6.9*	106	*10.8*	250	*6.6*
Canada	13	*1.2*	45	*1.1*	10	*1.0*	31	*0.8*
Japan	10	*0.9*	52	*1.3*	7	*0.7*	30	*0.8*
Other OECD countries	124	*12.0*	459	*11.6*	157	*16.1*	611	*16.3*
Planned economies	64	*6.0*	231	*5.8*	60	*6.1*	202	*5.3*
Developing countries	270	*26*	1,204	*30.3*	178	*18.2*	892	*23.7*
of which OPEC	124	*12*	753	*19*	45	*4.6*	480	*12.7*

4 Regions and regional policies

The comprehensive study of economic and demographic statistics introduces the fundamental issue of spatial inequality which seems to be the major problem besetting Italy in the twentieth century. This is not a new situation, for regional imbalances began to be felt straight after the unification of the country had been achieved. The problem, however, was only really apprehended after the Second World War.

Regional structure and spatial organisation

Economic and political inequalities should not let us lose sight of the basic fact that the State has, relatively, lost power to local and regional authorities. The resulting diversity can be seen in the regional structure and organisation of economic space.

Regional systems – theory and practice

In the traditional regional hierarchy of Italy, with communes, provinces and regions, the province plays a relatively minor role in the system of spatial organisation. This situation is basically due to the fact that there is a relatively large number of provinces (ninety-five) which are often indistinguishable from a hinterland dominated by its capital, upon which economic and political life focuses. As a sign of their higher status, communes have more employees on their payrolls than provinces. For example, Milan has 31,000 communal employees and only 4,000 provincial.

At the other end of this administrative hierarchy, the twenty regions play a vital role because of their size and of the range of responsibilities and services they offer. (In fact, there exist two small regions, Aosta and Molise, defined by special circumstances and problems.) The constitution stipulates that the regions cannot do anything that goes against the State or another region, but it leaves them the right to legislate in numerous fields including agriculture, fairs and markets, transport, tourism, urban planning and education.

The specific status of some regions has been sanctioned by special regulations, and an autonomy status accorded Val d'Aosta (substantial French minority), Trentino-Alto Adige (considerable German minority in the province of Bolzano), Friuli-Venezia Giulia (centres of Slavic population and problems of regional integration following the transfer of the Upper Isonzo valley to Yugoslavia), and Sicily and Sardinia due to problems related to their insular situation.

Finally, there are intermediate levels that link town and country. These are the small-scale natural regions corresponding to a type of landscape (Brianza, Langhe) or to valleys (Val Trompia, Val Sugana). Though lacking existence as administrative units, these regions are, none the less, very much alive, especially in mountainous areas.

Apart from the diversity of administrative arrangements, the state of the budget varies considerably, especially among communes. Some are deeply in debt, others less so; some employ vast numbers and others not; some support football teams, others construct hospitals.

The structure of economic space

Unlike a country such as France, the regional level in Italy fulfils an essentially political and administrative role. The urban hierarchy is not centred on a single city with regional capitals gravitating around an acknowledged and unmistakably dominant capital. An examination of the eleven major Italian cities (Rome, Milan, Naples, Turin, Genoa, Palermo, Bologna, Florence, Catania, Venice–Mestre and Bari), based on various criteria, will elucidate the nature of this hierarchy (Mainardi 1973). The results of this are far from being in Rome's favour, since it only clearly comes out on top in the number of employees in administration, entertainment, luxury commercial activities and airline connections. Rome is almost able to equal Milan in terms of external employment because of its para-administrative sector (IRI, ENI, ENEL, etc.). Lastly, the role of the capital is insignificant in terms of exports (3.4%) where it only comes fourth. In short, then, it is a city of employees and shopkeepers, unable to hold first place even in the realm of newspapers, since its 13 daily papers with a circulation of 1.7 million copies cannot beat that of the 9 Milan dailies with a 2.2 million circulation.

The reverse of these Roman inadequacies is Milan which heads the list in a number of ways: in employment, *per capita* income (3.2 million lire, as in Turin, compared to 2.3 million in Rome), foreign trade (30% of imports and 24% of exports, and even more if one takes into account its role in placing orders), finance (30% of the capital of credit institutions and insurance brokers, compared to Rome's 22%) and publishing houses. Its importance in placing outside orders provides work for 450,000 people outside the province, mainly in the industrial sector. Finally, if more qualitative aspects are included, there are its prestigious educational institutions and cultural establishments like La Scala. Dalmasso's title of 'moral capital of Italy' is easily understood (Dalmasso 1973).

Yet this does not mean that the urban hierarchy can be reduced to a competition between two cities, where the northern one produces and works and the southern one administers and decides policies. Other cities also stand out, foremost among them Turin, a rival with Milan in *per capita* income. It provides work for 100,000 outside the province, a greater number than that provided by Genoa, which is the headquarters of Finsider. Turin also comes second in wholesaling and transport, and third for field of influence. For its part, Genoa comes third, and ahead of Rome, in terms of foreign exchange; its *per capita* income is also higher than Rome. Bologna too is very important, particularly in transport and wholesaling.

In this diverse and complex hierarchy, southern cities consistently occupy the lower positions. Of course, Naples occupies fourth place in the hierarchy of zones of influence due to its population and location, but it only comes fifth in the provision of employment outside the province and seventh in foreign trade. Only its university function is in keeping with its size. The same applies to Florence which scarcely retains any of its prestigious past, apart from its university; it has a modest role as a regional capital and its hinterland seems more and more split between Milan, Rome, Bologna and Genoa. Among other southern cities, Bari manages to supply 0.5 per cent of Italian exports (barely more than Catania, 0.3%), and this appears to be a just assessment of the regional influence of the Bari–Brindisi–Taranto development complex.

It is easy to understand why Mainardi (1973) views the hierarchy as assymetrical – complete in the North, with gaps in the rest of Italy – so that the sixteen main centres are distributed in the following way:

(a)   two dominant metropolises – Milan, Rome;
(b)   eight regional capitals – Turin, Genoa, Venice–Padua, Bologna, Florence, Bari and Palermo;
(c)   six secondary regional capitals – Brescia, Verona, Taranto, Messina, Catania and Cagliari.

Mori and Cori (1969) have also studied the nature of the urban hierarchy, especially the zone of influence of large Italian cities (Fig. 4.1). Here too, there is a marked contrast between the coherent, dense, interlinked northern network, and the weaker, fainter boundaries and more fluid, less connected regions elsewhere. Thus, once again, regional analysis emphasises the contrast already noticed in other domains between the North (Piedmont, Lombardy, Trentino, Friuli, Veneto, Emilia-Romagna and Liguria), whose spatial organisation, once its specifically Italian characteristics are discounted, corresponds to a European model (one is tempted to say Rhine model, given the intensity of exchanges and numerous centres); and southern Italy whose boundary passes between Rome and Naples. The South's basic features are a restricted

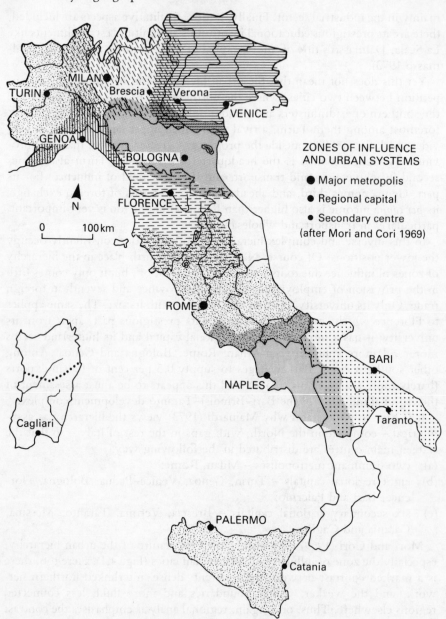

ZONES OF INFLUENCE
AND URBAN SYSTEMS

● Major metropolis

● Regional capital

• Secondary centre

(after Mori and Cori 1969)

Fig. 4.1   Zones of influence of the major Italian cities

zone of influence and weak links with the rest of the hierarchy outside those
derived from administrative functions.

As in all other countries, the development of different regions is uneven.
The weighty triangle of Piedmont–Milan–Liguria, industrial and wealthy,

presents a contrast to the mainly agricultural areas where the low level of industrial activity has led to chronic unemployment and emigration. Undeveloped areas certainly exist in the North, for example in northern Friuli, but they cannot compare with the South, a problem area which, since 1945, has been one of the major issues confronting the Italian Republic. In effect, this is no ordinary problem of regional development, for solutions to it depend not only on socio-economic planning but, to a greater extent, on the complete realisation of the process of unification, begun in the nineteenth century and still not fully achieved.

Fundamental aspects of the *Questione Meridionale*

What is the Mezzogiorno?

The term Mezzogiorno, apart from the fact that it designates regions in the South, does not have a simple definition covering both an administrative entity and a geographic region in its various aspects. The Mezzogiorno's components are mainly economic, but they also include social and psychological aspects, and a great deal of diversity.

The official Mezzogiorno

This applies to the territory in which the *Cassa* can operate; its boundaries have been fixed by law with all the problems that this implies. Some wanted to be located within the area to benefit from its advantages, others considered it an affront (Rome lies outside it). The Law of 10 August 1950 drew a line which started at the Adriatic mouth of the Tronto near Ascoli Piceno, and then crossed the Apennines to the west of Fucino, to meet the Tyrrhenian at the mouth of the Garigliano. Soon afterwards, the perimeter of the *Cassa's* operation was extended to southern Latium, encompassing the Pontine marshes and, for the purpose of reclamation, a small area of Tuscany in the Maremma.

Characteristics of the Mezzogiorno

This is a classic problem region, the problem in this case being its underdevelopment in relation to the North. It needs to be stressed that this is a question of relative underdevelopment in comparison to the North, rather than an absolute low standard of living. The Italian South is rich and has a high standard of living when compared to much of Spain and Greece, and even more so, compared to the really underdeveloped countries of the Third World.

Economic characteristics of the South

These are evolving so rapidly that in order to understand them it is best to describe them as they were around 1960. At that time, the most striking feature was the weakness of industrialisation. The South had 14.4 per cent of

Italian manufacturing employment, restricted to a few towns such as Naples, and comprising traditional activities like wool and clothing. The corollary of this was that agriculture everywhere occupied more than half the working population and produced low returns despite the employment of an abundant and badly paid work-force.

Economic underdevelopment went together with poor communication networks. Only the port facilities of Naples, Palermo, Taranto and Cagliari were not significantly worse than the North. It was, and is, well served by railway lines (Basilcata and Sardinia have the highest ratio of railway lines per 10,000 inhabitants in the country), although the network is of very mediocre quality and the model of slowness and slack use. The normally winding roads are also slow.

The distinct social characteristics of the South

The population still displays a marked individuality in terms of language and dialect, especially Sardinian, Sicilian and Calabrian. The autonomy granted the two islands sanctioned the two most distinct cultures, although the Mezzogiorno is not homogeneous in terms of regional mentalities, and antagonism between different areas is still strong.

Besides these differences, the major factor of similarity is demography. The South is a region of demographic surplus. In the 1950s, the average increase of around 13 per thousand per year was three times that of the North and, although it has decreased, it still retains the same relative proportion. The birth-rate is higher than the national average (Campania has the highest rate, 19 per thousand), while infant mortality, a sign of bad health conditions, also exceeds the national average. However, the mortality rate, often lower than the Italian average, has fallen considerably. In 1976, the natural increase of the South reached 180,000 persons, or four-fifths of the national increase; in the same year Liguria lost' 74,000 people.

To these statistics should be added a long history of emigration. Originally emigrants went abroad – North and South America, then northern Europe and neighbouring countries (France, Switzerland and Germany). As a reservoir of cheap labour, the South has facilitated, to some extent, Western industry – in Boston, São Paulo or Buenos Aires, for example. The loss of manpower was enormous; probably 15 million southerners have left for overseas and 7 million for other Italian regions, with the yearly maxima recorded in the years 1909–13 and 1944–50.

Southern underdevelopment mainly persists in the low rate of economic return, the standard of living, social infrastructure and, now less and less, certain types of behaviour. The average income per inhabitant is everywhere less than the national average. In 1975 it only reached 56 per cent of the national average with a peak of 77 per cent in Sardinia (Lombardy was 135%). Indices of services and of infrastructure are all lower than the average – consumption of energy, number of cars, televisions, telephones, hospital beds, etc. Finally, education is less widespread despite the abundance of unemployed graduates in towns. Technical education has hardly penetrated this area and illiterates are common: on average double the percentage of the North, the highest level recorded in Calabria, with 15.2 per cent compared to 4 per cent in Italy as a whole.

The boundary of the South and its diversity

The problem of defining limits is always tricky. It is clear that the South does not suddenly begin at a demarcated frontier: a transitional zone, or a pre-South, begins further north. Many researchers and politicians are in agreement over the area belonging to this southern transitional zone. It contains Latium, the Tuscan Maremma south of Leghorn, the agricultural provinces of southern Tuscany and Umbria, and the greater part of Marche, whose southern province of Ascoli Piceno belongs to the 'official' Mezzogiorno.

Inevitably in such a vast area, differences cannot help but exist. There is obviously a deep South, more agricultural, less industrialised and poorer than the rest. All the economic indices point to an area that includes the mountainous zone of Calabria, Basilicata, Molise and southern Campania, all of which are situated at the bottom of the ladder of indices for gross product and provision of infrastructure, and among the top in illiteracy and unemployment. The landscapes around Naples, Apulia and Abruzzi, as well as Sicily and Sardinia, are different again. Here, industrialisation has made considerable progress, at least through large-scale projects; net product everywhere exceeds 70 per cent of the national average, and amenities attain an even higher level. This is possibly the area of the South which has succeeded in 'taking off'.

Fundamental causes of underdevelopment

Inadequate deterministic explanations

The influence of the natural environment has occasionally been invoked to explain the level of underdevelopment. Indeed, mountains are to be found almost everywhere in the region, erosion has been very severe, climatic vagaries are frequent and destructive, and soils are often thin and nearly always unstable. There are virtually no natural resources, except for small quantities of zinc, lead and sulphur, and, of course, agricultural products. While all these statements are correct, they are no more so than for a good part of northern Italy where, for example, in Emilia, soils are as threatened by erosion as those of Sicily. However, more significantly, it can be pointed out that this supposedly inevitable, predetermined situation has not always operated with the same effects. Naples was one of the largest cities in the Mediterranean in the eighteenth century, Sicily was one of the most prestigious centres of civilisation in the Mediterranean under the Arabs and Normans. The absence of natural resources is not a handicap for modern industries, nowadays more and more footloose.

A shaky economy after unification

It is not our intention to write a complete economic history of the South but merely to outline some of the main stages. For several centuries most of the South was governed by a centralised monarchy. The Bourbons in Naples, as well as the papal sovereigns, erected an economic system based on principles of Colbertian protectionism that encouraged industry and commerce so that foreign products were almost entirely excluded and industries managed fairly well within very effective customs barriers, despite an already active smuggling trade, the memory of which is not always entirely forgotten. Absolutism reigned supreme, as in the France of Louis XIV, where all activities revolved around the Court which had the power to dispense titles and favours and was the centre of the world. This had two basic consequences. Firstly, the influence of the nobility and the bourgeoisie, who had been granted titles through the acquisition of property, was maintained and extended. Where else did the latifundia reach such dimensions and cover such a large area? Secondly, a belief in initiative and the virtue of effort was lost.

In many cases confidence in the State itself was undermined. Numerous traces of this attitude persist in people's mentality, as the example of Sicily illustrates. Here, nearly all large landowners lived in the capital or in other large towns, leaving the estate manager to cope with harvests and revenue. In northern Italy, on the other hand, estate owners generally managed their properties themselves, often very ably, as did Cavour in Piedmont.

At the time of unification, the already weakened South was literally unhinged by its integration, without any transitional period, into a larger and different system. The major effects were the following. The administration of the new nation was entrusted to those who had the experience and capability of doing so – in other words, the northerners, especially the Piedmontese, who sometimes only poorly understood the languages under their administration and assumed a tactless, colonial attitude. Economically, the same incomprehension of local problems and lack of concern about the consequences of general measures characterised this period. Thus, without the help of internal customs barriers, southern industries were quickly ruined. The previous fiscal system was replaced with high direct taxes on items of everyday consumption, such as cereals. Furthermore, many of the landowners, who had lost out under these new conditions, realised some of their assets by cutting down substantial areas of woodland. In these circumstances the population was reduced to poverty, resulting in large-scale emigration and the desperation that lies behind banditry in Calabria and Sardinia.

From then on until the Second World War, the inevitability of the unchecked economic mechanism was allowed to run its course. Only occasional token efforts were made to alleviate the most flagrant poverty, as in

Naples. No concerted effort was made to eradicate the underlying causes so that no lasting or effective solution was possible.

Programmes for the development of the South: policies and results over thirty years

After the Second World War, and in response to the threatened unity of the nation, political (autonomy) and economic measures were passed in favour of the disadvantaged regions. However, a coordinated programme only really got off the ground when the existence of the Mezzogiorno was acknowledged and a special Ministry with responsibility for the South was created on 10 August 1950. This was the *Cassa per Opere Straordinarie di Pubblica Interesse nell'Italia Meridionale*, known as the *Cassa per il Mezzogiorno*.

Range of policies

If the objectives are clear – reduce the gap between North and South and raise the latter to a level of development comparable to the North – the means need to be discussed. In general, the two principal, opposing positions were the free market doctrine and directive socialist planning. At present the former serves as the reference for official policy. Infrastructure has been improved and incentives have been offered, particularly financial ones which will encourage industrial enterprises, generally private, though there is also state capital (Finsider for metallurgy at Taranto, Alfa Romeo in Naples). Upholders of the second position consider that this programme is not sufficient (although it has admittedly created more employment), and that it has not reduced (if anything, it has *increased*) economic dependence upon the outside: the firms are from the North or are multinationals, because the South has not managed to develop its own industrial base. Given this situation the unions and left-wing parties once again feel that the North has reaped the advantages and has only exported activities which anyhow it would not have been able to keep. In these circumstances, then, directive planning is a necessity. It is highly significant that strikes throughout a sector, as in the chemical industry, broke out both in northern and southern plants in summer 1979, to demand expansion in the latter. This is a rare example of a social protest concerned with regional development.

The actual programme

The development Acts

All the finance of the *Cassa* is, of course, voted by Parliament which passes an act determining the amount and use of the funds. There are two types of Acts. A large number specify particular measures or conditions but have little to do with funding. The most important ones are those operating for a period of several years which allocate an overall budget broken down into individual projects. The most recent budget was passed in Law 183 (2 May 1976) and allocated 18,000,000 million lire for a period of 5 years to end in 1981.

The institutions
The Cassa per il Mezzogiorno

The *Cassa* is a unique institution, for it is a legal public entity, separate from the State, and receiving from the latter funds voted by Parliament. It is fairly independent in the detailed implementation of measures and possesses its own research services, but it never undertakes the work to be carried out and instead puts out tenders.

Distribution agencies

There are three agencies which distribute funds bringing together local capital with that of the *Cassa*. They are: ISVEIMER (*Istituto per lo Sviluppo Economico dell'Italia Meridionale*), with 40 per cent *Cassa* capital and 40 per cent Banco di Napoli; IRFIS (*Istituto Regionale per il Finanziamento alle Industrie in Sicilia*), 40 per cent from the *Cassa*, 20 per cent the Sicilian Region and 20 per cent Banco di Sicilia; and CIS (*Credito Industriale Sardo*), 40 per cent from the *Cassa*, 20 per cent the region and 20 per cent Banco di Sardegna. They were all created on 11 August 1953 and, until 31 December 1977, had lent more than 4,000,000 million lire of the 10,600,000 million lire advanced to industries to set up or expand in the South. In addition, IASM (*Istituto per l'Assistenza allo Sviluppo del Mezzogiorno*), established in 1961, can give technical advice to firms.

Major projects

Management of the natural environment has been the object of numerous works relating to the control of water resources at all scales from small gullies to large rivers, and including reafforestation. The results of this programme can be seen in the barrages across streams and rivers. By the end of 1977 26 reservoirs had been completed with a capacity of more than 1,800 million cubic metres, and 15 others were in progress with another 900 million cubic metres. There are many other works more or less in progress with less spectacular, though no less useful, results concerned with the improvement, reafforestation and terracing of slopes: 141,000 hectares of forest have been newly planted, 148,000 hectares replanted and 718,000 hectares improved.

Transport has been the field of the most spectacular projects, though not financed only by the *Cassa*. Railways have been modernised where it was feasible (new lines, double tracks, electrification). Ports have been improved, some almost totally transformed for industrial use, as at Taranto and Cagliari. Above all, the road network has been completely transformed. Domestic trunk roads have been resurfaced, their alignments improved and shifted to bypass winding stretches; many, in fact almost too many, new roads have been built. Motorways and high-grade roads enable rapid and safe movement.

Industrial infrastructure has also been one of the most costly investments. Areas selected for development have been connected to water and electricity systems and have been linked with the transport network.

Agriculture has been considerably modernised; cereal yields have frequently doubled and the use of fertilisers has greatly increased. Irrigation works undertaken by the State now cover 657,000 hectares, of which more than 300,000 hectares are due to the efforts of the *Cassa*. The conversion and storage of agricultural products have been largely modernised. It is sometimes difficult to distinguish what is due to the efforts of individuals and what has been implemented by the *Cassa*, but all are part of the same impetus.

Tourism has also played a role in development, since *Cassa* financing has contributed to the construction of 14,000 hotels and 65,000 rooms.

Industrialisation was the principal objective of policy measures in the South. How is it to be evaluated today?

Industrial activities were established in isolated places, especially in areas and nuclei of development. These nodes or poles are numerous, forty-eight in all, and have been dispersed according to the aims of development planning. Not all have been successful; in fact, far from it. More than 1 million jobs were aimed at in the various projects that were to be completed by 1978, a target that was probably attained. Of these a little more than half were created by new firms; the rest resulted through the expansion of existing firms. Although in principle this is an excellent start, it is insufficient to soak up the demand for employment.

Only in theory is it a sound idea, for the industries which have been established are of a certain sort; they are large-scale establishments (generally more than 1000 employees) in steel, oil refining, chemicals, and more rarely, in textiles. These industries have contributed a great deal to the development of Italian industry but are, for the most part, imported activities, employing not much labour and without the ability to generate other industries. It is now clearly understood that, after thirty years of effort, the South is still not capable of developing its own industrial base. This neo-colonial industrialisation has not put out a network of local initiatives able to diffuse development.

Improvements in the standard of living

The social improvement is evident everywhere, for the South has closed the gap with the North in all the aspects we previously mentioned at the beginning of this chapter. Depopulation has inevitably occurred in mountain areas, but everywhere salaries and incomes, which we should not confuse with economic return, have drawn closer to those in the North, while the infrastructure has perceptibly improved. The policy in this domain has been an unquestioned success, although it is more the result of a transfer in the form of government funds derived from largely northern tax contributions rather than a real economic transformation.

Regional systems

There are numerous ways of ranking regions using demographic and economic criteria, but they always produce an identical regional polarisation, notwithstanding certain nuances, at the upper and lower ends of the spectrum – an economically healthy space in Piedmont–Lombardy–Emilia and a depressed area including the islands and the regions south of Latium and the Marche. The problem is to know whether these larger areas are continuous or could be divided into sub-regions and, if it is possible, to discern a transitional zone, a central Italy which needs to be defined and delimited.

An answer can be found in Tagliacarne's more detailed provincial analyses (Tagliacarne 1971 and 1975), but, in fact, the analysis of gross regional product which we have used is based on a composite index that can be mapped by provinces (Fig. 4.1). Three economic spaces can be distinguished from this index:

(a)   a highly developed economic region, where the index always exceeds 115 (100 is the national average). This region includes Liguria, excluding the province of Imperia, Piedmont outside the Cuneo–Alessandria area, Lombardy except Sondrio, and Emilia-Romagna excluding Forli. Even within these less wealthy zones, the index never falls below 100. On the other hand, the centres of greatest economic activity (index higher than 130) occur in the provinces of Genoa, Turin, Milan, Reggio Emilia, Modena and Bologna. Without any doubt the economic heart of Italy lies within this polygon.

(b)   a depressed space, where the index never reaches the national average. This area covers the whole of Umbria, Marche, (excluding Ancona at the provincial scale), Abruzzi, Molise, Campania, Apulia, Basilicata, Calabria and the islands. The province of Frosinone in Latium can be added to this list. This analysis can also be differentiated since the index never descends below 85 in Marche and Umbria but, elsewhere, only a few provinces rise above this figure (L'Aquila, Taranto, Matera and Syracuse).

(c)   a transitional zone consisting mainly of areas with indices slightly above the national average (100–115), with some anomalies above and below this figure. Within this category are Trentino-Alto Adige; Veneto, split exactly between a wealthy sector (Vicenza, Treviso, Rovigo and Verona), and a poorer area (Belluno, Venice and Padua); and Friuli-Venezia Giulia where the average index is raised considerably (134) by the presence of economically rich Trieste. Separated from this transitional zone by Emilia-Romagna, there is a southern extension (Tuscany and

Latium)with less variation around the average, either slightly above (Pisa)
or slightly below (Massa Carrara).

It is understandable that this pattern should lead economists and geographers, such as Muscarà (1978) to suggest a radiocentric division with an epi-
centre corresponding to the Lombardy–Piedmont–Liguria–Emilia-Romagna
region, a 'central' Italy which includes Trentino-Alto Adige, Veneto, Friuli,
Tuscany and Latium, and a southern Italy which can itself be divided into a
transitional and a deep South.

Though sound in principle, this regional division has to be compared with
other ways of classifying regions. Our analysis of demography, trade and spatial organisation leads us, however, to propose for two reasons a different
division, more in line with traditional geographical analysis. The first relates
to the organisation of trade and the structure of economic space. It would
seem that all the regions of northern Italy, from Turin to Trieste, from Como
to Genoa, and from Bolzano to Bologna, are connected by the exchanges
between them and by a whole set of interdependencies of which we shall say
more later. In contrast, the various regions of the Centre and South are characterised by a lower level of interregional trade, most of which is directed
towards, or comes from the North. Thus the flow between northern regions
is replaced further south by enclosed regions that have little to do with one
another in terms of trade and migration. So, if Veneto and Friuli clearly belong
to the northern system, this is not the case with Latium and Tuscany which,
in this respect, function less as transitional zones than as part of the southern
system.

The case for a single, large, northern region is reinforced by another set of
arguments relating basically to problems of regional planning. These are concerned with mountain regions, ranging from Alpine passes to the maintenance
of economic life in high, isolated communities; the problem of the complex
relationships between mountain and plain; the problem of water resources
including energy policy and the organisation of a vast area of irrigated agricultural land.

We would, therefore, propose a fourfold division – a large region corresponding to northern Italy, a transitional zone stretching from Tuscany to
Latium and Abruzzi, a deep, mainland South, and the islands which form a
world in themselves due to their insularity.

5 Northern Italy and its regional system

It is of course difficult to regard as a single region an area as extensive as northern Italy. Defined statistically, it has 120,000 sq. kilometres and 26 million inhabitants, accounting for 40 per cent of the territory and 46 per cent of the Italian population, with an average density of 215 persons per sq. kilometre. It is also a highly diverse area. It encompasses both the Alps and the Po plain; it experiences the severe climate of Central Europe and the mildness of the Mediterranean fringe; and it combines the wealth of Lombardy and the real poverty of the upper Alpine valleys (see Fig. 5.1). This diversity does not, however, diminish the simplicity of its spatial organisation based on the influence of six cities, with zones of influence that include coast, plain and mountain. The linkages between these zones are too strong and the networks too dense to be able to ignore them and introduce some other basic division. First, it is necessary to examine the nature of the spatial integration of northern Italy.

The spatial network

Relationship between plain and mountain: population

The relationships between plains and mountains have been very well outlined by Dematteis (1973) for the western Alps; the same types of relationships, though more complex, operate for all the Alpine flanks.

The closed system of the mountains, opened up progressively by the diffusion of the textile industry from Turin, still utilises hydroelectric energy and manpower supplied by the upland areas. This equilibrium was later broken by the attraction Turin exerted on the valley populations. In respect of this, one may distinguish between the lower valleys, where Turin's industry expanded and from where daily commuting took place, and the upper valleys. The latter were literally depopulated and their economies disrupted by migration toward the plain before some of them were able to benefit from the second urban discharge, this time in the form of tourism, principally in winter resorts and mountaineering areas.

More generally, the Italian Alpine valleys have not given rise to the organisation of modern economies, as has occurred around Grenoble in France, because of their smaller size, and this has made the cities of the plain more attractive. The influence and autonomy of the economic and urban systems of the valleys remain mediocre, varying in proportion to the development and importance of the valleys – weak in Piedmont, but more substantial in the Upper Adige.

On the other hand, the small size, the immense contrasts in relief and the proximity to developed and densely populated areas, have now helped the growth of tourism, nationally and internationally, thanks to the development of the Alpine passes.

Relationship between plain and mountain: the system of Alpine passes

Alpine passes have always played a considerable role in the growth and dynamism of the large northern cities which, in turn, have contributed to their development. It is a complex relationship, since the flow of people and goods has increasingly operated to the advantage of the cities and the disadvantage of the passes, due to three causes. Firstly, there is trade, which was the origin of Milan's prodigious wealth during the Middle Ages and which has now reached previously unknown levels. Secondly, a number of passes, now only of secondary importance, such as the Little St. Bernard, Stelvio and Tonale, were opened up for strategic purposes (frontiers, alliances and military operations). Thirdly, the present political system, which favours trade with northern and western Europe has led to the eastern passes, such as Mt Croce and especially Tarvisio, losing much of their significance.

The significance of these three factors is now overshadowed by the magnitude and direction of the flow of exchanges which, in the space of a few years, have undergone major changes. Now, in addition to light goods, which consisted mainly of manufactured products. there is large-scale transportation. A new type has appeared, that of crude oil, distributed through three pipelines: the Great St Bernard, from Genoa to the Swiss refineries of Aigle and Collombey; the Splügen towards Ingolstadt; and from Trieste, the Mt Croce, which leads to Ingolstadt and Vienna. The pipeline from Trieste alone has a capacity of 25 million tons per annum.

Technical progress in civil engineering and expansion of road traffic for goods and passengers have meant that the railway system has lost the quasi-monopoly which it had for a long time enjoyed. Traditional routes have only benefited from this switch in areas where feeble trade flows meant that no new railway construction was needed, as in the west (Mt Genèvre, Mt Cenis, Larche) and in the east (Tarvisio, Mt Croce, San Candido). The maintenance

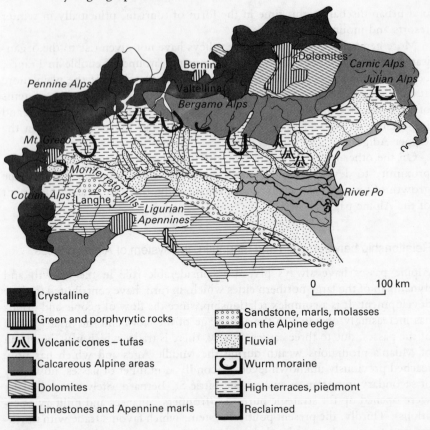

Fig. 5.1 Northern Italy: relief

of the road system in good condition also highlights the secondary importance of certain passes in the central Alps (Splügen, Maloggia, Bernina and Resia). Otherwise, the need to keep the Alps open for the entire year has required the construction of large motorway tunnels, which have been completed, some very recently (St Gotthard). Brenner is an exception, for here the uncovered railway has been supplemented by a motorway through the pass.

In the course of this evolution, and at the present time, the flow of traffic is divided into three very unequal sectors which correspond very roughly to the traditional regional classification of the Alps. A western sector, without much activity, extends from Tende, where the tunnel has not been reopened, to Mt Cenis, where the railway tunnel is to be supplemented from Modane to Bardonecchia with a road tunnel which, for the present, is not going to include a motorway. In the east the only properly equipped pass is Tarvisio, a situation that has remained unchanged for years. Most of the traffic and infrastructure thus remains concentrated between Mt Blanc and the Brenner, with a marked concentration on the Swiss St Gotthard pass, which carries a considerable rail traffic and the most important flow of road traffic connecting Milan and the German motorway network.

These motorway routes have brought distinct advantages to the series of small towns at the foot of the passes, and each one possesses its own international railway station, transit facilities, customs, highway maintenance and hotels. Aosta, particularly, has benefited from the opening of Mt Blanc and the Great St Bernard, there is also Bardonecchia, Susa, Domodossola and Bressanone. The future of these small towns, nevertheless, remains uncertain. What will happen, for example to Susa after the opening of the tunnel under the Fréjus? On the other hand, some of the present development of the large cities of the plain is linked to transalpine traffic. The case of the Bolzano–Verona–Bologna urban chain is a clear example, but the construction of motorway slip-roads around Turin and Milan indicates that the large metropolises also feel involved.

Relationship between plain and mountain: water management

Northern Italy holds 54 per cent of Italy's water resources. Thanks to the North's topography, this proportion includes the most regular, the easiest to store and the richest in potential energy. It is, therefore, hardly surprising that this region produces most of the nation's hydroelectric power (45,000 million kWh of a total of 52,000 million), consuming most of it in industry, and contains, with 2.4 million hectares, 70 per cent of Italy's irrigated land.

Despite this impressive record the region is facing several difficult hydraulic problems. In terms of energy provision, the potential for production from existing major sources has been practically exhausted by the construction of large power stations such as Soverzene, Ponte-Murandin and Turbigo. Most of the new and future resources depend on the utilisation of pumping basins, the largest of which is Delio which now operates in conjunction with Lake Maggiore to produce energy of 1,000 MW.

Yet the energy problem is assuming crucial proportions to the extent that the hydroelectric potential is far from being able to meet a regional demand which is continuing to grow and already reaches 81,000 million kWh per annum. In terms of regional planning we should note that the Alpine valleys only keep an insignificant proportion of this energy. Certainly there are in the large valleys – Dora, Adda, Ticino, Adige – electrometallurgical industries (Aosta, Varzo and Darfo) and electrochemicals (Rumianca and Ardenno), but, on the whole, the distribution of power has mainly benefited the nearby lowland, endowed with a long industrial tradition.

As with the supply of energy, water for agricultural purposes comes from the mountains and benefits the plains. Not that irrigation techniques are unknown in the mountains; for modern methods are often used (sprinkler irrigation which serves equally as protection against frost) in the upper valleys of the Adige and Adda. However, this system only covers at most 100,000 hectares.

Two factors, one positive (the system of *fontanili*), the other negative (low altitude and bad drainage in the plains), explain the significance and diversity of irrigation techniques. Possibly too much attention has been devoted to the *fontanili*, for they only irrigate a relatively small area, but they constitute an unusual element in the landscape due to their linear positioning at the foot of high terraces and pro-glacial features, from which they gather and release the water which has percolated to the surface. These slow, regular water sources exude a constant flow whose temperature never falls below 10 °C. This remarkable characteristic has for a long time been utilised in the cultivation of *marcite*, irrigated grasses that are even harvested in winter. Unfortunately, the line of springs, particularly abundant in Lombardy, yields less plentiful quantities of water in Veneto and supplies only very irregularly distributed sources in Piedmont. It is a fact that due to problems of altitude and drainage, the lower plain of the Po would still be in the process of infilling if it were left in its natural state. The process of raising the level, except where it is prevented by the construction of a system of dykes, leads to serious flooding downstream of Verona. When this happens, there is hardly any alternative either to leaving it in marshes or completely developing the land and water by a system of dykes and drainage ditches which collect the water from the higher ground and channel it downstream to the lower lands, after it has been used for irrigation.

Elsewhere on the piedmont, water problems are of a different sort. On dry, stony, porous terraces, the naturally infertile *brughiere* and *barrage* lands have only become more fertile by the construction of canals dug from supply sources to drainage channels on the left bank of the river.

The various types of improvements, together constituting the largest and most complex hydraulic planning for agricultural purposes in Europe, do not form a unified whole, but rather an organic entity constantly expanding and in evolution. The oldest part of the system probably dates from the Roman period, and much was accomplished by Benedictine monks after the seventeenth century. As for the large canals, this system was started in 1177 with the Ticinello, and this work continues today with the completion of the Canal Emiliano-Romagnolo. Between times, remarkable canals, such as the Naviglio Grande (fifteenth century), the Villoresi and the Cavour, finished in 1891 to irrigate 50,000 hectares, have been dug.

From the supply of electricity to the construction of irrigation systems, and including the supply of water to public bodies and industrialists, there are hardly any aspects in common other than the operation of the same hydraulic potential and the continual increase in demand. Until now all these demands have been able to be satisfied without there being any great need for coordination, although one notes attempts to regulate, for example, the automatic adjustment of seasonal river levels by storage in reservoirs whose capacity reaches 2.3 cubic kilometres with an estimated total flow between 130 and 210 cubic metres per second. The ability to regulate will be increasingly employed in the years to come in order to satisfy demand. It appears, none the less, that the operation is proving difficult since needs and seasonal demands do not necessarily coincide between the supplies of energy (winter demand and autumn storage), farmers (summer demand and spring storage) and those responsible for civil protection who are worried about the high autumn levels and would prefer the barrages empty at the beginning of this season. Naturally, the differences in these demands could be covered by additional barrage reserves situated in glacial and intramontane basins, but these are areas which have for long been used by mountain farmers. Thus the conflicts between mountains and plains are tending to become very acute.

Uniform mountain areas

There are no comparable relations between mountain regions as there are between plain and mountain, for what have mountains to exchange among themselves? Yet some similarities, as shown by certain examples, allow one to define an Alpine culture, whose chances of survival vary from one area to another. The open, small valleys of Piedmont are not easily able to guard their identity and cultural autonomy against the attraction of an all too close metropolis. On the other hand, the extent and spatial hierarchy of the Val d'Aosta enable it to reaffirm its cultural identity. A basic distinction is also to be made between regions (Val d'Aosta, High Tyrol) which, while maintaining their originality, are highly integrated into an exchange economy, and other regions (Sette Communi, Val Sugana) whose identity is derived from a kind of withdrawal into picturesque, though vulnerable, customs.

Furthermore, some original features are adapted to the economic demands of a mountain existence. This is the case particularly of the *masochiuso* or *Hof* of the Dolomites and the Tyrol, where large farms function under a patrilineal group directed by the eldest who is the sole owner. This system avoids the typical fragmentation of land in the mountains, while guaranteeing some sort of livelihood for all members of the family, though admittedly in a subordinate role. There is no other alternative but emigration. Another Alpine institution is the *malghe* system, fairly similar to the Swiss *mayen*, since it involves the exploitation of high Alpine pastures and functions from an enormous building, the *malga*, characteristic of the eastern Alps and situated usually at about 1,500 metres. The herd is looked after by a full-time shepherd paid in kind. The owner only goes up to the chalet for the harvest and to bring down hay cut from the high fields, and the animals, leaving the lower pastures in spring, are only driven down to the villages in autumn. This system is in the process of breaking up or of moving towards a cooperative structure.

In Italy, as elsewhere in the Alps, these institutions form part of a system of land use based on the changing environments at different altitudes. This vertical system consists of three elements:

(a) the *fondovalle*, where the arable fields and permanent habitat are;
(b) the *mezzacosta* on the slopes and terraces with woods in which there is often a mixture of chestnut trees, pastures for hay and haylofts;
(c) the *parte alta*, the high Alpine pastures.

These complementary zones were formerly integrated with certain technical functions (mills, workshops for the spinning of wool, sawmills using water-wheels) which no longer have any role to play. Similarly, certain aspects of the landscape, such as the cereal fields, are no longer economically viable. It follows, then, that there has been a complete revaluation of the traditional economy which has resulted in several types of solutions.

1. Total abandonment due to the impossibility of harmonising the various elements of local society. Emigration occurs to the plain or neighbouring countries (France and especially Switzerland).
2. Specialisation according to local environmental conditions: vines and fruits in the Adige and Adda valleys, forestry in Upper Friuli.
3. Orientation towards a second complementary activity in tourism (High Tyrol) or industry (Val Camonica).

At a more general level, there is finally an originality that lies in the dis-crepancy between political and linguistic frontiers. The fact is that the cultural groups in the upper valleys are nearly always similar on both sides of the frontier, especially when it coincides with a watershed. This symmetrical division is easily explained in the ease of movement provided by the passes. The areas that impede movement are the natural frontiers which are usually found lower down in the zones of narrow gorges and rockslides and in the transverse valleys. This explains the diffusion of French beyond the two St Bernard passes and its penetration into the Val d'Aosta as far as Pont Saint Martin as well as to Pinerolo and Saluzzi. In the Upper Tyrol, German groups settled in the Middle Ages and were protected by the Habsburg administration which controlled the area between Val Pusteria and Val Venosta. Further east there appear groups of Ladins and Slovenes who imprinted their cultural dis-tinctiveness in Upper Friuli where Slavs, Germans and Latins still come into contact with each other.

These national minorities, who locally constitute the majority, have always posed real and imagined problems in political terms since the delimitation of summit frontiers, which is, after all, a recent thing. The Tyrolean problem, partially resolved since the granting of an autonomy statute, has given rise to numerous dramatic incidents since the integration, without prior consultation, into Italy, the voluntary migration agreed by Mussolini, its return in 1945 and the terrorist incidents of the 1950s. In any case, the German minority remains little affected by Italian culture in spite of the numerous civil servants of south-ern origin in Bolzano. The same cannot be said of the French-speaking Pied-montese who, given the similarity of Latin languages, often use Italian. A sign of this displacement is that religious services at Torre Pellice in the Vaud are now delivered in Italian.

There is less frequent local contact on either side of the mountain crests. The inhabitants of Crissolo no longer pass through the Traversette Pass to cut hay at Saint Véran; likewise the inhabitants of Oetztal wade much less frequently through mud in crossing the snow-covered slopes of Mt Re in order to socialise with their cousins in the Upper Adige. Little by little, outside influences are penetrating this way of life and the Alpine world in Italy, as elsewhere, is losing its cultural identity.

The development of a Mediterranean megalopolis?

At a conference held in Bergamo in 1976 (Muscarà 1978), a group of Italian and foreign geographers projected the development of the urban system of the Po plain in order to work out whether the centres now form, or would form in the future, a polycentric megalopolis comparable, though less extensive, to the megalopolises defined by Gottmann (1961). This question is not irrelevant considering that 22.6 million inhabitants live at a density of 268 persons per sq. kilometre in an area of 85,000 sq. kilometres, and that the heart of the Po region, situated in the plains west of Venice, exceeds the theoretical minimum population of 15 million (see Fig. 5.2). However, these statistics in themselves do not necessarily permit a comparison with the northern European megalopolis, but it is obvious that the Po plain is evolving in this way, and unless there were to be no growth as a result of a major crisis, it represents at present the largest conurbation in the Mediterranean. For this reason it is interesting to analyse it functionally and critically.

The latter objective would be meaningless without being situated in a very specific cultural context of a region which, for a long time, was characterised by the persistence of political, and therefore customs, boundaries, and in which manufacturing and commercial traditions have a long history. Small and medium-sized towns multiplied; artisanal trades, commercial activities and industry reinforced government and administrative functions which were often out of proportion to the population and importance of the towns. This fertile terrain encouraged the development of a powerful bourgeoisie whose interests extended into all sectors of the economy from local agriculture to international commerce. In spite of these flourishing activities, no metropolis stood out and extended its sphere of influence permanently over the plain. The Duchy of Milan could never gain control over Genoa or Venice, while the latter limited its ambitions to firm land. Meanwhile, economic dominance continually fluctuated between the thalassocracies and the large cities of the interior. In this respect the dominance of Milan is recent, for, at the time of the foundation of the kingdom, Turin held 55 per cent of the share capital compared to Milan's 4 per cent and Florence's 32 per cent.

What remains from the past is an urban tradition found elsewhere only in

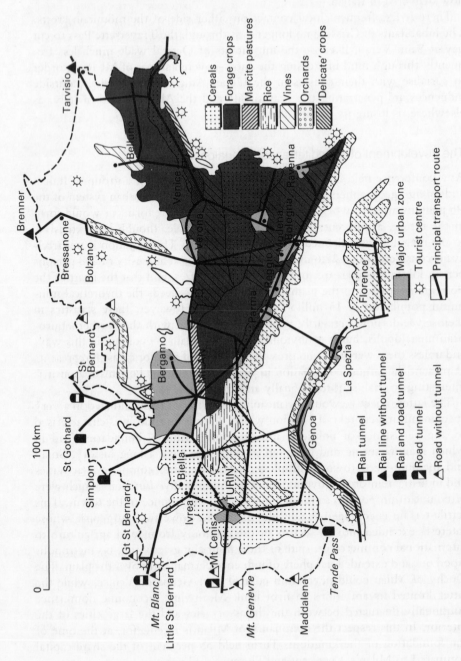

Legend:
- Cereals
- Forage crops
- Marcite pastures
- Rice
- Vines
- Orchards
- 'Delicate' crops

- Major urban zone
- Tourist centre
- Principal transport route

- Rail tunnel
- Rail line without tunnel
- Rail and road tunnel
- Road tunnel
- Road without tunnel

Fig. 5.2 Northern Italy: major routes, urban fields and agricultural regions

the Rhinelands; a tradition that has influenced the functional organisation of the region through a remarkable diffusion of quaternary activities (management, tertiary education, dissemination of mass media) and that often involves towns of barely more than 100,000 inhabitants. Industrial activities are also dispersed and located in very small towns which often specialise in a certain branch of production, whether it be in textiles or in ceramics. On the other hand, no large metropolis has managed to emerge as the central city, despite Milan's recognition as the economic leader and its important role as transmitter, for the North of Italy, of administrative power emanating from Rome. It should be noted that this pattern tends to change eastward where the medium-sized towns sometimes have an industrial sector that is, in employment terms, much less significant than the service, and especially administrative, sectors.

In addition to a functional analysis, an examination of the pattern of flows also brings out the distinctiveness of the large cities. Thus Milan and Turin differ not only in their population and the quality of their infrastructure, but also in the type of relationship they maintain with their hinterlands. Turin draws in activities and is partly responsible for the decline of certain regions like the Monferreto hills; Milan, on the other hand, redistributes functions and acts as a regional catalyst. In other respects one can compare Turin and Milan, which are largely independent, to other cities, such as Genoa, Venice and Trieste, which owe much of their expansion to Milan and Turin (industrialisation of Porto Marghera and Mestre due to Milanese capital) or to the State, especially noticeable at Genoa (Italsider) and at Trieste (ENI). Finally, Bologna commands a unique position in the urban hierarchy due to its historical continuity and its route location, formerly based on the Via Emilia between Piacenza and Cattolica, and today on the transport facilities provided by the motorway.

Thus, in analysing the urban system in several different ways, we have noted the absence of a uniform model; a certain dispersal of growth poles; a variety of situations which encourage the maximum of initiatives and identity. All of these are extremely vital for small towns and regions – a fortunate situation that cannot fail to encourage a democratic system. Yet it is also a precarious situation, continually threatened by the encroachment of the centralising State; threatened also by urban expansion which reduces the role of urban centres and impedes the acculturation of new immigrants who now form a large part of the population. It is understandable, then, that Italians are highly conscious of the choice now posed between the 'super-growth' of several large centres and the dangers this policy implies (one need only think of the dioxin disaster at Seveso) and the alternative policy favouring small and medium-sized towns so that they would form an expanding ring eastward, and possibly southward. It is within this perspective that any regional analysis should take place, that is, by contrasting regions organised around dominant centres (Milan, Turin, Bologna), with coastal regions, which while remaining somewhat marginal in this system, complement them and lead them to participate in their growth.

Turin and the Piedmont desert

Turin is the capital of Piedmont as Paris is the capital of France, by the pleasure of the prince and the continuity of a dynastic policy. The Prince in this case is Emmanuel-Philibert and the dynasty, the House of Savoy, whose move from one kingdom to another, shifting the capital to Florence (while waiting to go to Rome) in 1867, dealt a severe blow to the city. The choice of Turin as the site of the capital of the kingdom of Savoy, which extended over both flanks of the western Alps, is explained basically by the combination of a defensive site and easy crossing of the Po. In fact, Turin does not completely command the passes leading to the western side between the Great St. Bernard and Tende, except for the road network which obviously did not exist in 1566 when the decisive choice was made. Previously, it had been frequently supplanted by other towns in the spatial hierarchy: Ivrea, well situated at the entrance to the Val d'Aosta; Asti, situated half-way on the Roman road from Piacenza to Aosta; and Alessandria, a new town commanding the route from Liguria to the Po plain. The choice of Turin is no less suitable, for the city is at once situated on the route to passes and on the dry hillocks of the Piedmont, and equidistant between the hills of the south-east and the low plain of the north-east. But the potential of this location was only realised after the establishment of a network of good communications linking the small kingdom.

The excellent network and the small size of Piedmont initially combined to put a stop to the development of other towns, including Novara and Vercelli. Turin, where business affairs were settled, was easily reached. Once its political functions were definitely lost and its industrial role was confirmed, the process of centralisation assumed a different aspect and continued to aid Turin's growth until the urban system made its way up the Dora Riparia valley, spread towards Ivrea and drew in labour from even further afield. At the same time, however, this expansion destroyed to some extent certain activities in the areas which did not fall within its direct influence and were not in Milan's orbit. This contrasting pattern is by no means simple, for certain regions, like the Val d'Aosta, have come out of it well. Of course, Aosta is admittedly already at the limit of Turin's zone of influence which does not fully extend its administrative hold to the north-east.

A surfeit of short Alpine valleys

From the Tanaro to Dora Baltea there are at least fifteen valleys in an area whose width reaches at most 50 kilometres in the north and barely 20 kilometres in the south. These narrow valleys are virtually without tributaries apart from the Dora Baltea, hollowed out of rocks that are softer than the gneiss-hardened schists that occur further south. The numerous small networks and the narrow expanse of the eastern face are explained by the double movement that tipped the Po at the same time as the internal section was being uplifted before the Pliocene. If, to these youthful landscapes, is added the fact that there was less glacial action south of Val Clusone, it is understandable that these valleys rarely interconnect and that many of them end up in steep, insurmountable faces. There exist, however, six passes that are sufficiently wide to be endowed with a more or less complete infrastructure (Tende, Larche, Mt Genèvre, Mt Cenis, Little and Great St Bernard).

The number of passes does not really compensate for the lack of development. There are few real towns south of Val d'Aosta: Susa, Bardonecchia and Clavière are only customs posts. Finally, it also explains the weak development of agriculture, which is deprived of land. Still, the valleys do bear the imprint of a previous demographic pressure: abandoned terraces, diseased chestnut trees and deserted villages. The only remaining life outside the villages at the base of the passes are a few ski resorts: basically Sestrière (the resort frequented by *Torinesi*), Susa, Bardonecchia, and recently, the upper Ellero valley above Mondovi.

Most settlement is now concentrated in the lower valleys, at an altitude slightly higher than the line of piedmont towns upon which they are dependent. There is a textile industry at Susa and Perosa Argentina, a foundry at Susa and Bussoleno and, lastly, mechanical engineering with RIV SKF at Pinerolo and Villar Perosa where there is also a Fiat workshop. All this is fairly insignificant. As for the production of hydroelectricity (1.8 MkW and a capacity of 6,000 million kWh), it is only used locally by the few steelworks mentioned above and is essentially for Turin industry.

The Val d'Aosta is very different because it is broader and has better links with surrounding areas. This has enabled local life to survive and prosper. Even so, agriculture is clearly in decline, despite extensive Alpine pastures and the survival of several good vineyards below Saint-Vincent. The mountain dwellers are much more involved with forestry, industrial work and tourist activities than with agriculture as such. The production of electricity (3,000 million kWh) has permitted traditional industries, for example metallurgy at Val de Cogne, to continue and to go on and make high-quality products. To this may be added aluminium and electrochemicals at Verrès and Pont Saint Martin, as well as synthetic fibres at Châtillon. Finally, tourism has acted to develop scenic spots and has encouraged new access routes which bring in French, Swiss and German tourists. With the aid of Turin capital, local dynamism has modernised old resorts, such as Courmayeur, and developed new ones such as Breuil-Cervinia.

These advantages have particularly favoured the town of Aosta which, thanks to its administrative and transit functions, now has 40,000 inhabitants and extends out beyond the Roman walls and the old town. A tangible sign of this prosperity is the *per capita* income which equals that of Piedmont. Yet, there is a dark spot in this picture for, if the population has increased from 100,000 to 115,000 inhabitants between 1961 and 1977, this has arisen through an essentially Italian immigration which replaces the French language and culture.

The Piedmontese 'Mezzogiorno'

To the east of the Po and south of a line through Casale, Alessandria and Voghera, the meeting of the Po plain and the Apennines engenders an infinitely complex series of small-scale landscapes. The lowest zones corresponding to marls, sands and Pliocene molasses (Astian) form small, open plains (Alessandria), basins (Asti) and a series of crumbling hillocks and cuestas. There appear, to a varying degree, the first outlying Miocene limestone hills of the Apennine system. Topographically, all the high areas fall into three systems: the Turin hills, the Monferrato hills and, between the Tanaro and Bormida rivers, the Langhe hills.

The complexity of landforms is coupled to a fragmented human landscape. Even after initial attempts to restructure it, property is still fragmented, the average size barely reaching 3–5 hectares. Production is also fragmented, divided between small fruits, nuts, white truffles and cereals. There is little irrigation, the *fontanili* being few and of small flow. Toward Alessandria specialisation begins to make an appearance with wheat, but wine remains the main activity with the vineyards of Alba and Asti. Here also the properties are too small; the vines are often mixed with other crops and wine-making is far from being fully rationalised. Commercially a whole series of distinctions between types of grapes and *appellations* relating to the vineyard are blurred. As a result, the wine is not selling as well as it should and the vineyards are losing area. Many vineyard properties are being sold. In this way, the beautiful landscapes of mixed vineyards together with leafy trees on the upper slopes of hillocks, are in the process of permanently changing.

Further north, in the hills around Turin, these landscapes are simply disappearing, due to urban expansion in what is a difficult terrain for urbanisation. The people who take advantage of this situation are the wealthy. As for the towns to the west, for long prosperous because of their military location, they receive the leftovers of Turin's expansion. On the other hand, the region between Novi Ligure and Tortona has managed to make the most of its position on the only route from Genoa to the Po plain. Here there are now wholesalers, fruit and vegetable markets, and chemical factories using methane and petroleum which is piped through in transit.

The ricefields of Lomellina

Beyond the Po, and in complete contrast to the dry plain of Alessandria to the south as well as to the high, flat lands of the *barrage* to the north, stretches a hollow zone, badly drained and underlain by clay soils. This is Lomellina, a poor country, of late settlement, still sparsely populated today. This basin, shared by Piedmont and Lombardy, has been carved out into large estates that have evolved a system which combines water-fed pastures with ricefields in the lower lands. The labourers from Lombardy who carried out the work of transplanting and weeding until the 1960s (the *mondine*) are no longer needed, their work replaced by seeds that can be planted directly and by selective weedkillers. The large buildings with their dormitories, which were a fundamental element of the rural landscape, now stand empty, threatened with destruction in a region which has remained prosperous. With 10 million quintals of rice in 1978 in Piedmont and Lombardy, the production is only profitable in relation to prices paid in Europe, so that the part of the harvest which does not meet with consumer taste has to be exported at a loss.

These factors explain the relative decline of rice. Tonnages have stayed constant or increased, but the area under cultivation has given way to pastures as well as poplar growing, which is carried out intensively with ploughing, fertilisers and irrigation by flooding.

The Turin Piedmont

Between the river and the Alps, and above the valley bottoms, stretches a vast area laid down by glaciers, fluvio-glacial deposits and ancient, often pebbly, alluvia. This *alta pianura* of permeable soils, except along the layers of *ferreto*, is also a zone of poor soils of the *vaude* and *barrage* type. On the other hand, irrigation began very early on the cones where Alpine torrents emerged and where it was easy to tap these waters immediately downstream from the mountain zone. The small plain of Pinerolo admirably demonstrates the nature of the first gravity irrigation and the good use that successful farmers made of it on land planted with wheat, corn, mulberry trees and pastures for hay and sundry types of grasses.

Later on, in the nineteenth century, the elaboration of irrigation techniques and the contribution of industrial capital which could not be invested in land enabled this system, originally to the south of Turin, to be extended northward and eastward. In the course of this evolution in space and time, the land holdings progressed from small to medium to large properties. Today, this agriculture is becoming more intensive.

In short, this is a zone more remarkable for what men have been able to do with it than for its intrinsic qualities. It is also noteworthy for its regular line of towns of a similar size which are located at the mouth of each valley at the point of contact with the plain. Thus, within Turin's zone of influence, this scattering of towns stretches from Mondovi to Biella, passing through Cuneo, Ivrea and smaller towns such as Pinerolo. If this system seems to be similar, notably in terms of a growing population as a result of immigration from the valleys, it is, nevertheless, not entirely homogeneous. The southern part (province of Cuneo) has for some time remained outside Turin's expansion; an example is Verzuolo with its textile industry and paper mills.

The situation has been somewhat modified in the past twelve years by the arrival of Italcementi and Michelin and later by the move outwards of Turin's clothing industry. The northern part (Ivrea and the Canavese) has experienced a simpler and more continuous development thanks to Olivetti whose head-quarters and a certain number of workshops (typewriters and calculators) are located at Ivrea. Finally, to the very north, at the boundary of Milan's field of influence, Biella profits from its pure water and humidity for the production of wool.

The industrial belt around Turin occupies the area between Carmagnola in the south to Chivasso in the north. As it moved out of Turin, though still centred on the town, industrialisation first reached the banks of the Stura di Lanzo (Venaria, Robassomero), before spreading along the motorway to Settino Torinese and Chivasso. The whole system encompasses 1.6 million people, of whom more than 700,000 have settled here in the past 20 years.

It is not therefore surprising that the problems of growth, mentioned above, figure as the major preoccupations of the city council. These problems are all the more acute because the city has achieved, since the end of the nineteenth century, a twofold demographic and functional transformation; until 1865 its main activities were administrative and military. With the departure of the Court and the administration, a period of stagnation set in and lasted until the development of hydroelectric power and the motor car industry. The estab-lishment of Fiat in 1899 marked, without any doubt, the key date, since the city and firm have grown at the same rhythm until Fiat was forced to pursue a policy of decentralisation. In his book on Turin, Gabert (1964) has shown the limits and dangers of expansion based on industry rather than serv-ices, on a single industry rather than an extensive range, and on a single firm rather than many. The diversification of the Fiat group into the area of the daily press adds further to this one-firm concentration.

Have things changed since Gabert's book? A rapid perusal of the list of industrial activities in the area leads one to believe not, for the percentage of mechanical engineering industries and those associated with the car industry has tended to increase. Out of a total of 90 factories employing more than 500 workers, only 2 are in textiles, 1 in clothing and none in the food industry (there is, however, Cinzano and Martini-Rossi). On the other hand, 74 are in mechanical engineering industries with Fiat figuring directly under 10 dif-ferent headings. It also occurs under different names, such as Lancia, Mag-netti-Marelli and RIV SKF, the latter arising four times. Furthermore, many large firms, like Philips and Westinghouse, work exclusively for Fiat. Others are linked to the car industry, such as Viberti and Pinin-Farina, among many. Furthermore, the car industry recurs in sectors outside the mechanical engi-neering industries with the manufacture of tyres by Pirelli and Michelin. Of course, it is not possible to equate Fiat totally with the car industry, for the group is diversifying its activities, notably in the aeronautical industry (two factories in Turin), but it would seem that in one form or another, Fiat is more than ever identified with Turin, where, apart from the references given by Gabert, the only expansion to be noted is that of CEAT into cables, the growth of Nebiolo (printing machines), the reinforcement of Indesit and, especially, the take-off of telecommunications.

One should also mention that a good proportion of the industrial activity is still located within the commune of Turin itself, while the population lives in the suburbs, some of which are far out. As a result there is extraordinary congestion in the old city centre, despite efforts to improve the situation by peripheral bypasses. Otherwise, the city centre preserves its traditional face of a grid-iron pattern and baroque monuments, often with a severe façade; here one is definitely at the frontiers of Italy.

Lombardy dominated by Milan

In devoting a major study to Milan, Dalmasso (1973) has paradoxically almost given us a geography of Lombardy. The city, however, does not overwhelm the region, for the proportion between 1.7 million inhabitants in the city and 8.5 million inhabitants in the region (1 : 5) is less unbalanced than the relationships of Turin (1 : 3.5) or Rome (1 : 1.7) to their respective regions. Milan is unique in giving rise to a region of 5.7 million inhabitants in an area of 3,500 sq. kilometres with an average density of 1,600 inhabitants per sq. kilometre. Here, therefore, one may speak of a city-region. The zone of commuting extends beyond the zone of high densities and includes an area between Milan, Busto, Como and Bergamo. People work in Milan from as far as Brescia in the east, Cremona, Piacenza and Pavia in the south, Novara to the west, Varese and even Sondrio in the north. In fact, Milan's zone of attraction, pushed out westward, extends beyond Lombardy.

This regional domination is expressed in activities covering all fields and means that Milan's *per capita* income is the highest in Italy, as is its share of foreign trade (Milan alone handles 24% of exports and 30% of Italy's imports). Yet other towns also attain almost the same high standard of living and have an equally admirable range of activities. The relationship is thus one of osmosis rather than domination; in this Milan differs from Turin. We shall now examine how this system, which does not preclude considerable regional diversity, operates.

A recent success

At the end of the eighteenth century Milan, with 130,000 inhabitants, was only the fifth city in Italy after Naples, Rome, Palermo and Venice. Its economic take-off did not properly begin until after 1880 and its supremacy was only established at the end of the last century. How does one explain the rapidity of this rise? It appears that, aside from the physical environment, a whole series of factors played a part.

Among these factors, one should cite Milan's location in contact with rich and complementary regions; for the city, the Alps are less an obstacle than a gateway between northern Europe and the Mediterranean. The agricultural fertility of Lombardy has also played a positive role in several ways. Firstly, at the beginning of the industrial period, it was able to supply itself with foodstuffs which other Italian cities were certainly not capable of doing; secondly, it transferred capital at the time of the agricultural crisis in 1882 to underwrite the bulk of the monetary operations which laid the foundation for industry and the basis of financial power; thirdly, it provided the necessary manpower for industry, so that after the introduction of mechanisation, the high agricultural densities became high industrial densities without much movement taking place.

A second series of factors arises from the location and development of a regional junction. However, there is nothing special in Milan's location in the extensive flat area between St Gotthard and Piacenza which, itself, is situated at the best crossing-point of the Po between Tessino and Adda. Certainly there was a nodal tradition, originating at the end of the Roman Empire, which, on several occasions, has facilitated Milan's expansion, but it was only able to take full advantage of this in modern times as a result of the construction of the St Gotthard railway tunnel, and the development of a railway network giving quick access to the Simplon, Genoa via the Novi Ligure gap, Bologna and Venice. More recently, the development of a motorway system (Turin–Aosta–Milan–Venice, Varese–Milan–Piacenza) has brought further advantages.

Lastly among these positive factors, Milan has had the advantage, in a country poorly endowed with energy sources, of both hydroelectric energy and gas hydrocarbon deposits. With respect to the first, the Alps ensure for Lombardy an annual capacity of 12,000 million kWh, insufficient for a total consumption of 30,000 million kWh, but still enough to play a decisive role in attracting large-scale industry and generating new activities at the beginning of this century. With respect to the second form of energy, the regional production of methane has continued to decrease after a peak production of a 1,000 million cubic metres in 1960. However, in this period it attracted a good proportion of ENI management and new petrochemical complexes which then installed a supply network that maintains their continued presence here.

Finally, it should be borne in mind that none of these factors were as decisive in their own right as coal seams or major port locations could be. If Milan had not succeeded in organising its surrounding area on three levels – conurbation, urban region and peripheral plain and mountain zones – it would not have been able to stamp its presence definitively on this area.

Milan, centre and conurbation

As a city of a plain that crosses no river, Milan has expanded without encountering constraints other than a series of rings, firstly ramparts then ring roads, over which it has constantly jumped. The Milanese conurbation could nowadays be considered to include Sesto San Giovanni to the north-east, Rho and Buoto to the north-west. The basic reason for its present growth is the replacement of factories in the city by residential areas and their location in larger premises in the surrounding countryside. For some time this movement only involved the higher and dry areas above the city, but, during the past few years, it has also affected the south and the low plains, now occupied by dirty factories which create pollution and cause many environmental problems.

Thus, it is within the peripheral zone that the industrial might of the city is to be found, a strength that is based not on a dominant concern as in Turin, but on a very comprehensive spread of industries. The oldest element is naturally represented by the textile industry which has undergone a decline in the traditional sectors (cotton, jute, linen), but has held up in the finishing, dyeing and printing of fabrics. On the other hand, there has been a growth in factories producing clothing, hosiery and leather goods, particularly in north-western area around Legnano and Busto Arsizio. To the north-east, it has been mainly mechanical engineering industries which have expanded around Cinisello and Sesto San Giovanni; here metallurgical factories, belonging to the European multinational firm Falck, are located. These have survived because of the quality of their products and the size of the local market. The mechanical engineering industries are at present the largest employers – cars (Alfa Romeo, Innocenti, Autobianchi), railway stock (Breda), engines (Franco Tosi) and electromechanical (Magnetti-Marelli). A good proportion of these industries are controlled by the State or by Fiat, but Milan keeps more control of the regional chemical industry, of which the major plants are Montedison at Rho and Sesto (polymers, resins and perfumes), Carlo Erba (pharmaceutical products) at Bergamo and the Viscosa plants. Also near Milan, at Biocca and Cusano, are Pirelli's research establishments. All these newest developments are based on the presence of oil refineries in the city or nearby (Rho, Vilasanta). Finally, the diversity of Milanese industry includes a whole series of food products (Motta) and publishing (Mondadori, Rizzoli).

However remarkable the industrial growth in the region, it only gives a partial picture of the dimensions and importance of the major firms. As firms progressively spread out, firstly benefiting Lombardy, then the neighbouring regions, and now the whole of Italy, Milan itself concentrates more and more on laboratories, management and senior staff. Nearly half of Italian firms, in terms of shares, have their headquarters here, and this proportion rises to 70 per cent in chemicals, 75 per cent in rubber, plastics and electronics. Milan's stock exchange alone handles 70 per cent of the Italian share market. Lastly, it is in Milan that the headquarters of the main banks (Credito Italiano, Banco Commerciale Italiana), insurance firms and import–export companies are to be found. It is astonishing, then, that, strictly speaking, there is no central business district, but that the major headquarters are dispersed throughout the city, in the renovated areas near the station (Pirelli) and on the ring roads (Metanopoli, ENI). It is no accident that these two headquarters have produced two of the best architectural creations in Italy.

Milan is also an ordinary city, where the old town between La Scala, the Galleria and the cathedral, occupies only a very small area. The other public building, including the castle and its enormous cemetery, is spread out in a concentric shape (Roman, medieval and Spanish walls), beyond which stretch vast and monotonous housing estates: middle class sectors in the north-east, lower-middle-class in much of the rest, while the working class squeeze into overcrowded areas (Lambro) or are banished to outlying suburbs cut off from factories. Some secondary centres such as Monza occasionally stand out in the midst of the urban mediocrity.

Between Milan and the lakes: an urban region

Traditionally, and now more and more, Milan maintains constant and multiple links with a series of towns which, as in Piedmont, mark out the meeting of the plain with the Alpine world. In Lombardy these are Varese, Como, Bergamo and Brescia. Other towns, on the dry, stony and well-drained lands of Brianza and along the routes connecting the above-mentioned towns with Milan, are also expanding. Until recently this area could still be considered agricultural, based on cereal production, sometimes using dry cultivation (wheat), sometimes irrigation (mainly maize and fodder crops); but urban growth, including the construction of new towns like Zingonia to the south of Bergamo, has put an end to rural life. Properties have been divided by the proliferation of roads, irrigation networks have been disrupted by urban expansion and soils have been polluted by industrial waste and toxic material as at Seveso.

Thus industrial and urban activities predominate everywhere, although always with a major difference between the towns at the line of Alpine contact, which are in themselves of some importance, drawing in administrative functions and still retaining a grand appearance, and the small towns of Brianza, such as Trezzo and Lissone, that have grown so rapidly that their development has not been properly planned. Of all these cities, Brescia (215,000 population) is the major one. Its relative distance from Milan has given it scope to acquire commercial functions not found to the west, while it extends its own economic influence over a series of valleys and Pre-Alpine lakes.

Milan's influence is much more evident in Bergamo which is at the centre of an industrial region based on cotton and wool and whose activities have been revived by metallurgy (Dalmine), tubes (Montubi) and cement (Italcementi at Calusco). The same balance occurs around Lecco (mainly mechanical) and Como (mainly textiles and sawmills). Milan's influence is even stronger at Varese where the traditional industries (cotton, paper) are losing ground to electromechanical, mechanical (Marchetti) and hosiery industries which are linked with Milan. Finally, Milan's influence is felt as far as the Piedmontese region of Novara with the same sort of industrial links in hosiery, clothing, mechanical engineering and petrochemicals. Novara is also one of the outposts of Fiat and is expanding in traditional industries such as printing.

The low plain: the wealth and problems of an agricultural region

To the south of the line of *fontanili*, the low plain between Lomellina and Mantua has remained for a long time in agricultural use. Although well drained and irrigated by numerous canals, of which the largest is the Muzza irrigating 55,000 hectares, the region does not escape from Milan's influence. The bourgeoisie, religious orders and companies own most of the land which is divided into fairly large properties varying from 50 to 100 hectares. If rice still forms the major crop to the west at the border with Lomellina, it is clearly replaced between Padua and Mantua by grasses and crops for livestock. There are now 800,000 dairy cows in the southern part of the Milan region and this has meant a decline in wheat and corn which for long had covered the Mantua region. It is here that the large Milanese dairies which make Gorgonzola, Locatelli, Galbani and Invernizzi, are located, as well as manufacturers of processed meats (Negroni) and pasta. There is also an industrial sector associated with agriculture in the manufacture of fertilisers, agricultural machinery, etc.

Downstream of Milan, this region no longer receives irrigation water as pure and reliable as in the past, and its young population is attracted by the city so that this flat and fertile region is undergoing depopulation. The compromise solution, which is to retain an industrial population that will maintain regional services, is progressing rapidly with the establishment of shoe factories at Vigevano, the specialisation of Pavia in agricultural tools and, above all, in sewing machines (Necchi), and mechanical and clothing industries at Lodi (Cimbali) and, finally, petrochemicals at Mantua.

The mountains: agricultural and industrial valleys

To the east of the Val d'Aosta and within Milan's zone of influence, the system of crystalline peaks reaches, in the Lepontine Alps, Ortles and Adamello, considerable proportions, reinforced by the limestone Pre-Alps, which protrude in the Ossola valley and are highly developed around Bergamo. These high mountains, with considerable rainfall, and covered with chestnut trees, are deeply incised by glaciation which has left behind broad valleys, such as the Adda, in addition to a series of lakes strewn between Orta and Isso.

Towards the upper reaches, these valleys, despite their size and the low altitudes of the valley bottoms, present serious problems for development. For example, although the Toce valley contains the Simplon Tunnel, it is so short that it lacks economic autonomy. Beyond the Swiss Ticino, the Adda valley (Valtellina) leads only to the poorly accessible passes of Splügen and Resia. Even Tonale and Stelvio, which command passes to the Alto Adige, can only be used with difficulty. Given these conditions, it is understandable that these culs-de-sac have not attracted industrial investment outside Sondrio and Morbegno, and that most of the energy produced is exported to Milan. Yet the valley floors support maize and pastures, and the sunny, rocky deposits are covered in orchards and well-known vineyards. Activities connected with spas and winter resorts are also present.

Further south two types of landscapes alternate: lakes and valleys. Only a few valleys, such as the Oglio and Chiese, give access to the large opening of the Val di Sole. Otherwise, these are culs-de-sac closely dependent on the situation at the valley openings (Val Formazza, Val Brembana, etc). The lakes give an impression of having been victims of their mild climate and their not excessive rainfall. Olive trees grow on their banks as do citrus trees with flowers in among them. Unfortunately, these features are counterbalanced by the steep slopes which make necessary unusually high terracing, more Mediterranean than one would expect. These agricultural landscapes resemble gardens, often too small to be economically profitable. There remains tourism, although the lakes still appeal to a fairly sedate and well-off clientele which is becoming less common. These problems are, to some extent, balanced by a certain amount of industrial activity in the towns at the opening of valleys, such as Como, Lecco and Varese.

The influence of Brescia and Bergamo is felt in the valleys with the manufacture of cotton in the Val Brembana, small steelworks and mechanical engineering industries in the valleys within Brescia's influence, with amazing specialisation as in the manufacture of cement tubes in Val Camonica, light-arms manufacturing in Val Trompia, taps, electroplating, engraving, etc. All these activities give an air of dynamism which is in complete contrast to the difficulty of access of these narrow valleys. There is an admirable will and a policy to keep the population in the region and this must, indeed, be credited to Milan.

From the Brenner to Emilia: axes and crossroads

In the second century BC, the Roman colonisation of Cispadane Gaul took place from the road which bears the name of its builder and whose linear path, from Fano through Bologna to Piacenza served as the Roman military line, dotted with soldiers' posts and laying out centuriation. Twenty-two centuries later the Via Emilia is still there. It crosses the ancient resting places, uniformly distanced from a central point which restores the *cardo* and *decumanus*. It serves equally as a basis for land division. This is a remarkable permanence, and is now emphasised by the path of the motorway and the railway line exactly parallel with the Roman way.

This continuity should not let us lose sight of another major route, also built recently and which joins up with the Via Emilia at Modena; this is the motorway from the Brenner through Verona and Mantua. Another major route, the Autostrada del Sole splits off from the Emilian route towards the south and links Bologna to Florence and Rome. Connecting these cities has entailed a slight detour to the west; the railway goes directly from Brenner to Bologna via Verona. The pull of the Modena–Bologna junction is such that it modifies the pre-existing nodes in the Po valley region. Trade between the Adige valley and Milan, which had greatly developed during the period of Austrian domination, has now become relatively less significant, as have the exchanges between Venice and Austria. However, the Brenner–Emilia route continues to grow in importance. This evolution is thus bringing together economically regions which are physically separate.

From Alto Adige to Emilia

The Adige valley introduces a fundamental break in the Alpine system, for it is here that the insubrien fault, which runs from Domodossola to Val di Sole through the Valtellina, stops; here also is the vast Bolzano plateau of Permian porphyry. Lastly, this valley marks the western limit of the Triassic dolomites. Though a major physical break, this does not, nevertheless, entail an important meeting-place for exchanges and economic activities. If the Brenner constitutes the most notable pass due to its altitude (1,327 m) and its size, if the upper and middle Adige valley forms a broad and sunny basin, the same does not apply south of Trento, where the valley narrows, leaving only a narrow pass (the banks of Lake Garda have only recently been opened up for traffic) for routes from Verona and Val Sugana.

The region has thus remained for a long time open in the north and enclosed in the south, a fact that explains its distinctive identity and its division between, on the one hand, Italian Trentino and, on the other, Bolzano, where the language and architecture (houses with oriel windows) bear witness to German influence. Besides the linguistic division, its physical orientation also explains why, despite its strategic importance, the Brenner Pass did not experience for a long time an economic growth comparable to that of St Gotthard. Constriction in the lower reaches partly accounts for the low degree of industrial investment, virtually limited to wood, electrochemicals and electrometallurgy with two principal centres, Merano and Bolzano. On the other hand, the ease of communication with Austria and Bavaria explains the origin of the vineyards and apple orchards which cover an area of 25,000 hectares.

To the north and east, the Adige valley opens out either on to pastoral valleys, such as the Val Pusteria, or towards the different world of the Dolomites which combine long, gentle slopes conducive to pastures as well as winter sports, with dolomite blocks with steep sides which are the dream of rock climbers. These features explain the growing popularity of Alpine sports both to the west of the Adige (Madona del Campiglio) and, more so, in the east in Val Gardena and Cortina d'Ampezzo. This activity has recently brought new wealth to a region that had previously to contend with problems of difficult access to the higher valleys, with movement cut off by the haphazard arrangement of limestone blocks. The persistence of a distinct group which employs a dialect derived from Latin, Ladin, can be explained by this pecularity of isolation.

At the mouth of the Adige, Verona has for a long time acted as a defensive site as well as a commercial and administrative city. However, for some time its role as a routeway had reoriented agricultural land use towards high-quality vineyards on the lower slopes of Mt Lessini (Valpolicella). However, in the past thirty years, orchards have multiplied to meet export markets from northern Europe, taking advantage of the well-drained soils of the piedmont and relying on the organisation of specialised markets with warehouses and cold-storage facilities, telexes, motorways, etc. These orchards have moved on to the Basso Veronese, invaded Padua and spilt over into the Ferrara region. The entire region now forms the northern part of the largest orcharding area in Europe for peaches (on raised gravel terraces of the Po and Adige), pears (on sandy soils) and apples (on the heavier, well-drained clay bottoms). Intended to win the German market, this strongly organised commercial network has made inroads into the French market, so that one now sees peaches from Verona competing with regional products on the Lyons market. This prodigious development has also had an effect industrially with the emergence around Verona of industries relating to agriculture, including pulverisers, weigh bridges and cold-storage plants. The town of Verona now has a population of 270,000 inhabitants.

From Rimini to Piacenza

The landscapes around the Via Emilia fall into parallel bands of differing richness. South of the road, long outlying fingers of hills with unstable slopes, dissected by series of streams and rivers which flow towards the Po, provide a transitional zone between the Apennine mountains which reach their peak at 2,000 metres at Mt Cimone. These long crests interspersed with woods and grassland are virtually deserted, for it now seems that the economic and demographic decline has truly hit the hill zone, which for too long was overpopulated and overworked, a situation that has generated the proliferation of *frane*. For the most part, the landscape remains as it was: small, owner-occupied farms combining wheat, vines and sheep. The quality of some wines (Albana di Romagna, Sangiovese, Lambrusco) enabled some farms to concentrate production in homogeneous plots. In other sectors producer cooperatives tried to supplement vines with small fruits.

In the very north and along the Po stretches a zone of low-lying land which broadens out towards the delta and now manifests the opposite development to the area mentioned above. Once deserted because of the risk from flooding, it began to attract population once it was drained and improved. Starting from the alluvial banks which flank the river and afford protection, the settlement of this area has moved on to the lands between this line and the higher terraces, already for a long time under cultivation. Poplar plantations still form a major activity although the new, large farms are tending to replace it with maize and forage crops. However, the low plain remains almost empty and isolated; the river repels settlement contrary to the road, which attracts it.

Between these fairly unattractive zones lies the high plain with its numerous advantages; its well-drained, pebbly and silt soils, its protection from flooding due to the steep sides which channel the streams descending from the Apennines and its favoured position away from the fogs and temperature inversions of the low-lying alluvial plain. It is not surprising, then, that this zone has retained its population and contains much of the economic activity of the area.

Among these activities, agriculture occupies an exceptional place in terms of its share of the regional product (along with Verona, the province of Bologna has the highest agricultural income in Italy, ahead of Ferrara and Forli), as well as an unusually high proportion of people actively employed in agriculture. This wealth is traditionally based on the preponderance of direct cultivation in properties of about 20 hectares (in the eastern provinces their size is larger and share-cropping is less significant). The division of land based on centuriation and the number of mixed plots are possibly excessively traditional, although this is modified by the highest consumption of fertilisers and mechanisation in Italy. The number of homogeneous plots, which is a sign of the willingness to change, is increasing yearly. However, there remains a deep-rooted suspicion of any monoculture among Emilian farmers; the dominant crops – vines in the Romagna region, fruits on irrigated lands, cereals on dry land, beef cattle in the west – rarely occur on their own. This characteristic occurs even within the major crop zones; a fruit producer always mixes peaches, pears and apples and it is rare if he does not own a small bit of vineyard as well. Overall, regional agricultural revenues are fairly evenly divided between the two major earners, fruits and grazing, and then between the two secondary incomes, vines and cereals. A not inconsiderable extra source of income is derived from the sale of vegetables from small properties. Finally, it is worth noting that the products from grazing are themselves fairly varied, milk being less important than butter and cheese (especially Parmesan).

This wealthy agricultural system, well served by cooperatives, also supports some industry, notably the large Fiat tractor factory at Modena. There are other large enterprises in the Piacenza region, of which some are already in Milan's zone of influence. On the whole, Emilia-Romagna is the region *par excellence* of medium-sized firms that have recently expanded on the outskirts of towns and along the motorways: clothing, furniture, household appliances, small electrical motors, mechanical parts, prefabricated construction material, canneries and food industries.

This dispersion of industry explains the present growth of the many towns between Cesena and Piacenza. It is very rare to find a town with only a single function like Rimini whose summer population reaches nearly 600,000. On the contrary, one always finds a mixture of administrative, commercial and industrial activities. This equilibrium is particularly strong in the case of Bologna whose 550,000 inhabitants derive their livelihood as much from commerce and artisanal activities as from an industry that is highly diversified apart from the manufacture of railway material. The most remarkable feature is not so much this balance, but the proximity of Modena, Reggio and even Parma (180,000), which tend to form with Bologna a sort of linear city whose communications are provided by road. One is rightly surprised by the functional character and modernity of this urban system which has evolved without interruption from the oldest urban cluster in Europe.

The Ligurian lattice

From Ventimiglia to La Spezia the continuity of landscapes – cores of hard rocks and erodable slopes of marls and sandstone – hide subtle tectonic changes between the Apennines and the Alps. Overall, this system looks like a gigantic lattice divided into two unequal parts. Towards the west, the Riviera di Ponente has less steep slopes and, above all, a sheltered orientation which gives it a climate more like that of Campania. It is here that most of the cultivated lands are found, bearing in mind that these account for 5 per cent at the most of the area of the region. In contrast to the wooded higher slopes, the lower slopes are terraced and covered in olives, fig trees and vines, with islands of specialisation of which the most noteworthy is the Riviera di Fiori, or the flower production area. Much of the flower area is under glass, geared to supply an out-of-season market. To the east, on the other hand, the Riviera di Levante is more exposed to westerly winds, and slopes are also steeper. The most striking feature in the succession of landscapes is the Cinque Terre, a group of villages perched on dizzying terraces and virtually isolated from land communications until a very recent date.

Liguria's wealth owes as much to the agricultural development of these terraces as to the tourist sites between San Remo and Rapallo and the ports, of which there are more than can be easily used. All of them, including Genoa, are sited in rocky bays; their harbour bottoms are excellent but inadequately sheltered from winds from the open sea. On the landward side the ports are hemmed in by nearby highlands and communications with the interior pass through narrow, steep valleys. These are 'thalassocratic' sites, harking back to when Genoa knew a great period of prosperity. But times have changed and Genoa has had to respond to the needs of its hinterland and construct a communications network which is still too recent to have had a profound impact on the regional balance of forces.

For a long time the communications network worked particularly to Genoa's advantage, thanks to the railway system established by Cavour and then the construction of the motorway to Milan via Alessandria. The completion of a direct route with Ivrea and Aosta further adds to this good network which will soon acquire a new motorway directly linking Genoa with Lake Maggiore via Novara. However, we should note that on a regional scale two new motorways now directly link Savona and Turin in the west and La Spezia and Parma in the east. Together with the coastal motorway and the Genoese spur of Polcevera, this makes an interconnected system. Given that Savona and La Spezia also have rail links which have been considerably improved in the past few years, it would clearly seem that Genoa is far from enjoying a monopoly of good communications. Nor does it benefit from a monopoly of pipelines for, although Genoa can send its crude oil to Ingolstadt, Milan and Cremona, the terminal at Savona is also connected to this network and more easily serves the refineries of Novara, Volpiano, and within the Alps, Aigle.

Nevertheless, it is Genoa which has the largest share of the total regional freight flow with a total flow of 50 million tons as against 15 million at Savona and 13 at La Spezia. The latter port suffers from the lack of pipeline towards Parma. Apart from a substantial oil trade, La Spezia also handles imports of agricultural products to Emilia. However, the present crisis in shipbuilding has lead to the virtual closure of the yards modernised by IRI in favour of those at Monfalcone. There remains nothing but the arsenal to supplement the petrochemical industries. Savona seems to have a brighter future, as does Vado Ligure, since they are both supported by Turin. The industrial complex attached to the port of Savona has now regained much of its activity after being hit by IRI's choice of Genoa. This activity is partly the result of its excellent coal installations at Bormidda where a coking plant and steelworks still operate.

Compared to its competitors, Genoa is only moderately advantaged by its location near the mouth of the Polcevera which gives it access to the plain of Alessandria through the Passo di Giovi. The advantages of its site and the historic importance of its San Giorgio fort are more obvious, but the decisive factor was the historical circumstances of Genoa's past glory as well as its attachment to Piedmont which in the nineteenth century made it the port for Sardinia. Later on, Lombardy's growth pushed its relations with Piedmont into second place, while the development of the Alpine passes, notably St Gotthard, broadened its horizons to Switzerland and Germany which now account for more than 10 million tons of the volume of port activity.

Genoa's European penetration explains why its port function is more important than its industrial role, so that the product per person in the tertiary sector is double that of the secondary sector. However, the possibilities of further expansion around the initial site of the old port and the careenage basin are extremely limited. For expansion to occur westward, it was necessary to construct a channel to the open sea in 1936 and beyond there to Sestri Ponente in 1968. The current work is concerned with the integration of the Voltri site, a linear development of 18 kilometres in relation to the old port axis. These successive stages of expansion have allowed Genoa to cope with the increased size of oil tankers which are basically handled west of the port. It has also led to the construction of specialised quays right next to the maritime station and the old quays. Thus, in Genoa, unlike Marseilles, there was no reduction in the number of sites and the whole system became more integrated, except for the congestion and extreme pile-ups that occurred at the container terminals. One should point out, if only to underline the dominance of port functions over industrial ones, the excellent back-up facilities that the Genoese ship-builders, partially owned by the State, have been able to build up brokers, insurance agents, cargo offices.

The construction of the channel to the sea has enabled both the building of an airport, which handles 600,000 passengers annually, and an industrial complex including an oil basin to the west and a steelworks on the Cornigliano platform. This complex, the second largest in Italy after Taranto, includes a blast furnace, a Siemens oven and two rolling mills. It supplies associated industries among which shipbuilding now is less important than before since the take-over of the Ansaldo Group by IRI. In compensation, Genoa received several mechanical construction factories belonging to IRI through Finmeccanica and still retains control of maritime engines, iron parts, etc. Notwithstanding, the dynamism of the industrial sector depends very largely on IRI, even when the traditional sectors – leather, textiles, oil-mills, food – are taken into account. One cannot therefore speak of economic dynamism in Genoa as one can for Milan.

In fact Milan's influence tends to intensify progressively with the expansion northward of the industrial zones. Factories and warehouses intermingle well beyond the Scrivia valley as far as Novi Ligure. Despite this growth and the urban expansion on to the slopes of the Granadolo, Genoa still preserves the major part of its offices and headquarters within its walls. The expansion of the business district around the old port has resulted in the demolition of old areas and the rehousing of families in the peripheral areas. In some parts the morphology of the city has been appreciably altered, although the nature of the ancient centre, containing the old palace and main shipping companies, has not been changed as much.

Around the Gulf of Venice: a poorly integrated region

The area between the eastern Alps, the Gulf of Venice and the Po delta forms a somewhat distinctive unit in northern Italy. Despite the presence of three major ports, the interrelationships typical of other Po and Alpine regions are less strong here, but it would need much more to turn this independence into a positive factor. Indeed, in many ways, these regions require a better integration with the Po and adjacent parts of Italy.

Historical and geographical contingencies

On the macroregional scale, the Gulf of Venice, understood in a general sense, certainly forms a unique area, a sort of prolongation of the Mediterranean world into Europe, either through the penetration of the Po, or from Friuli and Trieste. This intermixing, to take up the expression and thesis of Brigitte Prost (1973), is evident everywhere: in the proximity of the olive trees of Monfalcone with the large Carnic forests, as in the settlement frontiers of Slavs, Germans and Latins. But if one looks more closely, it immediately appears that the physical orientation of the terrain is much less advantageous.

On the Alpine side there is no central axis raised and formed by glaciers, but only a series of ridges which, without being very high, are always a deterrent. North–south movement is always difficult, while from east to west the hollowed basins formed by the rivers Sava and Drava have helped both movement and invasion, depending on the period in question. At the line of contact between the piedmont and the coastal plains, the routes opened up by the large valleys are often very narrow and hemmed in by blocking peaks like Asiago.

On the Adriatic side, the region is no less closed in. The mouths of the Po and the Adige are not fit for navigation and even less for port installations: unstable soils, shifting bottoms and distributaries make any sizeable installation unthinkable. Further south, the Byzantine port of Ravenna now finds itself situated inland. Northward, the Venetian lagoons are unsuitable in their natural state for defence purposes or for port developments. Only Trieste offers a good site, but communications with its hinterland have always posed problems.

These variable factors have given rise to highly changeable situations in different periods. Ravenna silted up; it needs very little for Ferrara to return to its marshy state. The future of Venice is more complex, for the republic of the Doges knew how to develop, at the cost of enormous works (damming of the Po), a lagoonal port complex which was unique in its time, but today is merely something of the past. It is to the east that the historical ups and downs have been most acutely felt in the immense wealth and decline of Trieste, an Italian town whose fortune was, and today remains, potentially linked to its relations with central Europe and also with the fate of nearby frontier towns like Gorizia and Cividala which have been cut off from their former regional hinterlands.

The foregoing analysis indicates what are likely to be the main regional problems in this area. First there is the need to improve port facilities and revitalise the coastal economies in relation to the Po. Second, how is the reclamation of the marshy coast to be continued? The last issue is how to pull the peripheral and unbalanced economies of Trieste and Friuli into the national economy.

From the mountains to the piedmont

The main characteristic of the Friulian and Venetian mountains is their continuing depopulation, although certain areas, such as the Sette Comuni and the Val Canale, had been overpopulated for too long in an archaic, self-sufficient and fairly impoverished economy. Recent efforts to adapt through mountain cooperatives and grazing collectives have come too late to stem the highly organised flow of emigration which has emptied the valleys of the youngest section of their population. Yet, these cold and wet regions are not entirely without resources. There is hydroelectricity and Friuli is one of Italy's main reserves of workable timber. But all this is fairly small-scale; the area's lack of a real routeway function means that this is basically 'frontier country'.

Mountain depopulation has partially fed the piedmont towns which derive their livelihood from a successfully modernised agriculture based on cereals, pastures and grasses, with superb orchards in the area around Vicenza. The growth of these towns also owes much to a sericulture tradition which is still maintained through the raising of silkworms (1,600 quintals, virtually the entire Italian production, in Friuli). It is upon this tradition, and an emphasis on unusual local assets, that an industry dependent on the overpopulation of the area between the mountains and the *lidi*, was established. Several large firms have arisen from among small firms manufacturing cutlery, furniture or small electrical equipment, etc. In general, these various industries have led to some urban growth: Udine increased from 86,000 inhabitants in 1951 to 105,000 by 1978; Pordenone, designated a provincial capital in 1968, managed to make the most of its new advantage and also to preserve its industrial function. On the other hand, Gorizia has barely managed to maintain its rather average level of activity.

The maintenance or increased significance of coastal areas

To the north as to the south of the Po delta, the coast is in the process of being filled in; the coastal spits are building up seaward, and enclose still waters which river alluvia then fill in. These vast, badly drained areas are either lagoons and ponds, like those of Comacchio, or more or less peatbog marshes, like those which surround Ferrara, and are divided by layers of river alluvia. These are fringed on the seaward side by beaches with pine trees.

The utilisation of these difficult lands has long remained limited to extensive grazing, or fishing in the *valli* (ponds). Following the failure of several earlier attempts, the period of reclamation began at end of the nineteenth century, undertaken by large public companies who were the only groups able to install the big steam pumps needed for the drainage and raising of the level. Some of these companies still operate here and, after calling upon the services of a large number of *braccianti*, have developed a highly mechanised and specialised agriculture based on simple rotations: corn, sugar-beet, lucerne. The largest of them still operate with over 10,000 hectares. On the margins of these giant enterprises, and on firm land, other farmers, working on much smaller farms, have defined the eastern limits of fruit-tree cultivation. Finally, the Ente Delta Padano, after distributing about 50,000 hectares of land in small plots, continues to reclaim new lands, which are used to enlarge old estates or to form enormous cooperatives, which are unusual within the political context, and these also concentrate on sugar-beet and lucerne. It should be noted that rice-growing, which was formerly a pioneer crop during the period of soil desalinisation, is now merely an activity from the past whose importance is declining year by year.

Regionally, it is not rice specifically, but agriculture as a whole, which has acted as a pioneering activity giving life to large areas between the pine forest of Ravenna and the Gulf of Panzano. Maybe they have proceeded too far in this direction; some voices fear the excessive drying out of the Comacchio *valli*. Despite the impoverishment of the natural habitat, the coast has benefited from the reclamation for, with the newly acquired access to the *lidi*, large-scale tourism catering mainly for a German clientele, has emerged. It remains to be seen whether the beaches and the pine forests, an environment that is highly vulnerable, will be able to withstand these considerable invasions. As a result of this colonisation, the coast is receding in a number of places, notably at Comacchio (Lido di Spina) and Ravenna.

The growth of the ports only roughly follows the development of the low lands, principally in the case of Trieste whose volume of activity (35 million tons) should not deceive us. ENI and Italsider occupy a vital place, and private interests (Fiat, shipbuilders) are only there in so far as they are involved in Italian regional policy. There is otherwise little more than basic activities here: oil refining, metallurgy, mechanical engineering industries, and naval ship-yards which compete with Monfalcone. It is a far cry from the time when Trieste was the third busiest Mediterranean port (7 million tons handled in 1914) and dealt with maritime affairs for Austria, as well as maintaining many links with the Middle East and containing the headquarters of the powerful Lloyd Triestino. There now only remains from this period an urban landscape typical of that in Budapest and other posts of the Austro-Hungarian Empire. The improvements of relations with Yugoslavia only offer limited opportunities, and trade with continental Europe hardly concerns more than crude oil. Basically, urban activity seems most associated with frontier traffic: Serbs and Slovenes find products here unknown in Yugoslavia and give back to the town a little of the cosmopolitan ambience that it had. The population is stagnating or declining at 270,000 inhabitants.

On the other side of the Adriatic Gulf, Ravenna's future is totally different. The former Byzantine city is now flanked by a canal-port whose trade (12 million tons) has almost doubled in a period of about twelve years. The oil refinery supplies the chemical industry which is dominated by Milanese interests more than local interests, which have assigned Ravenna the role of an importer of agricultural products. Although all this is still on a modest scale, it contrasts markedly with the not-too-distant past when Ravenna reminded one of a dead city.

If Ravenna has benefited from a division between the old city and the industrial port, the same cannot be said for Venice, despite appearances. The historic town and Porto-Marghera are, in effect, part of the same lagoon basin whose delicate balance is endangered by modern developments. Until this occurred, a complex system of diversion canals and graded channels prevented sedimentation, swept out the lagoon and acted as a brake against sea tides. The establishment of an industrial platform has modified the flow of currents and aided the infilling of part of the lagoon. Furthermore, the dredging of a large channel has helped tidal penetration and increased the number of high tides which invade the historic city. Finally, the pumping of water deep down results in marked subsidence. Environmental problems are made worse still through pollution caused by industrialisation that is not adequately controlled. The lack of decisive action and control is at the root of a very serious deterioration of monuments as a result of sulphur dioxide fumes. However, awareness of this problem came too late. The worst is that the deterioration of the rich historical environment has not even been compensated by a working population that has remained there; the latter have now basically moved to Mestre (270,000 out of 365,000 inhabitants) and along the road to Padua, thus abandoning the historic town to tourists and service personnel.

One is thus witnessing a sharp split in the use of land. A steel complex, refinery and petrochemical complex with a satisfactory rate of growth are located on dry land. A growing conurbation is firmly integrating Venice to the Po urban network through the intermediary of Padua. On the other hand, there is rapid degradation on the lagoon more in terms of the abandonment of buildings than in peeling exteriors. Supposedly, the water-levels have now been stabilised and there exists a plan for saving Venice under the auspices of UNESCO. Yet, despite these reassuring views, there seems really no other future for the city than to survive as a museum. But Venice deserves much more. Urban planners ought to remember that it was here that industrial zones, with restriction of the arts of fire such as glassmaking to the island of Murano, were thought up. It was also here that urban health conditions in the form of quarantine were implemented. Furthermore, there still exists a perfect system which permits two circulation networks – on land and water – to intersect and yet never cause any obstructions. The layout of Venice acknowledges a hierarchy of urban districts possibly without any other equivalent in the world. All these aspects deserve to be taken into account.

6 North-central Italy: a transitional zone towards the real South

Oh, how happy I feel in Rome as I think back to the times when a greyish day surrounded me up there in the North.

GOETHE

As we have already mentioned in the chapter on regional problems, a line from La Spezia to Ancona separates two very different domains. South of this fairly fluid line of demarcation, in Tuscany, Umbria, Latium, Abruzzi and Marche, there is a distinctive region which is very much 'central' in Italy and whose major geographical characteristics, though certainly original, are mainly related to its transitional nature. There are some truly southern features: agricultural and industrial underdevelopment, emigration and land reclamation – these occur mainly along the Tyrrhenian coast, extending as far the Tuscan Maremma, and in the Umbrian and Abruzzian mountains. Yet, there are also somewhat more 'northern' features in the small properties, *mezzadria*, a long-standing wealth in the wine-growing areas, and cities such as Ancona, Perugia and, above all Florence, which have been active for a long time.

Northern Tuscany

Tuscany possesses the most unquestioned historic unity in Italy. This does not mean, however, complete homogeneity; it quite definitely juxtaposes a southern part that begins in the area of Siena and Chianti, and a northern part based on the Arno valley starting from Florence. While the former is highly agricultural with a low level of economic development of a 'southern' nature, the latter largely forms part of the 'northern' type of economic development mainly diffused through a dense urban web whose most prestigious names are Pisa and Florence, Lucca and Pistoia.

Fragmented and deserted Apennine mountains

The degraded Apennines

This zone belongs to the northern Apennines and its system of overthrusting layers pushed towards the north-east, but what is important is the extent of the hollow basins which have left very little of the original edifice. These become more common southward and, on the latitude of Florence, constitute a degraded and broken system, which from Mugello to the Tyrrhenian Sea clearly reduces the Apennines to a low partition. Thus the highland, chopped up in this fashion, forms corridors in a north–west, south–east direction, and out of line with each other. The Apuan Alps have a limestone core with sharp peaks rising to 1,954 metres in Mt Pisanino, a double backbone culminating in Emilia at Mt Cimone and with Mt Falterona fairly unaligned (1,654 m). Between the barriers of these intermontane basins there are the peaks of Lunigiana (Magra valley), Garfagnana (Serchio valley), Mugello (Sieve valley) and, cutting through all the southern part, the basins of the Arno where there remain no more than 'islands' of the Apennines like Mt Pisanino.

The wet and wooded Apennines

These mountains receive a high rainfall; above 1,000 metres more than 1 metre of rainfall falls and more than 2 metres on the Apuan Alps. The sheltered parts support magnificent stands of oak forests, then beech, larches and pines as on the slopes of Abetone. People and herds have largely eradicated the vegetation cover, but with the helping hand of depopulation, more and more slopes are becoming covered with coppices which are slowing turning into forests as in the valleys of the Apuan Alps.

Depopulated mountains

In spite of the steep slopes, these mountains were once densely populated, although there was never really a mountain way of life of an Alpine kind. The harshness of life and the attraction of the basins have resulted in a very rapid depopulation, so that many villages are largely deserted. This decline has not been checked by the development of summer and winter tourism. In the Apennines, there are still marble quarries which leave white scars right up to quite high altitudes. Now that these quarries are increasingly mechanised, they employ fewer people.

Intense human activity in Tuscan basins

A fairly benign physical environment

The plains and hills framing the southern flank of the northern Apennines seem to be part of the mountain system, so close are they to it. Coming south down peninsular Italy, these are the first flat landforms of the Mediterranean climate. Summers are now dry, rainfall average and the brightness incomparable. Columns of cypress trees mount guard near dispersed residences in a countryside whose landscape was long ago fashioned by men. However, climatic rigours remind one of the latitude, for winters are wet and also often quite cold: Florence has an average January temperature of only 5.6 °C as against 8.4 °C at Genoa. The violence of the Mediterranean is demonstrated by the Arno's maximum flow. The annual average is only 100 cubic metres per second, but at its greatest it can be highly devastating, as in 1966 when it so damaged Florence. The coast, formed mainly by the alluvial plain of Versilia, bordered by a very long sandy coastal fringe where several stands of pine remind one of what was such a beautiful forest, has a climate which is a milder version of the Ligurian Riviera.

A prosperous agriculture

The *mezzadria* crisis here affects mainly the hills and interior basins. Tuscan polyculture mixes cereals, beef raising, fodder crops, fruit, olives and vines in *coltura promiscua*. The fragmentation of the fields and the dispersed habitat create an infinitely varied landscape; its charm is part of the emotional charge of everything which is Tuscan. Share-cropping is decreasing rapidly. Properties are growing larger and people leave, yet a new equilibrium seems close. In Versilia, on the plains of the Arno and downstream of Florence, agriculture has already become more intensive and specialised: cereals in the reclaimed land of the lower Arno, vegetables and flowers in Versilia, coupled with enormous nurseries and tree crops in the interior plains of the Arno.

A ubiquitous yet unobtrusive industrial activity

The textile tradition is old here although it has been diffused and followed by a large number of modern activities. The latter, as in Emilia-Romagna, are hardly evident because they are small scale. It is difficult to distinguish artisanal activities, home production and industry. The dispersion in terms of activities is reflected on the ground and, if there is a relative concentration by town or sector, as with textiles in Prato, dispersion is, however, the rule. There is, therefore, both a great density of population and yet no all-consuming large city. The principal industrial branches can be briefly listed. Among the heavy industries, there are oil refineries at Leghorn and near La Spezia, steelworks at Florence (Bagnone) and Piombino, chemicals at Rosignano and glass manufacture at Pisa. Among lighter industries can be named vehicle manufacture (Piaggio-Fiat at Pontedera, Fiat at Marina di Massa), machines (Olivetti at Massa, Galileo at Florence), textiles (wool) at Prato, clothing at Florence and Empoli, shoes of all qualities at Monsummano and Fucecchio, and furniture at Cascina. Artisanal activities, strictly speaking, have flourished in all towns, but especially in Florence, which has been highly successful in jewellery, leather and fancy goods. It is due to all these activities that this part of Tuscany has not experienced long-distance emigration, for the countryside has supplied, without too much uprooting, a labour force for the lower lands.

A remarkable urban organisation

Tuscan cities are among the best known in the world. Florence and Pisa are universally known; for centuries they competed with each other for primacy.

The position finally fell to Florence, but now it does not completely over-shadow the others, either in its population or its administrative superiority.

Modern ports

The rapid advance of the coast has condemned the old ports to the interior. In the Middle Ages, Pisa rivalled Genoa, but it is now 11 kilometres from its *marina*. Northward, the port of Marina di Carrara serves the twin towns of Massa and Carrara (133,000 inhabitants in the two); its trade is based on marble. To the south stretches a line of beaches with maximum density at Viareggio (57,000 inhabitants). The real port, aside from La Spezia (navy and oil), is Leghorn, created by the Medicis. Leghorn's old port, fortress and ancient core, rebuilt after the Second World War, are surrounded by charmless suburbs, but the town has much activity, with more than 10 million tons of port traffic, varied industries and a tertiary function. It has 177,000 inhabitants.

Interior towns

Lucca (91,000 inhabitants), Pisa (103,000), Pistoia (94,000) and Prato (150,000) have many things in common. They are all ancient cities with a glorious past, and each has a centre surrounded by ramparts which more or less enclose an old quarter with a dense network of narrow and tortuous streets harbouring medieval monuments of great value – witness the cathedrals in each of the cities, the Commune at Prato, the baptistry, cemetery and Leaning Tower in Pisa. All are surrounded by newer characterless districts, and it is here that industrial activities are located. These have given economic life to towns which, though museum pieces, are also living organisms and where, except for Pisa, tourism is only a supplementary element. These cities have thus managed to adapt to the present without sacrificing their past.

Florence

With its 464,000 inhabitants, Florence is clearly larger than the others, but it is in many ways simply an enlarged version of the typical Tuscan town. The basis of Florence's power, its situation and its site characteristics are not different from those of the others. Florence is situated on the communication routes which cross the Apennines from Bologna to Rome. Its direct links with these centres by the Autostrada del Sole and a railway which uses a tunnel of more than 18 kilometres are of relatively recent construction, that is 'a posteriori' to its emergence as an important city. Its site is asymmetrical; the right bank of the Arno is on higher ground while the lower left bank, though prone to flooding, has facilitated easy settlement. There is nothing unusual in its location; it is basically its recent history, principally its choice as Italy's capital from 1865 to 1870, which gave it a start in its administrative and commercial role and finally assured it a leading position.

Its present functions are as diverse as those of its region. The tertiary sector is the most important due to a highly developed commercial sector, ranging from numerous administrative services to intellectual activities (university, National Library) and a very important tourist industry. Its metropolitan role is evidenced by the publication of a newspaper, *la Nazione*, widely read in central Italy. To that, as we have said, should be added important artisanal and industrial activities. In fact it is the diversity of these activities which provides the mainstay of its livelihood, and not tourism which, in this highly visited city, is only a superficial phenomenon that has not stultified the Florentine way of life. There are few cities that have succeeded so well in totally preserving their identity in the face of such external pressures.

The old town, with the same original line of houses, the San Jacopo and Pitti palaces and the Boboli Gardens on the bank, contrasts with the flatness of the right bank where, from a maze of narrow streets, Piazza della Signoria, the Palazzo Vecchio, the Duomo decorated with its polychrome façade, the Campanile of Giotto, Saint Mark's Baptistry, through which one reaches the convent where Fra Angelico painted, all stand out. The same sort of asymmetry exists in the recent developments. The hills to the east and south, as far as Fiesole, are the site of beautiful houses and gardens; the plains to the west have received, without much planning, a mixture of activities and housing of all types.

The Apennine mountains and basins

For more than 200 kilometres from the Metauro valley to Molise stretches the highest and most truly mountainous part of the Apennines. Variations in economy and landscape are many, but these are less significant than the unifying factors. Parallel limestone alignments give it a rigidity which is interrupted by numerous collapsed basins. These cold and inhospitable mountains, lacking agricultural potential, are being depopulated despite tourism, and most habitation is clustered in the lower parts in Umbria and the Abruzzi.

Two contrasting natural environments

The cold limestone mountains of the Apennines

Alignments at different altitudes

The disorderly overthrusting of clays, characteristic of the northern Apennines, no longer exist here, although there are still unsolved geological problems. The rather rigid limestone material forms fairly regular folds, aligned from north-north-west to south-south-east in parallel anticlinal and synclinal bands. These are asymmetrical, pushed towards an east-north-easterly orientation, and forming on this side a curved arc which overlies the end of Tertiary formations on the Adriatic side. However, in this general schema two variations appear from north to south:

(a)   The Umbro-Marche Apennines, as they are typically called, form the section between the Abruzzi and the Tuscan Apennines. The altitude and significance of limestone increases as one moves southward.

(b) The Abruzzian Apennines are the typical Apennine mountains, particularly in the shape of their peaks. The action of levelling has created a generally heavy appearance and contrasts with the steep rock faces of glacial cirques hollowed out above 2,000 metres in the Gran Sasso and Maiella and the long linear slopes of periglacial mud screes.

The raised blocks, separated by basins, are aligned in a fairly regular and identifiable way. To the east, the Gran Sasso reaches 2,912 metres and is matched beyond the Pescara valley by the enormous mass of Maiella (2,795 m). A second chain passes through Mt Terminillo, Sirente (2,349 m), the heights of Marsica and ends beyond Mt Greco in the mountains of Matese. Finally, to the south-west, a shorter and lower chain is formed by the Simbruini and Ernici mountains; the highest point is Mt Viglio, 2,156 metres.

A pastoral economy that is being abandoned despite tourism

Besides the veritable stony deserts at the rocky summits, forests and pastures cover most of this area. The forests are among the most extensive in Italy; in the middle-altitude zones up to 1,200 metres the slopes are covered with oaks, especially in Umbria and Marche. Higher up, beeches and then conifers form the next zone of mountain cover, beyond which there are only extensive mountain pastures on the higher slopes of the peaks, as on Gran Sasso. Vast areas are only thinly wooded and remain covered by scrubland.

Pastoral lands are, however, too limited to be able to support dense grazing; pastoralists have only been able to organise a full-scale system of transhumance with the aid of outside political power. This only happened during the Middle Ages when, in order to encourage the production of wool, Swabian, Aragonese and then Bourbon rulers forced the agriculturalists of Apulia to receive mountain herds during the winter months. Since the end of the nineteenth century the decline of this *pastorizia* system has stopped these transhuman movements and the *tratturi* (communal sheep trails) have been abandoned.

Thus today grazing is confined to the mountains; the movement of herds only occurs between the mountain pastures and the neighbouring lower slopes. More than 1 million sheep grazed these uplands in the nineteenth century; there are now no more than 700,000.

Agriculture locally reached extremely high altitudes in the mountains, taking advantage of platforms as high as 1,600 metres; but, in the last twenty years it has completely disappeared from these niches, an abandonment explained partly by the rapid rate of depopulation. From 1951 to 1971, more than 50 per cent of the inhabitants left the area for the interior basins and more distant towns, principally Rome.

Tourism has not been able to stop the depopulation. The Abruzzi National Park, established in 1923, straddles three regions and covers 300 sq. kilometres. There are small protected regional parks at Mts Sibilini, Sirente, Gran Sasso and Mt della Laga. Winter sports and holiday resorts are to be found almost everywhere although they are fairly small: Terminillo, the closest ski resort to Rome, Rocca di Mezzo and especially Bonaraso.

Basins and interior hills

Tectonic basins are found everywhere. Most important is the upper Tiber or the 'Val Tiberina' extending beyond Perugia. The Topino and Clitunno rivers form the *valle umbra* as far as Spoleto. Other basins include Gubbio, Norcia, Aterno, L'Aquila, Sulmona, upper Liri, Rieti and Avezzano–Conca del Fucino. This system, parallel to the line of folds, is clearly cut off by recent faults that emerged in the Pliocene period. Having been thrust forward spasmodically, the basins now contain lacustrine deposits and continental detritus and are often badly drained like the Val Tiberina or Conca del Fucino. The sunken nature of these basins gives them a distinctive climate. Their sheltered positions result in lower rainfall, in general less than 800 millimetres (L'Aquila 720 mm).

The hills are very extensive. In Umbria, hills between 500 and 900 metres comprise half the area, especially in the west and centre, but they are also common around the Abruzzian basins of Avezzano and Sulmona. They are incised into soft rocks (marls, clays and badly consolidated sandstone) and form a distinctive milieu. A considerable amount of water erosion has carved out numerous orientations. Their altitude endows them with a specific climate, wetter (Perugia 892 mm) and less continental than the basins. The best forests of broad-leaved trees are found here.

The primarily agricultural Umbrian countryside

Umbria's percentage of the working population engaged in agriculture is still higher than that of Italy as a whole, although major changes are taking place. Depopulation has struck, not only in the mountains but also on the plains and especially in the hills, particularly in the period 1950–70, although it has now stopped. Depopulation has coincided with a major change in the pattern of land ownership. Mezzadria, or share-cropping, which works basically to the benefit of urban dwellers and which used to involve more than 42 per cent of the holdings, declined by 50 per cent from 1951 to 1971.

Today the modernisation of holdings and the adoption of new techniques and crops are continuing. This process has produced a variety of tree-clad landscapes (Desplanques 1969). Polyculture is still typical, especially on the hills where pigs are traditionally raised for fattening by industrial piggeries in the Po plain. Olive trees on the slopes below 700 metres supply a highly rated oil, and almost everywhere, vines, cereal fields and pastures are mixed without any apparent pattern.

The medieval past of this region is one of the most eventful in Italy. The thirteenth and fourteenth centuries are especially famous for well-known religious figures such as Francis of Assisi, and artists such as Giotto. Charming towns with monuments and memories remain from this period.

Assisi, despite an unequalled richness of Romanesque monuments decorated with Giottesque frescoes, and a considerable flow of tourists, has only 24,000 inhabitants. Gubbio, with 31,000, is slightly larger. Spoleto, an art centre that supports a famous opera festival, and centre of a prosperous agricultural region, has 36,000 inhabitants, smaller than Foligno (51,000), the major agricultural centre of the region.

Perugia is larger again with 131,000 inhabitants. It is capital of the Umbrian region, seat of a famous university and the major centre for services in this region. Industry is slowly expanding with food processing (Perugina), textiles (wool and cotton) and, less significantly, metallurgical industries.

On the other hand, Terni (108,000 inhabitants) owes its origin to industry. The location of a metallurgical industry in the town is due to two factors. The first is physical: an abundance of water and the hydroelectric energy produced on the rivers Nera and Velino. The second is historic, being the necessity at the end of the nineteenth century (1888) to find a safe location, away from land and sea frontiers, for the manufacture of military goods. Only energy remains as a positive location factor, for access is not terribly easy: here is a case that is exactly the opposite of coastal location! Metallurgy, specialising in steel production, employs more than 15,000 people and is supplemented by chemicals (Montedison), synthetic fibres and paper mills. Terni remains a vulnerable exception.

Changes in the Abruzzian basins

The Abruzzian basins have evolved differently from those in Umbria for basically accidental reasons. Their development has occurred at a more rapid pace because, besides the presence in Rome of important people from the region, Abruzzi is administratively part of the South, with all the policies that this implies.

Agriculture on the plains, less extensive than the Umbrian hill–basin system, has remained in polyculture, combining cereals and fruit trees, especially olive and almond. The reclamation of Lake Fucino, undertaken after land reform and the expropriation of the largest landowner, Prince Torlonia, paved the way for the settlement of 5,000 families of small farmers. The small fields, without houses or villages, form a regular geometrical pattern and carry varied crops dominated by sugar-beet.

The breaking of the isolation of the region was achieved by two motorways: Rome–L'Aquila through Rieti and, since 1976, Rome–Pescara. Industrialisation has occurred in the towns. These manage to survive after each earthquake (L'Aquila 1908, Avezzano 1915.), and have, despite everything, preserved their ancient monuments. For a long time, as centres for an agricultural and pastoral economy, these towns have fulfilled administrative and commercial functions, but the three most important towns (one in each depression) have recently experienced some industrial development. Sulmona (21,000 inhabitants) has a large Fiat factory. Avezzano (31,000) has cheese production and a sugar refinery. L'Aquila has more than 61,000 inhabitants thanks to its service functions as capital of the region, its tourist attractions, but also its industries (Siemens electrical appliances).

The Adriatic flank: from Pesaro to Molise

Despite the division into several regions – Marche, Abruzzi and now Molise – a geographical unity results from a fragmentation of activities and landscapes.

Dissected hills fringed by a linear coastline

The remarkable parallelism of the coastline and the Apennine edge produces a long region with a consistent width of about 20 kilometres.

The coast is nearly linear; the only interruption is due to the re-emergence of limestone in a hook-shaped promontory at Ancona (the town's Greek name alludes to this physical feature). Elsewhere, the coast is quite low, cut into soft Tertiary layers and sometimes worn down into clay cliffs, but everywhere fringed by large sandy beaches. The linearity of the coastline is obviously due to tectonic action and the sea. The action of the latter is apparently mainly determined by the force of storms from the north-east which straighten out the coastline not by bringing down deposits from the coastal strips, but by pushing it back.

Hills cut into strips

Throughout the region the geological material is fairly uniform. The Miocene and especially Pliocene materials, which constitute most of it, are formed by very soft rocks, clays and sands. The Pliocene sea helped to shift these deposits at the beginning of the Quaternary period by rocking them and this action lifted all the layers of this mound towards the Apennine edge. It was on this surface, slightly undulating transversally from north to south, that rivers then began to cut down. The latter (Biferno, Pescara, Tronto, Potenza, Metauro, Foglia) are thus parallel and perpendicular to the coast. In a transitional climate with average, though irregular, rainfall (Pescara 763 mm) and hot summers, these rivers have very low water discharges which fall below 2 cubic metres per second, except for the Pescara. In fairly non-resistant rocks these rivers have carved out their main valleys several hundred metres deep, with a large number of small valleys and tributary river gorges.

Polyculture and small farms

Agriculture is the principal activity everywhere; the region of Marche has the highest percentage employed in agriculture in Italy. Agriculture is generally fragmented and holdings are small, most of them less than 5 hectares. Direct ownership is increasing, but it still comprises less than half the farms. Tenant farming is also increasing. *Mezzadria* shape-cropping is decreasing, but not as rapidly as elsewhere. So, although the latter diminished from 59.1 per cent in 1961 to 32.3 per cent in 1971, it still represents the highest percentage of all Italian regions. Fragmentation also occurs in the agricultural landscape: fields are small, sometimes very small (0.5 hectare on average), and with a highly diversified production which generally has low yields. Wheat is the most important crop (9 million quintals, of which 1 million was hard wheat in 1976), though the yield of 34 quintals per hectare is not very high for Italy. Maize produces 1 million quintals and fodder crops in conjunction with beef raising are increasing on family farms. Wine production is considerable even if the better vintages, apart from Verdicchio, are not well known. Table grapes comprise a quarter of the Italian harvest and wine production exceeds 5.5 million hectolitres. Olive trees, fruit trees, especially peach and apple, complete this attractive picture of Mediterranean polyculture.

Utilisation of the coastal fringe

Fishing is an important activity thanks to the strip-like ports sheltered behind the small sea-walls at Pesaro, Fano, Ancona, Porto San Giorgio, San Benedetto del Tronto, Pescara, Francavilla al Mare and Termoli. Fishing boats and land installations are modern and the fish – tuna and sole – often command high prices.

Seaside resorts are developing as an extension of, and modelled on, the Rimini Riviera. Hotels and restaurants line the sea front, multi-coloured cabins and lines of parasols gently descending towards the Adriatic. This coloured landscape is fleeting, for from October to May the sand is deserted, the facilities are closed, the pedal-boats are pulled out of the water and the sea is able to clean the beaches. Thus little employment is created. All the ports mentioned above have become beach resorts. However, Senigallia (35,000) is the only real tourist town.

Sleepy old towns and more dynamic coastal towns

The small interior towns are towns of the past. This is firstly because they have had their hour of glory: Urbino, the seat of a brilliant ducal court that embellished it, Ascoli Piceno which was a very powerful medieval community. Secondly, due to their location far from the main communication routes, they now only live from administration, tourism and some highly specialised activities. Urbino, with only 16,000 inhabitants, is the joint capital of the province with Pesaro and has a university near the ducal palace. Loreto (10,000) manufactures rosaries, Castelfidardo accordions. Fabriano (27,000) specialises in electrical household appliances and high-quality paper. Campobasso (42,000), Teramo (47,000), Ascoli Piceno (55,000) and Chieti (52,000) are all more important; together with their administrative services as capitals of provinces they have modest industrial activities: paper at Teramo, sugar and paper at Chieti.

The development of ports with industrial activities is uneven. Termoli, despite the arrival of Fiat, has only 16,000 inhabitants. Fano (50,000) derives its livelihood from tourism and fishing. Pesaro has 86,000 inhabitants, due to the combination of tourism and activities arising from its role as a service and industrial centre (furniture, Benelli motorbikes). Ancona's larger size (107,000) reflects its role as regional capital as well as its naval yards and oil refinery. Pescara (122,000) is larger again and the only one to increase its population by a large number since 1961. It is one of the industrial development nodes of the Mezzogiorno, very well placed at the exit of the cross-Apennine motorway from Rome, and an important junction for lines of communication. It has an oil refinery, metallurgical and mechanical engineering industries, textiles and a canning factory and is an important agricultural centre and fishing port.

The Tyrrhenian flank of central Italy: the Mezzogiorno advances north

South of Leghorn and the plains of the Arno, from Siena and Grosseto as far as the northern part of Campania, is an extensive region covering southern Tuscany and the major part of Latium. Its unity is not always very clear-cut. Undoubtedly Rome's influence is the major factor, but this is reinforced by equally obvious natural and human factors. The relief includes three elements of a structure responsible for dissecting and, consequently, splitting up part of the Apennine system in the process of tectonic subsidence: interior plains of subsidence and hillsides; thick, not very high, limestone and schist mountains; and volcanoes. Human activities occur in two parallel regions. The zones bordering the coast are empty areas of marsh, malaria-infested for more than a millenium and a half before being the scene of large-scale reclamation. Away from these infested lands, in the interior, deserted mountains contrast with zones of dense population associated with intensive agriculture, often based on viticulture.

The interior: deserted areas and islands of dense population

Deserted hills and mountains

This zone is mostly unattractive due to its transitional, fairly wet and harsh, climate and the thinness and poor quality of its soils developed on a structurally varied relief. A discontinuous line of peaks is composed of different types of rock. To the north, broad-based, metal-bearing hills in Primary schists, the Chianti uplands and clay hills cut into crests in the Siena region, hardly rise above 1,000 metres. In the centre, old, acidic, volcanic material reaches 1,738 metres at Mt Amiata, while more to the south, the three volcanic cone massifs of Volsini, Cimini and Sabatini each retain a lake in their craters: Bolsena, Vico and Bracciano. To the south, beyond the Tiber valley, and after the volcanoes of the Alban hills, the chain continues with the Lepini, Ausoni and Aurunci ranges. These are not very high, between 1,000 and 1,500 metres, but they have abrupt fault edges, and because they are formed of large masses of Jurassic and Cretaceous limestone, they have little arable land. Although the limestone peaks of these mountains are bare, they are generally well wooded. Agriculture occurs in clearings; its typical range of crops is nothing original: cereals, even on the clay slopes most exposed to erosion in the Siena area, plots of fruit trees and vines, a little cattle, pig and goat raising.

The vineyard hills

In this region of low densities, some intensively cultivated and densely populated islands, which are among the most beautiful areas in central Italy, stand out. To the north, in the Chianti hills, on well-drained soils of clay and sandstone origin that prevent gullying, are vines which have for long clung to the slopes. This area produces famous red wines, light-bodied and with a strong bouquet, sometimes compared with Bordeaux wines. The properties, which are mainly in the hands of noble families who have given their names to the best-known wines (Ricasoli, Brolio), can be more than 5,000 hectares.

South of the Chianti region a small area specialising in white wines centres on Orvieto. A much more famous wine-producing area is the 'Castelli Romani', south-east of Rome. Here there are relatively recent, cone-shaped volcanoes, over 20 kilometres in diameter and rising to 998 metres above Rocca di Papa. This 'mini Etna', adorned with two crater lakes (Nemi and Lago Albano), has for a long time been densely settled. There are numerous advantages for human occupation: good-quality volcanic soils, diverse aspects, cooler temperatures than in Rome, no malaria, abundant sources of water.... . The slopes are intensively cultivated in fruit trees, cereals and forage crops, as well as vines which produce well-known wines of which the best known is Frascati.

Agriculture in the depressions: a step towards progress

Between the mountains and hills mentioned above there are irregular corridors running from north-west to south-east. The presence of these depressions, which have sharply cut into the structures that preceded them, is explained by the fact that this zone is part of the interior Apennine system. To the south, there is the large trench of the River Sacco which runs for more than 50 kilometres from Cassino through Frosinone to Castel Ferrato. The western side of this trench bears the name of Ciociara. In the north, the basins are more numerous and more discontinuous. In Tuscany, these are found in the upper Arno, south of Florence, and then in Val Casentino. The southern extension of the Val d'Arno, the Val di Chiana, crosses Umbria, and then rejoins the Tiber trench as far as Orvieto. In all these depressions, agriculture includes cereals, a little grazing, fruit trees, olives and vines. The only industrial crop is tobacco in the Val di Chiana and Ciociara.

Parallel circuits: small, prestigious but stagnant towns

For a long time major routes have followed these depressions: the Via Casilina through the Sacco rift, the Via Cassia through the Val Tiberina from Florence to Rome. The most characteristic aspect of these communication routes is their duplication and competition. From Rome to Naples, the Via Casilina is duplicated near the coast by the Via Appia; if the motorway from Rome to Naples passes through Frosinone, the most utilised, modernised railway line passes through Latina. Similarly, from Rome to Florence, there are separate, yet parallel, routes. The one that passes through Siena is the old route of the Via Cassia; the other, more direct, follows the Val di Chiana, today used by the motorway and the main railway line which is being modernised. This dichotomy, together with the competition from Rome, is one of the reasons for the absence of major towns.

In Latium, Tivoli has 40,000 inhabitants due to tourism, tyres and paper, and Frosinone the same population due to its administrative, agricultural and industrial (mechanical engineering and paper-making) activities. Cassino has only 25,000 inhabitants.

In southern Tuscany the towns are a little larger because their zone of influence extends beyond the basins into the hills and surrounding mountains. The majority have had a glorious past and still preserve many fine monuments. The number of tourists they receive is commensurate with their beauty. Siena is the best example. Almost without any industry, this town owes its 65,000 inhabitants to its role as centre of services and tourism. Arezzo's main attraction are the frescoes of Pierro della Francesca. But, in addition to its service functions, it also has a fairly clearly developed industry which has given it a larger population (88,000).

Reclamation work in the Tyrrhenian marshes

The Tuscan Maremma, Roman Campagna and Pontine marshes share many features in common. Foremost among physical environmental restrictions is an excess of water. All of this coastal sector is composed of sunken zones with a few rare exceptions in Mt Circeo, Orbetello and the volcanic deposits of the Roman Campagna. Powerful watercourses from the interior have created infilled plains left untouched by sea action. The Ombrone, and especially the Tiber, have built up deltas that are being rapidly extended, old Ostia is now

4 kilometres inland. The sea reorganises deposits and lengthens the *lidi* with long strips built up in a south-easterly direction.

Without a firm economic base all these areas remained virtually empty for more than a millenium and a half; pastoral lands reached as far as the gates of Rome and even into Rome itself. Roman latifundia reigned supreme and extensive grazing occupied vast areas. In the marshier parts the most common animal was the curved-horn buffalo which was used to the mud. On dry zones, such as the plateaux of the Roman Campagna, sheep roamed through the meagre pastures.

Attempts at transforming this area date from way back, yet the first to succeed were those of the Fascist period, associated wtih the 'battle for grain'. The Pontine marshes were the first large-scale reclamation project, lasting from 1926 to 1935. A system of channels and pumps removed the water, several thousand colonists were settled in isolated farms, and the town of Littoria, which later became Latina, was built. The farmers, mainly from Romagna and Veneto, succeeded remarkably well in growing new crops. The area produces cereals and specialises in fruits and vegetables.

A similar economy is being introduced in the Maremma, but the lands involved, corresponding to small alluvial plains, are more restricted and are interspersed with zones of traditional cultivation. The reclamation, partly private, is leading to the development of large properties as in the Roman Campagna.

Few activities take place along the coast. Tourism, despite the large beaches, is not highly developed. The resorts are small except for Orbetello, Piombino and Santa Marinella; only the island of Elba has a wide range of facilities and a large tourist influx. Fishing, from the ports of Ostia, Anzio, Piombino and Orbetello supplies 35,000 tons of seafood of which 10,000 tons are mussels.

Finally, port and industrial activities are fairly unimportant, despite the availability of considerable resources. There are minerals, notably iron on Elba and mercury at Mt Amiata (the biggest producer in the world). Salt is obtained at Tarquinia. A small amount of energy is produced from a geothermal station at Larderello and from the refineries of Civitavecchia and Gaeta. There is a chemical industry at Anzio, Piombino and Civitavecchia.

Thus the towns are not large. The biggest is Grosseto, situated in the interior, an agricultural centre for 65,000 inhabitants. The ports have remained small even when they had industrial development, as at Gaeta and Orbetello. The only ones to have grown rapidly are Piombino (40,000 inhabitants), which has industry and tourism and is the port of embarkation for the island of Elba, and Civitavecchia (49,000) for the same reasons (it is the port for Sardinia).

Rome: Italy's capital

Rome's 2,911,671 inhabitants (1979) make it the largest city in Italy, well ahead of Milan. If this order is reversed in terms of conurbations, it is, none

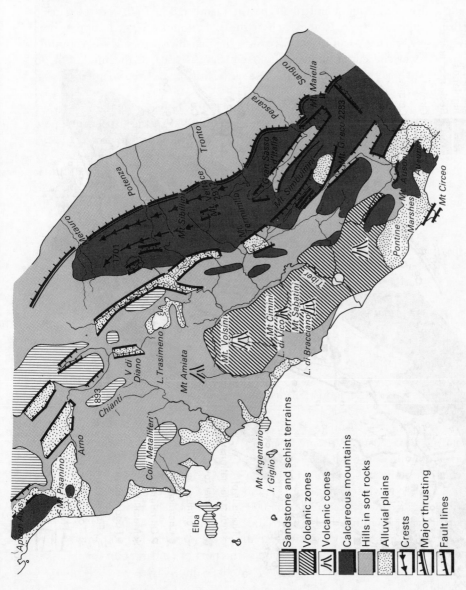

Fig. 6.1 Relief of north–central Italy

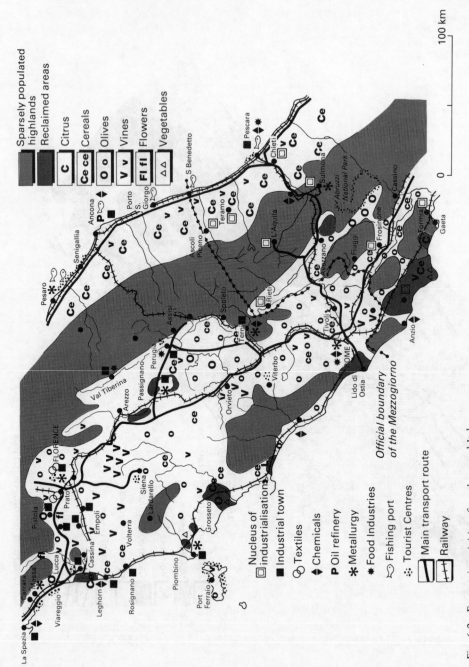

Fig. 6.2   Economic activities of north–central Italy

the less, the case that Rome has a considerable impact on Italian life, and, not only politically. Having grown twelve times since 1870, a growth unequalled in Europe, it has become an enormous organism where economic activities have gradually taken over from purely administrative functions. It has, however, paid the price of an excessive, uncontrolled growth in its urban problems which are becoming more and more difficult to overcome.

Factors and stages in urban development

Topography and its consequences

The Tiber as the major element

The Tiber is the largest river in the peninsula. It flows even in summer and never has the appearance of dry *fiumare* usual elsewhere. With its high water-levels contained by raised and very beautiful quays, it is an adornment to the city – a highly unusual accolade for a Mediterranean river! Although it meanders several times, its width never exceeds 100 metres, so it has been easy to construct bridges. Even in the beginning this was not much of an obstacle, particularly as an island, the Tiberina, still there today, was a site of settlement. Finally, although it is not deep, it has been possible for small boats to make their way upstream from the sea 20 kilometres away. All in all these factors have been fairly positive.

The hills

Rome is built on recent volcanic material, essentially tufas, upon which there sometimes appear, as at Mt Mario, Pliocene clay deposits. In this somewhat non-resistant material, fairly broad, and sometimes badly drained, valleys, such as that of the old Forum, have developed. These are isolated, depending on the degree of resistance of the seven famous hills: Capitolino, Aventino, Esquilino, Gianicolo, Palatino, Celio and Viminale. Though not very high, the 'seven hills' played a vital role as defensive sites and as features shaping the urban landscape. They obstruct movement but multiply the different aspects and views, sometimes aided by panoramic promenades such as the Passeggiata Gianicolo.

The peripheral plateaux

Outside the centre, the topography is simpler and one moves on to the more open horizons of the Roman Campagna. These too are composed of volcanic tufas (though much less dissected) and lava flows like those followed by the Via Appia Antica. On these vast spaces where there is no natural obstacle to urban development, large housing estates have been able to spread out like an encroaching oil slick.

The stages of development and their impact

Rome is literally a stratified city, the constructions of each brilliant period being superimposed on those of the preceding one.

Ancient Rome

The original core, in the depression of the Roman Forum between the Capitol and the Palatine hills, is close to this centre of activity. Growth was continuous from the fifth century BC to the fourth century AD, after which the city was abandoned. In 538 the two symbols of the city, the Senate and the provision of water by aqueducts, disappeared. From this period certain urban features of primordial importance have still persisted. One of them is a substantial reduction in the difference between levels as a result of the accumulation of debris (from 3 to 20 m). Others are the vestiges of monuments in the urban physiognomy, as evidenced in the nearly undamaged ancient buildings such as the Pantheon, the Sant'Angelo Castle, the former mausoleum of Hadrian, the Coliseum, etc. There are columns and triumphal arches. Excavated ruins leave empty spaces in the urban fabric.

Rome from the Renaissance to the modern period

In terms of the control of land, an urban *latifondo* in the hands of the Pope, feudal princes, religious orders and congregations is the rule, given the quasi-absence of a bourgeoisie. This fact had two consequences: the construction of prestigious buildings and gardens, of which many traces still remain; and, in the nineteenth and twentieth centuries, ease of land speculation which did nothing to help the balanced development of the agglomeration.

The urban framework slowly took shape during this lengthy period. The most ancient, and disorderly, network of streets was laid down before the fifteenth century, together with the lanes and small squares that can still be seen at the foot of the Capitol and in Trastevere. The first organised attempts to push through straight and broader streets began with the Corso, then, from the sixteenth century, the streets of Coronari, Lungara, San Selso and Giulia. The Renaissance, and later the seventeenth and eighteenth centuries (the baroque period), contributed an enormous number of civil and religious monuments which today constitute the architectural heritage of the city.

Rome in the nineteenth and twentieth centuries

A real transformation occurred as a result of unification and the designation of Rome as capital. Suddenly, all the necessary administrative services had to be created and room had to be found for them. A property boom, both for administrative buildings and housing, took hold of the city. Large estates were divided into building lots (Villa Ludovisi, Esquilino) and despite the conservation of the Villa Borghese, the Eternal City lost most of its open spaces.

Urban planning was no more successful during the Fascist period. The EUR area (Esposizione Universale Roma) was erected for a world fair which never took place. Although the architectural merits of the scheme are debatable, it is today considered a success. Ancient quarters, such as the Borgo and a part of the Palatine Hill, were, however, destroyed in order to make room for the Via della Conciliazone which leads to St Peter's Square and for the Via dei Fori Imperiali which goes from Piazza Veneto to the Coliseum.

The present functions of Rome

Its role as capital

Rome is three times a capital – of Italy, Christianity and the headquarters of the Food and Agriculture Organisation (FAO). The two latter functions create 5,000 jobs but really these are of little benefit to Italians. Rome as the national capital is by far the largest generator of employment. It has been calculated that the number of state employees living in Rome, and including those in retirement, is as high as 250,000.

To this political and administrative function may be added its role as a major business centre; for many years capital and headquarters shunned the city, but the rapid expansion in the influence of the State and its involvement in economic affairs have brought in headquarters and offices.

There are also in Rome the largest Italian university with 100,000 students, establishments associated with the Church (including the Gregorian University) and numerous foreign institutes. The museums and libraries are visited not only by tourists but also by artists and researchers. This extends to industrial art, fashion design (Pucci) and especially the cinema which has at its disposal the Cinecittà studios. All these activities supply the Via Veneto with a flow of stars.

Finally, there are the activities related to visitors which are very important. There are often several, not entirely separate, reasons for visiting the city; tourism, pilgrimage and business are rather difficult to distinguish in the statistics, but the figures speak for themselves. Rome partly lives from the revenue it derives from visitors, often from the informal sector and its small trades (including some disreputable ones): manufacture and sale of souvenirs, postcards, religious objects. And, in a more official manner, there is the income from restaurants, hotels, boarding houses and convents.

Industrial functions

Although Rome is principally a city of white-collar employees, its industrial function is gradually gaining importance. The oldest, and for a long time, the only one, was building. Today construction employs 60,000 people to which must be added all those who work in related industries, such as cement, bricks, ceramics and glass. Similarly, there are the industries which exist as a result of the large population; for example, food storage and processing, furniture and wood, textiles and clothing (35,000 jobs in these three sectors).

At another level, there are publishing industries linked to the cultural life (4,500 people at the Government Press for example). Furthermore, the labour market and proximity to decision-making has brought in some high-technology industries: chemicals associated with the two oil refineries, pharmaceutical products and cosmetics, mechanical and electrical appliances.

The Romans and the physiognomy of the city

The Roman population

Romans who have been there for generations hardly exceed 10 per cent of the city's population. It should be remembered that the conurbation has increased by 1.6 million people since 1940, of which 1 million are probably new arrivals. The origin of migrants is diverse, although those from surrounding districts of Latium form the largest group, probably a third of the arrivals since 1945. Most of the other immigrants come from the Mezzogiorno, particularly the regions of Abruzzi, Campania, Calabria and Sicily. As a result, the city's inhabitants exhibit a southern demographic pattern. The old and young are the largest groups. The natural increase is large due to a birth-rate still above 17.5 per thousand and a mortality rate which, though increasing slightly, is no more than 8.5 per thousand. For the past fifteen years the natural increase has been almost the same as immigration.

Basic characteristics and problems of the city

The centre: disorganised and beautiful

In the centre, or that which is essentially within the Aurelian town, the most significant feature is the absence of a regular plan; old, narrow streets and modern avenues coexist without any overall principle and with a traffic circulation that is one of the most chaotic in the world. Other notable characteristics are the existence of open spaces: gardens such as the Villa Borghese; ancient ruins which are also empty spaces; and an exceptional architectural density. There are monuments almost everywhere. Specialised areas and streets include those with a single purpose. There are commercial streets – Via del Corso, Vittorio Veneto, del Tritone, Nazionale. Working-class areas include Travestere and the lower part of the Quirinale. Streets with hotels crowd round the main station. Another feature is the depopulation resulting from the inconvenience of living in old buildings, the noise and congestion; part of the original population leaves and is not replaced, leading to a certain commercial decline.

The edges of the city centre extend out to a distance of 5 or 6 kilometres. These 'central peripheral' areas are closely linked with the core functionally and in terms of the urban system, for there is no organisation of services in these areas.

A suburban structure still in the course of formation

The area of the 'World Fair' (EUR) is the first type of suburb and includes, within the context of a grandiose plan, high-level tertiary activities (ministries, *Cassa per il Mezzogiorno*, research offices), de luxe residences and well-established commercial activities.

The *borgate* are working-class areas, all with a similar regular plan, without open spaces and, for a long time, without adequate facilities. Examples are Tiburtino, Trullo and Pietralata.

Worse still are the *borghetti*, full-scale shanty towns which house more than 50,000 people in shacks without even the most elementary amenities. The city authorities are trying to get rid of them but they still exist.

Finally, beyond the city itself, but still forming part of the urban system, are the seaside districts of Ostia, which is like all other urbanised resorts, but contains more year-round activities due to its excellent communications by road and underground with the centre.

The major urban problems

Rome has all the major problems of a city of its size (provision of water, sewerage, education and crime) but two are extreme: the lack of any structure, and traffic.

We have discussed many examples of the lack of structure. To summarise more analytically, there is a congested centre with too many functions, and without easy access, where all the lines of communication are swallowed up; and secondly there are dispersed, peripheral zones without cross-town links and lacking their own activities, so that there is hardly any correlation of work and residence.

Finally, traffic problems are the most obvious, given the horrendous bottlenecks on weekday evenings. Train services out of the city are good, motorways have exits on external ring roads, and there are the two airports of Ciampino and Leonardo da Vinci. Leonardo da Vinci, also called Fiumicino, handles 8.5 million passengers and 1.3 million tons of freight per year; it is the largest passenger airport in Italy. However, as soon as one enters the city, everything is spoilt. This is due to a series of mistakes and omissions. Pedestrian areas and zones for public transport were created too late and there are no peripheral car parks, nor very many in the centre, so that the anarchic parking is quite extraordinary. Public transport by bus and tram, though reasonably priced, suffers from congestion and slow-moving traffic, thereby discouraging people from using it. There is certainly need of an underground system, for one cannot count the single line from the main Termini station to EUR and Ostia as constituting one. However, there would probably be problems in constructing one in the Roman subsoil.

Rome has not yet acquired an infrastructure in keeping with its population and level of activities. It adapts but does not progress. Possibly the recent realisation of the major deterioration of all the monuments in the centre from the effects of exhaust gases and the vibration of motor cars will sufficiently shock planners into action.

7 The Deep South
of the peninsula

And the bitter lemons where your teeth left a mark
G. DE NERVAL

Beyond Latium and the Abruzzi, as one moves southward, a different world is suddenly entered. The landscapes, colours and crops are definitely much more clearly Mediterranean; on the Tyrrhenian coast citrus fruits are now common while they are almost non-existent in the Pontine marshes. Light and heat erupt in a truly southern ensemble. Yet belonging to the South brings with it the expected economic characteristics: together with the islands, this part of the peninsula is the most underdeveloped in Italy.

Regions of the Adriatic and the Gulf of Taranto

The contrast of this region with the Marche and the transitional Abruzzian area around Pescara hits the eye. A narrow belt of deeply etched hills is replaced by a fairly wide zone which quickly reaches 40 kilometres, and is striking in its broad tabular perspectives.

Three very different environments

Mt Gargano

This is a spur which juts into the Adriatic and is part of a little-deformed shield, bounded on all sides by rift faults, and is formed of limestone more than 500 metres in thickness. The uplifting, which continued during the Quaternary and is probably continuing today, raised altitudes to just over 1,000 metres (Mt Calvo 1,065 m), but has practically left intact the summit erosion surfaces which cut the secondary beds. This block has been greatly worn away by the dissolution of underground water; dry valleys, grottoes and extensive cave systems abound.

The Gargano, a world apart, is a limestone plateau where the arable land, the *terra rossa*, composed of red clay, is collected in small depressions (dolines) or brought into poljes by streams. The block is therefore covered almost entirely by a magnificent, virtually natural, vegetation. In its central area rises the famous Foresta Umbra, where total conservation has been possible because it belongs to the State, an unusual situation in Italy where 94 per cent of forest lands are in private hands. As with Mt Circeo, but in a much larger area, the Gargano is a sort of botanical museum of the peninsula.

Tavoliere

This is almost totally a plain, at an altitude of 50 metres in the Foggia region, and extends from north-west to south-east for about 80 kilometres, being about half as wide. The main rivers which descend from the Apennines, the Fortore in the north and the Ofanto in the south, avoid it though they flow through hill areas at a higher altitude. The plain itself is composed of a mixture of Pliocene and Quaternary gravels and sands and is thus naturally rather badly drained. The principal interior watercourse, the Calore, only reaches the sea because of a recently constructed canal. All these features probably signify that this area is an extremely recent subsided fault.

The periodic high rainfall in the Tavoliere is in striking contrast to the dryness of neighbouring Gargano. The high rainfall is not constant, however, for the area is sheltered behind uplands which isolate it in the north-east from the Adriatic and in the south-west from the Tyrrhenian, so that the climate is actually very dry. But in winter, when the rivers cannot get out of the depression blocked by sandy coastal strips, they flood the plain. Recent changes have included the construction of an outlet canal and, for an ever-increasing surface, the organisation of an irrigation system using subterranean beds.

Apulia

Seemingly one of the most monotonous landscapes in Italy, Apulia is composed of plateaux descending from a height of 660 metres in the northwest to about 100–120 metres in the Lecce promontory. The limestone origin (Cretaceous then Miocene) of the material explains the almost complete absence of valleys, although karst forms as such are much less common than in the Gargano.

In the Murge there occur the fertile red clays of the limestones as in Gargano, but the topography is less dissected and the karst depressions offer some possibilities for development. Furthermore, the environment has been remarkably transformed in two ways. Soils have been protected against erosion, and the extremely plentiful clays in the depressions, especially in the region of *trulli*, were transported to the sides to form small, terraced fields built behind small stone walls.

Since surface water is totally absent, rain-tanks provided a supply which, for a long time, was sufficient for human consumption and herds, but at the end of the eighteenth century, a large aqueduct (Aquedotto Pugliese) was built to bring in the abundant waters of the Apennines, including those of the Tyrrhenian flank.

An agricultural production dominated by commercial crops

Social structure: over-extended villages and trulli

There are few such convincing examples as Apulia of the relationship between settlement patterns and land structures. In three-quarters of the region large properties remain the dominant form. They were hardly affected by land reform, because they were classified as being efficiently farmed. This structure has produced a distinctive agrarian landscape and settlement pattern. Land-owners hire their workers and get their tenants in the villages. There is practically no dispersed settlement. Village territories are extremely extensive and are divided by paths which converge from all directions towards the place of residence. Thus agglomerations of houses have grown up without much of a service function. They form villages of exceptional size – several have 30,000 inhabitants.

One zone, however, is without large properties, that of the Murge dei Trulli to the north of Alberobello and Putignano. The settlement pattern changes immediately and completely. This is probably not due to the greater extent of *terra rossa*, as some have cited. Villages diminish in population, and isolated houses in the midst of crops become more common.

Principal crops

Large properties have not generated a system of cereal monoculture every-where, though many have. The High Murge and especially the Tavoliere, despite recent changes, still have mainly hard wheat cultivation.

The vine is the second major crop, covering vast areas at the lowest elevations, such as the Lecce–Taranto peninsula, though it is widespread in other topographical zones as well. Apulia produces the largest amount of table grapes in Italy – half the total national area and production (581,000 tons). The wines, mainly highly alcoholic, are used for blending and represent in an average year one-tenth of Italian production with 6.5 million hectolitres.

The olive is the third cornerstone of Apulia's agriculture. It grows almost everywhere but forms virtual forests in the Bari and Brindisi regions. The right climatic conditions have meant that it has reached impressive proportions and most trees are big, several hundred-year-old specimens. Thanks to them, Apulia produces the largest quantity of olive oil in Italy (152,000 tons of a national total of 350,000 tons).

Characteristic southern economic and social problems

Soaring demographic increases, unemployment and emigration

Given the present state of its economy, Apulia would seem to be overpopulated. Its density is greater than the Italian average (185 as against 180 per square km) in a largely agricultural region. Its birth-rate remains high (18.6 per thousand), only exceeded by Campania; its annual natural increase, 10.8 per thousand or 41,000 people, is the highest in Italy along with Campania. For many years emigration balanced out this excess population, but it has been reduced a great deal due to the European economic crisis. Since 1976, according to statistics, which are admittedly imprecise, more migrants returned to Apulia than left it.

Insufficiently developed non-agricultural activities

For the 429,000 farmers in Apulia, there are only 358,000 people working in industry and 420,000 in other activities, particularly in the service sector. The official statistics show that during 1975–76 the number of people employed in industry declined by 1,000 and rose by 24,000 in agriculture. We shall not comment further on these obviously debatable statistics, except to state that they do reveal a definite tendency in the continuing domination of agricultural activities.

Tourist activities are also not adequately developed despite the undeniable attractions of the region; beautiful landscapes (Gargano), architectural heritage (*trulli*, fortified medieval castles, highly decorated baroque churches at Lecce....), mild climate and numerous, long beaches. Recent developments have taken place around Gargano and in the *trulli* region, but many tourists simply pass through.

Fishing, which takes place in the surrounding seas, the Adriatic and Ionian, is an important activity. With a catch of 45,600 tons, including 26,300 tons of fish and 17,400 tons of shellfish, the region ranks third after Sicily and Emilia-Romagna. Taranto, Brindisi, Manfredonia and Bari are the main ports and fishing centres. They are also the economically most important towns.

Industrial development

Primary resources are not many, though, of course, there are agricultural products for food industries, but the subsoil, apart from quarries (limestone in particular), yield few usable materials. Only salt is produced in large quantities in the salt marshes of Margherita di Savoia.

The *Cassa per il Mezzogiorno* has devoted large sums to industrial development. In the period 1951–77 fixed investments made by specialised institutes reached the remarkable total of 4,311,000 million lire, one-fifth of all investments of this type in the area of *Cassa* intervention. Only Sardinia received more than Apulia in this respect. The highest increase in officially created employment of any Italian region (157,000 in new establishments and 58,000 in the expansion of existing ones) except Campania was expected to arise from this investment, as well as from other secondary investments (loans, subsidies). On top of these direct investments, the State has provided communications infrastructures – railways, port facilities at Bari, Brindisi and Taranto, and finally, motorways. The double tracking of the coastal railway line is almost finished as far as Brindisi, as well as the motorways from the

North – A14 from Bologna to Bari and Taranto and the A17 from Rome via Naples and Bari.

Extremely different towns

Agricultural centres

Despite their size – Bisceglie (45,000 inhabitants), Trani (40,000), Molfetta (64,000), Andria (77,900), Manfredonia (48,000) and even Barletta (76,000) with its fishing port – these 'towns' are hardly more than enormous villages. They are the agglomerated houses of agricultural workers, interspersed with oil- and wine-processing plants and grouped around a monumental church. Recently, industrial workers have moved into these settlements' peripheries or into the open countryside. Services in these overblown agricultural centres are limited to the daily needs of their inhabitants.

Lecce and Foggia

Lecce (84,000 inhabitants) is the same type of town, but due to its role as provincial capital and presence of noteworthy monuments, such as the cathedral with beautiful baroque sculptures, it stands out from the others. The quiet, narrow, tortuous streets suggest a sleepy town, but this is belied by the presence outside of town of a large Fiat factory making caterpillar tractors and engines.

Foggia may appear to be different because of its larger population of 144,000 inhabitants, but it is not. In the centre of the Tavoliere, it was the ancient capital of transhumance but did not grow until the cultivation of cereals in the nineteenth century. Since it was never an important town in the past, it does not possess a centre with monumental buildings and so spreads out unattractively with its straight streets in a grid-iron pattern on to the large plain. It has a tertiary role in administration and commerce, particularly in the agricultural sector, and its industrial activities are growing. Chemicals and metallurgy (a large factory manufacturing diesel engines that belongs jointly to Renault and Fiat) have now been added to the traditional food-processing industries.

Ports in the process of being developed

Brindisi (83,000 inhabitants) has a slightly smaller population than Lecce but is economically more active. The highly diversified port lies in a sheltered position which gave it an important military role in past centuries. Today it is the port of embarkation for Greece thanks to its car ferries – almost 200,000 passengers used it in 1976. International freight accounted for more than 1,250,000 tons in the same year of which 1 million tons were hydrocarbons which came into the port for the oil refineries located near the town. Coastal shipping represented more than 2 million tons, including a considerable amount of refined petroleum products. These have introduced an important petrochemical industry.

Taranto has shared the same model of development, though of a different intensity. The town, now with a population of 229,000 inhabitants, has always depended on the fortunes of its port, even from earliest antiquity when it was a major port of the Greek Empire. The port contains two basins that form the Mare Piccolo, and these are separated from the open sea (the Gulf of Taranto) by a promontory on which the town is situated.

By building a long channel a new port was easily constructed in the Gulf of Taranto to receive large vessels. This is closely linked in with industry so that its traffic makes it one of the largest Italian ports with more than 20 million tons of merchandise. Its considerable activity is due to industrial development. East of the town an oil refinery is situated beside a large power station, a chemical plant (Montedison) and a large cement works. And foremost, Italsider has established a large steelworks with a production capacity of more than 10 million tons per annum of steel.

This rapid growth has had two important consequences for the town. The old town, enclosed on the promontory, remains partly abandoned, its old residences inhabited by the poorest sections of the population. The modern town beyond the revolving bridge spreads north-east, its grid-iron pattern streets bordered by two seafront promenades.

A regional capital: Bari

As a city of 362,000 inhabitants the variety of Bari's activities equals that of its zone of influence. Like Brindisi and Taranto, Bari was an ancient port; from here the First Crusade set off. To the east of the promontory upon which the old town is built is the old port, to the west the new.

The industrial development of the past two decades has been remarkable and, though less spectacular than Taranto, much more diversified. Chemical industries related to rubber production are coupled with mechanical engineering products, textiles and an important food-processing industry. These investments have received the support of the *Cassa per il Mezzogiorno* but, unlike in other towns, they have also resulted from local initiative. Bari is a town of entrepreneurs whose spirit of initiative principally manifests itself in the tertiary sector. It is by far the largest commercial centre in Apulia.

Mountains and basins of the southern Apennines: from Molise to Calabria, the poorest part of Italy

The southern Apennines begin south of the Abruzzi and continue till the Straits of Messina where they form the Aspromonte. They are divided into numerous provinces and regions: Molise, Basilicata, Campania and Calabria, but these entities are much more administrative abstractions than real geographical units, as with the case of Molise which was artificially created in 1962. However, the geographical units are clearly defined.

This is a country of strongly contrasting reliefs, of crests and high plateaux reaching more than 2,000 metres which overlook the sea, and of low, sunken plains, all of which create a veritable jigsaw puzzle. In these difficult conditions, people have managed to survive by putting in an inordinate amount of work, and have even multiplied, although this remains the poorest area of Italy from where people have had to emigrate *en masse*.

A naturally difficult environment

Despite the unremarkable altitude of the summits at about 2,000 metres (Mts Pollino 2,248 m, Sila, Aspromonte 1,995 m), there are few more mountainous regions.

Mountains damp and raw

The bare limestone peaks of Campania and Basilicata seem to be an extension of those in the Abruzzi, but only the sombre Matese (2,050 m), with secondary limestone domes scooped out by a superb glacial cirque really does resemble them. Beyond, towards the south-east and as far as the Crati rift, the features are different. The Triassic limestones are less dominating and more ancient, as well as being less sharp; above all, a more complex and older tectonic action has superimposed recent upheavals on transversal movements, including major thrusting which affects the basement and all its cover. This results in total discontinuity, accentuated by different orientations (the Sorrento peninsula, aligned south-west – north-east, is perpendicular to the general mass). The mountains thus form isolated blocks, small and very steep, with highly developed karst features: Cilento, Mt Cirino (2,005 m), Mt Pollino (2,248 m).

High crystalline plateaux covered in forest and pastures

Crystalline material appears gradually. In the coastal chain of northern Calabria schists coexist with Triassic limestones, but as from Sila and Aspromonte they dominate totally.

West of the Crati tectonic trench the coastal chain rises to 1,541 metres, but is no more than an alignment abruptly stopped by a maze of valleys. To the east, the Sila, divided into Sila Grande (1,928 m) and Sila Piccola (1,678 m), forms a distinctive series of high plateaux with a Hercynian type of undulating surface which corresponds to a Tertiary erosion surface. Beyond the Catanzaro Trench the third series of landforms are the bosses and ridges of the Serra San Bruno and particularly Aspromonte.

These mountains, more than the preceding ones, have a wetter, fresher climate, receiving more than 2,000 millimetres on their summits. The soils are sometimes quite deep on the crystalline plateaux which carry an attractive vegetation cover. The forest covers the Sila in a characteristic vertical zonation: evergreen oaks, then deciduous oaks, chestnut trees, beeches and, finally, conifers.

Bare clay landscapes

Clay soils reappear in force in the eastern part of the southern Apennines, especially in the provinces of Potenza and Matera, but they are to be found in nearly all the lowlands. Their age ranges from Jurassic clay schists to Pliocene white clays; structures are often chaotic and related to thrusting, but dissection has given them some unity in forming landscapes with landslips and gullies as in the characteristic landscape of Basilicata.

Tectonic trenches: long, dry corridors

Each section of the Apennines has its own type of tectonic trench: here they are small and narrow, from 3 to 4 kilometres on average but with edges well defined by still-active fault faces. Thus from north to south there stretch the Salerno plain, Val di Diano or Sele Trench, the Crati valley, the plain of San Eufemia, all corridors or openings rather than trenches. Their youth partly explains the bad drainage, the rivers flowing in enormous Primary beds, shifted from one side to the other by large alluvial cones originating in the rivers that have come down from the bordering slopes. The high rainfall, resulting from winter downpours, contrasts with the dry summer conditions in the sheltered interior basins

Inhospitable coasts

This coastline is not very suitable for maritime life, for here are the dreaded Straits of Scylla and Charybdis. The general shape of the coastline is irregular and swept in large curves, corresponding to recent displacements cutting into the interior reliefs. This produces an alternation of sometimes steep cliffs (Belvedere Marittimo, Palinuro) and sandy beaches bordered by small plains. The latter, except for Sele and San Eufemia are small and all susceptible to erratic rivers which are still building these plains.

Unfavourable social conditions and massive emigration

A society set in its old ways

The first relevant feature of the economy is the persistence until the land reform, and even after it, of large properties. Latifundia have decreased due to the reform, but very unevenly – a great deal in Calabria, little in Basilicata. Where land reform has occurred, it has not been able to create viable units. Emigration slowed down greatly in the period 1950–60 but then took off again in response to the attraction of high salaries in the North and abroad.

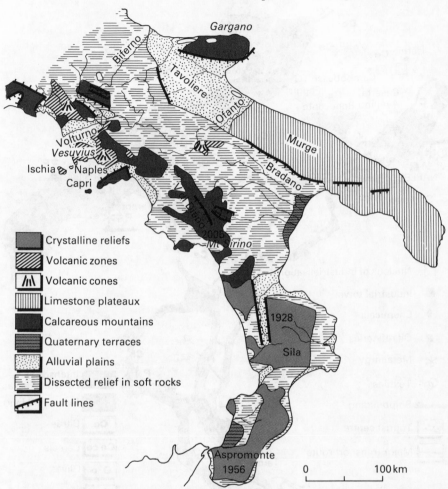

Fig. 7.1   Relief of the southern peninsula

These provinces are still among the poorest and most 'backward' in Italy. Poverty can be seen in houses without amenities, sometimes susceptible to the effects of erosion and partially buried in natural caves (the *sassi* of Matera). For long it has engendered violence, as embodied by Calabrian bandits who were stock theatrical characters in nineteenth-century Europe.

Society remains marked by the harshness of the conditions of life, generated by the violence of physical elements and human actions. For example, illiteracy reaches record levels in Calabria (15%). *Laureati* (university graduates) are better represented (7.9% in Calabria as against the Italian average of 10.2%), but we should have no illusions about this – educated people have rarely done technical subjects and there are many white-collar unemployed in the small towns.

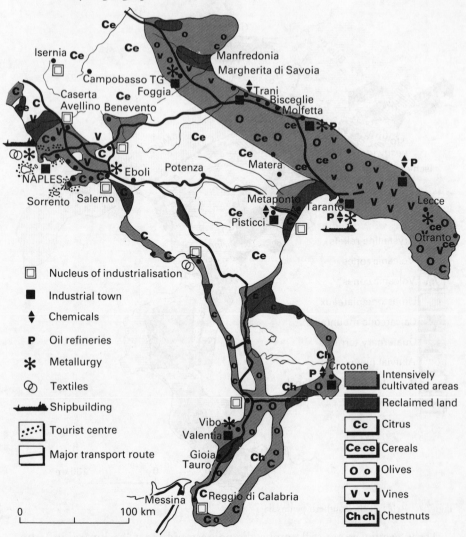

Fig. 7.2　Economic activities of the 'Deep South'

Massive emigration

Calabrians have for a long time emigrated. From the seventeenth century they were known in the towns of the South and in Rome as suppliers of wood and charcoal, workers who specialised in doing dirty and repellent tasks, players of bagpipes and *pifferari*. However, it was unification which provoked a mass outpouring from the mountain zones. The imposition of taxes on the consumption of foodstuffs and housing, a measure unsuitable for such a poor area, led to a full-scale exodus, sometimes less severe, but never absent.

At present the demographic situation is changing. The natural increase is not very great since, without young households, the birth-rate has declined (16.2 per thousand in Calabria which is clearly lower than that of the rest of the Mezzogiorno). In 1976 the natural increase came to no more than 25,000 people. However, there are now two contrasting situations – deserted villages in the mountains and small towns swollen with unemployed in the poorer parts.

The present economy: archaic dullness and attempts at development

Fallow land, cereals and extensive grazing

In the higher areas depopulation has left behind many signs of abandonment. More or less deserted villages are surrounded by vast areas where crumbling stone walls no longer keep back arable land and where fallow land is turning to scrub. Residual agricultural production still employs archaic methods. Cereals are still the dominant crop, even on steep clay slopes. Along the slopes fields of wheat and oats interweave as they follow the slow-moving path of the *frane*.

The area under forest remains considerable – 270,000 hectares, of which 74,000 are conifers, especially in the Sila. Here production of charcoal represents a third of the Italian total, not that one can get much joy out of this figure since 'finished' wood only accounts for 12 per cent of national production. In Irpinia, in the Benevento region, chestnuts and walnuts are of high quality and are mainly exported.

Development projects and current changes

In the area beyond Eboli, the *Cassa per il Mezzogiorno* has been unstinting in its efforts.

Its general programmes have involved improvement of the physical environment and attempts at ending isolation. Major programmes were undertaken in reafforestation, regularisation of river beds and the stabilisation of water flows. Basilicata took up half the money attributed to the South from 1950 to 1977 in the *Sistemazzione Montana* project where 130,000 hectares were reafforested as well as 115,000 in Calabria. The barrages on the Sila plateau, which form the Arvo, Ampollino and Cecita lakes, and those of the Ionian rivers (Agri) and Adriatic rivers (Fortore, Biferno and Suini), have meant that flows could be stabilised and water stored.

Isolation here took on two aspects, one in relation to the rest of Italy and, the other, the links between the different parts of the area. Much has been done about this state of affairs. Although part of the main railway line was converted into double track, nothing much could be done about the actual line itself, so that full-scale change depended on the road network. The majority of transverse routes, which bypassed the valley bottoms and constantly meandered, were replaced by shorter links which followed the hydrographic axes: the Biferno valley from Campobasso to Termoli, the Bradano and Suini valleys. At the same time the old Via Cassia was paralleled by an express route from Potenza to Metaponto and two motorways, the A3 and A16, linked Naples to Salerno and Cosenza to Reggio.

Local programmes and development zones

Not all the region was concerned with traditional activities. A developed agriculture, based on citrus fruits, had been in existence for a long time on coastal terraces, especially those of the Tyrrhenian coast. However, all these areas also came within the scope of the *Cassa per il Mezzogiorno* projects.

The Sila, which for twenty years has been the object of the Ente Sila's attention, was the domain of a set of coordinated programmes which aimed at water control, production of electricity, reafforestation of conifers, conservation of broad-leaved trees and an efficient organisation of cattle and sheep raising.

The irrigated sectors of the lowlands can be divided into two groups: coastal terraces which had already been irrigated, and the still marshy plains which are in the process of being reclaimed. The first occur discontinuously, depending on the possibilities offered by the terrain, especially in the very south, from Palmi to Locri through Reggio, then on the edges of the Gulf of Policastro. Two main crops dominate this densely populated area of large perched villages – olives in the dry parts, citrus fruits, lemons and oranges in the irrigated lowlands nearer watercourses.

A considerable effort has been put into controlling rivers, draining marshes and providing irrigation in the Crati and Liri valleys, at Cosenza and Sala Consilina, in the coastal basins of Gioia Tauro and Metaponto. From 1950 to 1976 the *Cassa* irrigated 71,000 hectares in Calabria and Basilicata and 1,300 hectares in Molise. Citrus fruits have been planted, especially on the Ionian side.

Efforts at industrialisation have been carried out, as elsewhere in the Mezzogiorno, in the framework of numerous nodes, but the results for the moment are fairly meagre. The interior centres (Benevento, Avellino, Potenza) have not been very successful, apart from the establishment of several mechanical engineering industries (Fiat at Avellino) and textiles. Pisticci, near the coast, has a small petrochemical plant due to the hydrocarbon deposits there. Development, however, remains primarily coastal with plans to develop nuclei at Reggio di Calabria, Crotone, Cornigliano Calabro, Maratea and Gioia Tauro. For the moment, development has occurred mainly in Crotone (chemicals, fertilisers, zinc refining), Maratea (textiles), Vibo Valentia in the Gulf of Gioia Tauro (metallurgy) where large-scale steelworks were intended before the crisis. Since 1950 all these investments have created little employment – 17,000 in Basilicata and 38,000 in Calabria.

Tourism is not an insignificant activity, but it suffers from distance and the fact that, on the beaches of the bays of Policastro, Gioia Tauro, Metaponto and Crotone, as in the mountains of Sila, its clientele is mainly national.

In these poor, yet densely populated, lands (130 inhabitants/km² in Calabria, 72 in Molise, 60 in Basilicata) there are many towns, none of which have had a sufficiently extensive zone of influence to be able to act as catalysts of development.

Despite their individual identity, several points in common are shared by these towns. Apart from Reggio, these are all inland towns for the coast was to be feared, a situation which is manifested in the insignificance of fishing (5,900 tons per year). All the towns are at some distance from the coast, as with Catanzaro which overlooks it from a hillock 10 kilometres from the shore. Nearly all are on two sites. Originally these towns were perched on hilltops surrounded by ravines, sometimes very deep (Catanzaro, Matera), which were good defensive sites, but inconvenient and even dangerous, so that the sites had to be moved down into flatter areas where it was possible: this has happened at Benevento and Cosenza.

Individualistic identities of towns

Ten towns have a population of over 40,000 inhabitants. There is an entire group of small and medium-sized towns, based primarily on administrative activities: Isernia (16,000) and Campobasso (44,000) in Molise; Avellino (56,000) and Benevento (60,700) in Campania; Potenza (60,000) and Matera (47,000) in Basilicata; Catanzaro (89,000) stretching between two ravines in Calabria.

The development towns are mainly in Calabria: Crotone whose 54,000 inhabitants owe their existence principally to industry, and the two towns of the Gulf of Gioia Tauro–Vibo Valentia (31,000) and Nicastro (58,000). Cosenza has more than 100,000 inhabitants, thanks to its excellent situation in the centre of northern Calabria. It now has a university too.

Finally, Reggio di Calabria has 174,000 inhabitants. It is part of a region in which Messina forms the other half of a symmetrical relationship. Reggio is a major commercial centre, based on small industries, and is a town without much charm since it was rebuilt after the 1908 earthquake. The low standard of living and the chronic unemployment are certainly characteristics of a South where, despite the efforts that have been made, little has really changed.

Campania and the Neapolitan region

Like Apulia, Campania forms a distinctive geographical region. Around the large city of Naples, still the third most populated in Italy, everything takes on extreme proportions. Naples and its surrounding area are a sort of caricature of the South: prosperous plains contrasting with the deserted highlands;

a Third World demographic pattern (highest birth-rate in Italy); a city with record levels of unemployment. All these features are amplified and magnified to a unique dimension whose disproportionate intensity often leads to dramatic conflict.

A region with a typical Mediterranean environment

A good climate and abundant water

As one descends from the North, Campania is the first area really stamped with a Mediterranean feel: hot, bright and highly coloured. What is important and is, in fact, conveyed by averages, is the mildness of the winter (January average of 8.7 °C in Naples, 7.4 °C in Rome) and a large amount of sunshine (87 days of cloudy weather in Naples, 105 in Rome).

This warm and sunny atmosphere is, nevertheless, not dry, for it rains a lot in Campania because of the land's blocking effect on moisture-laden air masses from the sea. Naples receives 994 millimetres, and the irregularity of it does not vary by more than 50%. The only thing to fear is the sometimes extreme violence of the downpours during the wet season in autumn and winter. Summer is dry, although the monthly rainfall does not fall below 10 millimetres. Anyhow, water is not lacking, for there exists not far down in the subsoil of the alluvial plains numerous and abundant water sources emanating from the neighbouring limestone and volcanic country. Streams are generally diverted. Only the too powerful Volturno, which for a long time was troublesome, was not, but even it has now been contained.

Steep mountains and low plains

The mountains form the distant horizons. In the east and north-east these are the fault scarps of the Apennine peaks (Mt Aurunci). In the south-east, Sorrento, extended by Capri, has a backbone rising to more than 1,443 metres above Positano, and is still at a height of 589 metres at Capri which has incredibly steep and breathtakingly high slopes that fall in vertical cliffs to the sea.

The volcanic terrain is varied in altitude and morphology, but it has in common youthful forms whether they be active or dormant like Vesuvius. The latter is a cone of 1,227 metres, formed at the summit by a sub-crater lodged in the semicircle of the older and, partially exploded, Summa crater. The Phlegrean Fields, west of Naples, and the islands of Procida and Ischia are composed of lava, tufas and ancient craters which, in the Phlegrean Fields, still emit gases. The Lake Arveno there was considered by the ancients to be one of the entrances to hell.

The plains contained between these landforms are obviously of small dimensions. They have been built by recent alluvial deposits and are of two types. Those near Naples, based on small rivers, are easily developed. But those at the mouth of large rivers, the Sele east of Salerno, the Volturno and the Gargliano, have for a long time been susceptible to flooding. All these soils have, after development, considerable agricultural potential.

Organisation of the Campanian countryside

Apart from its decline during the period of barbarian invasions, this region has always been densely populated. It is enough to cite Herculaneum, Pompeii, Cumae and Capua for evidence from antiquity. From the Middle Ages to the modern period, Campania was one of the most populated regions of Europe, and Naples, as capital of the Bourbons, was the largest city in Italy in the eighteenth century. Even the limestone peninsula of Sorrento and the lower slopes of Vesuvius were densely settled. And today it is still the same. A high fertility is the dominant demographic trait: Campania has the highest birth-rate in Italy – 19 per thousand as against 13.6 per thousand national average. With a mortality rate of only 8.3 per thousand, the natural increase is high. A dark spot on this picture of demographic vitality is the extremely high rate (26.3 per thousand) of infant mortality. It is a sign of underdevelopment and that this large population lives in poor conditions. This can be seen in indices relating to the standard of living – 166 cars per thousand compared to 250 in Italy, 163 telephones compared to 232, 147 television sets compared to 209, and so on.

Agricultural organisation

Terraced limestone and volcanic slopes

On the steep slopes of Capri, Ischia, Procida, the terrains of Amalfi and Sorrento and the slopes of Vesuvius, only the rocky summits have remained unused. The sides have been transformed into gigantic series of low walls containing tiny, but fertile, plots, continually worked by farmers. Everything is cultivated, though two crops dominate – vines yielding strong wines (Lacryma Christi) and citrus fruits, oranges and lemons.

Irrigated plains

Water is supplied by watercourses, springs and wells. The Nocera canal flows in the plain of Pompeii, the 'Regni Lagni', fed by the considerable springs of Morbito, in the plain of Naples. The dry periods have no effect on the crops which have created a varied landscape, of which the most striking is the *coltura promiscua* where vines, especially table grapes, reach almost 6 or 7 metres in height, suspended on strings attached to poplar trees and forming garlands that were described in ancient agricultural treatises. This type of view alternates with market gardens, large orchards and even, in the recently developed zone of the lower Volturno, with cereals and fodder crops. Everywhere, except in the final example, plots and holdings are small – 95 per cent have less than 5 hectares.

Agricultural production and current problems

Due to the high input of work, the yield is high. The vine supplies more than 2 million hectolitres, lemons provide the second largest quantity in Italy after Sicily, apricots 60 per cent, cherries 30 per cent and peaches 26 per cent of the Italian total. With vegetables there are aubergines (one-third of Italian production); cauliflowers and tomatoes provide the same percentage, peppers, etc.

But there are problems. These arise from external sources and from competition with other Italian and European regions, but above all through the development of other activities. There are conflicting uses for the land, arising from the numerous motorways here and industrial and urban development.

Industrial and urban growth

A tourism that is still alive

If industrial activities needed the programmes of the *Cassa per il Mezzogiorno* in order to give them the spectacular take-off, tourism has never ceased being very important, such are the attractions of this region's landscapes (Vesuvius, coastal areas, islands), its archaeological heritage (Pompeii, Herculaneum, Pozzuoli, Paestum) and architectural heritage (Palazzo di Caserta). The region has 70,000 beds available and, in 1976, more than 2 million tourists spent 7.6 million nights here.

Industrial activities

Old activities were established before 1950, and some have continued to develop. Food processing is among the foremost of these – flour milling and production of pasta at Gragnano and Torre Annunziata, canning and jam factories (Cirio) at San Giovanni a Teduccio. To these may also be added metallurgical plants which include steelworks at Bagnoli, naval shipyards at Naples and Castellammare di Stabia, mechanical engineering (Olivetti typewriters at Pozzuoli). Textiles for many years consisted of clothing factories but, since 1948, this has included synthetic fibres at Casoria. However, all these industries employ only about 20,000, which is very little considering the demand for work.

New industries

The infrastructure necessary for new industries was laid down first: electrification of the Rome–Naples line through Caserta; an almost too dense network of motorways that fans out from Naples in all directions; reorganisation of domestic and industrial water supply; improvement of port installations at Bagnoli. In short, the new industries have at their disposal all that is necessary. The Alfa Romeo plant at Pomigliano d'Arco employs more than 15,000, but its production raises many questions. Textiles (spinning mill at Aversa) and mechanical engineering have also been added, but these only provide 70,000 jobs which again is not enough to soak up unemployment.

Salerno, situated to the south of Sorrento, is very old, but disdvantaged by its restricted agricultural hinterland and its inconvenient port site. None the less, its population exceeds 159,000 inhabitants due to the commercial functions of its port, medium-sized industries (textiles and mechanical engineering) and work in the Neapolitan suburbs.

Naples

The city officially has a population of 1,223,228 inhabitants, but the conurbation has more than 1.7 million for the municipality of Naples, unlike Rome, is small. For example, Torre del Greco (92,000) is already a separate municipality.

The economic activities of the population are sometimes imprecise and do not correspond to the norms of developed countries. The proportion falling into the non-active category is high, due to a large number of children, unemployed and, particularly, those without any specified occupation (one-third of the population of working age!). The proliferation of small trades (dealers in second-hand clothes are a typical example) often reveals a surprising level of ingenuity. This is both admirable and yet a sign of underdevelopment, as Milton Santos (1979) has described in the structure of the tertiary sector in the Third World. In addition to the traditional industrial activities mentioned above, there is also a plethora of administrative functions and a traditional tertiary sector including an important tourist component. Fishing takes place at the port, as well as passenger traffic to Sicily, Sardinia and Africa (2 million passengers in 1976) and freight (10 million tons, of which 7.5 were international).

Apart from its distinctive activities, the population is also quite unusual sociologically. We have already discussed Campania's demographic characteristics which are dominated by Naples' role, but the urban poverty throws up astonishing features in twentieth-century Europe. Overcrowded housing and the bad state of many of the facilities are the cause of a health record unworthy of Italy, despite the efforts made to remedy it. The last major epidemic of cholera, which killed so many, was in 1883; it reappeared in 1973. Periodically, diseases specific to an urban environment break out, as with the mysterious illness which struck children in 1979. All this – unemployment, poverty, bad living conditions – is overcome with fatalism, some would say resignation and laziness, thanks to a deep-rooted courage which relies on family solidarity, neighbours, those on the street…but how long can it last?

Naples is thus a city of contrasts, of a beautiful site and poverty, of glittering façades in the major commercial streets and narrow sordid, tortuous alleys and rows of working-class housing. The old town is built in the innermost part of the gulf at the edge of the ancient port, now filled in; it is not a very hilly terrain, dominated by the bulk of the feudal Castel Nuovo and Bourbon royal palaces. It includes several major commercial arteries, one of which, the Corso Umberto I, was driven through in the nineteenth century, and old quarters within a generally irregular layout.

Beyond this core the city developed in all directions despite the obstacles. In the east the city extended along the coast to Torre del Greco (92,000 inhabitants) and then Torre Annunziata, in an industrial and residential suburb served by the Vesuviano railway line. Westward on a steep escarpment are situated the castle of Saint Elmo and the Certosa di San Martino. There follow, one after the other along the coast, the working-class district of Santa Lucia, and the seafront promenades studded with large hotels towards Pausilippo and Marechiaro. Above it rise characterless, tall houses in concentric circles in the Vomero district. Further west still, industrial suburbs go from Bagnoli as far as Pozzuoli (62,000 inhabitants). Finally, northward, there are rural areas, industries, towns with ancient centres ringed by working-class housing – Aversa (50,000), Caserta (65,000) alternate until the mountain edge is reached.

8 The islands: Sicily and Sardinia

The presence of two large islands is a distinctive feature of Italian geography. Sicily and Sardinia are practically the same size and have a number of points in common. Their unique patterns of settlement and social phenomena make them a world apart. Both are autonomous regions with a special statute. Isolation and distance from the rest of Italy, especially from the North, have led to a level of underdevelopment as severe as in the mainland South, but the recent expansion of heavy industrial activity is much more marked, based as it is on imported oil and a chemical industry associated with its by-products. As it should be in islands, the coastal location of industries took place in a spectacular manner.

However, these rather superficial shared characteristics can be contrasted with much more unquestionable, unique geographical features. In Sardinia, morphological landscapes, developed on a rigid shield, stand in contrast to Sicily's clay hills and the large volcanic cone of Etna. While the conflict between pastoralists and peasants dominates rural life in Sardinia, cereal and tree cultivators occupy practically all the usable land in Sicily. Furthermore, in Sardinia coastal settlement constitutes a complete rupture with the past which wanted to ignore the sea and deliberately turn its back on the outside world. In Sicily, on the other hand, it is only the modern version of an orientation towards the Mediterranean which, throughout history, brought foreign domination as well as the flourishing civilisations of the Greek Empire and Islam and enabled the flight to richer countries, such as the United States of America, to take place.

Introspective Sardinia, extroverted Sicily; this might seem a slightly simplistic and sketchily drawn contrast, but it nevertheless has the value of demonstrating that one should study the two islands separately. To group them together in a geographical study is arbitrary and distorts their fundamental personalities.

Sicily

As the largest island in the Mediterranean (25,708 sq. km), Sicily forms a world apart. On the map it seems just like an extension of the peninsula, separated by the Straits of Messina, which are deep but only 10 kilometres wide on average. If this impression is correct physically, for geologically the Peloritani mountains resemble a great deal the Aspromonte, it is totally false in social terms (see Fig. 8.1).

A varied environment constantly threatened by nature and by man

A typical Mediterranean climate with its characteristic extremes

Summer drought is the most basic feature of Sicilian climate. Summer is the season most commonly associated with this climate. Its dryness, heat and sometimes unbearable brightness have struck all observers, not least certain gifted novelists, such as Tomasi di Lampedusa (1963) who, in *The Leopard* speaks of the 'great mourning in summer'. July and August everywhere are extremely dry, normally receiving less than 10 millimetres on average, although, particularly after mid-September, there can be downpours, especially on the northern coast.

Compared to these two dry months, the wet season is a little more difficult to define, since it does not exactly correspond to the usual period. The wettest months are generally those which straddle autumn and winter. November is the wettest month almost everywhere. The rainy season from November to January coincides with the coolest season. This makes the relative abundance of snow at not very high altitudes understandable. One can also see why the drop in temperature and the rain appears so cold to people who could be bogged down in their clay paths or isolated by streams that completely fill their beds.

The rigours of winter are keenly felt by the population whose life-style is not adapted to it. In effect, Sicily has a mild climate so that, despite bursts of capricious cold, winter is warm, especially on the coast. Average January temperatures in Sicily vary between 8 °C and 13 °C – for example 11.3 °C at Palermo and 10 °C at Agrigento. Only the real interior and higher regions have decidedly lower temperatures – Caltanissetta at 600 metres has a 7 °C January average.

Irregularity, seen in cold spells, and especially in rainfall, is a basic aspect of Sicilian climate. Such irregularity may occur within the year and between years. The beginning of the rainy period never occurs at the same time so that, although it is usually in September, it may be as late as December or January. Rochefort (1960) has cited the drought in 1952–53 which lasted from 25 April 1952 to 25 January 1953.

Regional variations, due to different aspects and the effect of relief, are noticeable. On the whole one can distinguish the following climatic zones:

(a)   the wet north-east which receives more than 700 millimetres and more than 1,000 millimetres on Mt Etna and where, in winter, snow-capped mountains and mild coastlands coexist;

(b)   the arid south from Marsala to Syracuse where the summer is very dry and hot, the sirocco and the winter warmth reminding one of nearby Africa;

(c)   the centre, slightly continental and well watered in winter, but with very hot summers.

A massive triangular form which masks considerable morphological variety

The almost perfect triangular shape of Sicily has struck cartographers and sailors since far back in antiquity. The island was called Trinacria and was designated by the characteristic symbol of three legs coming out of the same body. This shape has nothing to do with its internal structure which is cut by almost straight lines; these are recent faults which have tended since the end of the Pliocene period to break down the Apennine mountain system.

The south-east: the Ragusa plateaux and the Iblean mountains

This zone forms the simplest and most tabular landscape in the island. Altitudes are fairly high – 600 metres on average, rising to 985 metres at Mt Lauro. Nevertheless, the topography is still composed of plateaux deeply incised by valleys. Movement is made difficult by the valleys, although there are many acropolis-like defensive sites, of which Ragusa is an excellent example.

The north-east: the Sicilian mountains

All the north-east is higher in altitude but there is no morphological unity. Of prime importance is Mt Etna. This is one of the largest active volcanoes in the world, since it rises from sea-level to 3,300 metres and its cone-shaped peak forms a circumference measuring more than 100 kilometres. The volcano itself is a mixed type. Its internal backbone is formed of resistant volcanic openings and acidic lava tongues and dykes. The shape of its cone is due to lava flows, especially basaltic ones, which pour out from scores of openings which exist, or have existed, around the volcano, and to all sorts of ejected material, of which ash is the main component.

All along the north-eastern Tyrrhenian coast of Sicily, deeply fissured mountains form a discontinuous line for 150 kilometres from Termini Imerese to the Straits of Messina. The watershed hardly ever drops below 1,000 metres. The structure splits this alignment up into the following landforms: in the east, the Peloritani Mts (1,279 m) high crystalline plateaux; in the centre, the Nebrodi and Caroni Mts (1,840 m) with massive schist summits; and in the west, the higher and steeper, limestone Madonie (1,879 m).

The mass of clay hills in the centre of Sicily

The major part of Sicily (at least 15,000 sq. km), that is the interior and the adjacent coastal zones from Megara to Gela, is composed of hills with an altitude of barely 600 metres. The dominant rocks of Tertiary origin are fairly homogeneous clays, though only those of the Miocene are gypsum and sulphur-bearing. Anyhow, the minor differences have little bearing on their resistance to erosion.

Dissected landscapes are dominant everywhere; the clays are gullied by *calanchi* while *frana* landslips are especially common. Everything is on the move in this apparently inert landscape of white, denuded hills glimmering in the summer sunshine. The only fixed points are the limestone blocks which seem to float and, in effect, probably 'swim' in the Tectonic ocean, swept along by Eocene clays and then surrounded by Miocene seas, but always forming blocks with bare, steep escarpments.

Limestone topography and alluvial plains in the west

The western part of the island has a very uneven relief. There are plains which support large areas of agriculture such as the Conca d'Oro of Palermo and the wide stretches of low alluvial plain behind Trapani, Marsala and Mazara del Vallo. However, these plains are surrounded and overlooked by steep limestone mountains including Mt Pellegrino to the west of Palermo and the rugged blocks of Montelepre and Partinico.

The volcanic islands around Sicily

These include the Eolian islands (Stromboli, Vulcano and Lipari) which are still active, and Pantellaria, half-way to Tunisia and the largest and Lampedusa, both of which have been extinct for a long time.

Natural and human dangers

Natural hazards

Seismic and volcanic activity are the most deadly, but the interval between disasters is long enough in terms of a human life span so as not to be greatly feared. The north and south-east are zones of disastrous seismic activity and, in numerous other areas, such as Palermo, it is quite intense. The island has been the scene of some dreadful catastrophies – Catania was practically destroyed in 1666 and, in 1908, 30,000 people were killed in Messina.

The erosion that is occurring at present is a far more immediate and visible danger. It has been helped along by deforestation, which they have only just begun to stop in the mountains, and by cereal cultivation on bare clays. This erosion occurs almost everywhere and threatens lines of communications, crops, soils and even houses. In theory the motorways are protected from this danger but, in the interior, many roads remain impassable for several weeks each year. In interior Sicily, the isolation in winter due to the clay is equal to the effect of snow in the mountains further north.

The river beds, everywhere disproportionate in size, build wide, pebbly obstructions which necessitate costly, large-scale works to allow clearance for maximum flows. In December 1936 the Simeto flowed at a rate of 8,300 cubic metres per second, yet its annual average rate is only 18 cubic metres per second.

The insecurity of the past and the present: internal and external domination

Since the beginning of history Sicily has never been under its own political control except fleetingly. It has constantly been dominated by outside powers who have shaped its civilisation. As Prince Tomasi di Lampedusa (1963) says in *The Leopard*, it is a 'government by others, we have never controlled it'.

For Sicilians, Unification was perceived only as the coming of a new intervention, this time of the northerners. Thus it is easy to understand the independence movements which, nevertheless, have not been deeply rooted. These began with the liberation of the island when it was seriously proposed to make the island the forty-ninth state of the USA! After some bloody incidents where social and political struggles and banditry were confusingly, yet closely, interrelated, they virtually ended in 1950.

The effects of outside domination were always negative. Large estates characterised all historical systems, ranging from the ancient Roman latifundia employing thousands of slaves, to the feudal domains were managers (*gabelotti*) intimidated the landless (*braccianti*). The influence of this domination is constantly encountered, usually in a negative manner, in the economy.

During some periods, the status of Sicily was definitely colonial. This occurred even during the Arab–Norman period, in many respects Sicily's golden age, but it was even more characteristic of the Roman, Bourbon and Neapolitan periods. The same applies, to a great extent, since Unification. Until the recent efforts of the *Cassa per il Mezzogiorno*, Sicily was the reservoir of raw materials and, above all, of labour for the North, with all the underdevelopment that this implies. Article 38 of the Sicilian regional autonomy law explicitly speaks of the 'reparation of economic injustices'.

Internal domination – the Mafia

It is impossible to mention Sicily without thinking of the Mafia. Its existence is real, verified by all unofficial and official enquiries. Its precise structure and its organisational links with political and social forces obviously remain nebulous. One only knows that the law of silence, *omertà*, applies to everyone, that the hierarchy is clearly connected with the all-powerful *capi mafiosi* and that all classes of society are implicated in it. It is significant that the parliamentary report on the Mafia finished in 1965 was not made public but was deposited in the national archive for a period of fifty years.

The origins of the Mafia go back to the eighteenth century. From the beginning, as a kind of lords' militia, it was associated with the interests of the ruling class whose property it protected against thieves and social unrest. It has retained these aims until today; the assassination of trade unionists, the firing on 2 May 1947 at Portella della Ginestra on peasants celebrating Labour Day, clearly show the hostility of the Mafia to any structural transformation.

Today things seem to have changed; progress in land tenure and particularly agriculture has taken place and is continuing. The Mafia has lost its social influence but it has definitely not reduced its criminal activities, including those outside Sicily. Nevertheless, it represents an element of social inertia which has held back necessary changes.

Sicilian society

The family remains the basic element of Sicilian society; it forms an almost closed universe, a self-contained cell, and of greater importance than external interests, including work. The woman in this type of family has an ambiguous role. She was formerly the most hidden object of all and, in all senses, the property of the husband. Twenty years ago in the villages, those who could went out as little as possible, except to Sunday mass. Since then, customs have changed. Outside influences have penetrated through the media, especially television, so that women are now much more independent.

The family is not simply the primary unit, consisting of husband, wife and children, but includes all the close relatives, ancestors, descendants and relatives by marriage who occasionally need to be looked after. One could mention households in Palermo occupied by extended families of more than thirty people. The patron–client system oversees that of the family; it may coincide with the Mafia, but it also exists in many other fields – jobs, gambling and politics, all superimposing parasitic structures on to legal ones.

Migration patterns

In 1980 Sicily reached a population of 5 million inhabitants, giving it a density of 195 persons to the sq. kilometre, slightly higher than the Italian average. Until very recently, the population was, in fact, slightly decreasing, despite a considerable natural increase. Although the birth-rate has diminished from 20 per thousand in 1960 to 16.6 per thousand (Italian average 13.3 per thousand), it still remains high. The mortality rate remains low (8.9 per thousand), lower than the Italian average (9.7 per thousand), while the natural increase accounts for around 35,000 persons per year.

Despite a constant natural increase since the nineteenth century, Sicily has not greatly increased its population; it had already more than 3.5 million people at the beginning of the century. The reason for this lies in the continual emigration to other parts of Italy and abroad.

It is not known exactly how many Sicilians settled in other Italian provinces. All one knows is that they are many, for all one has to do is to go to the stations in Turin, Milan or Rome on the eve of holidays and see the trains for Messina, Palermo and Catania.

Emigration overseas has been the major outlet for the demographic increase, particularly emigration to the United States. More than 100,000 left annually

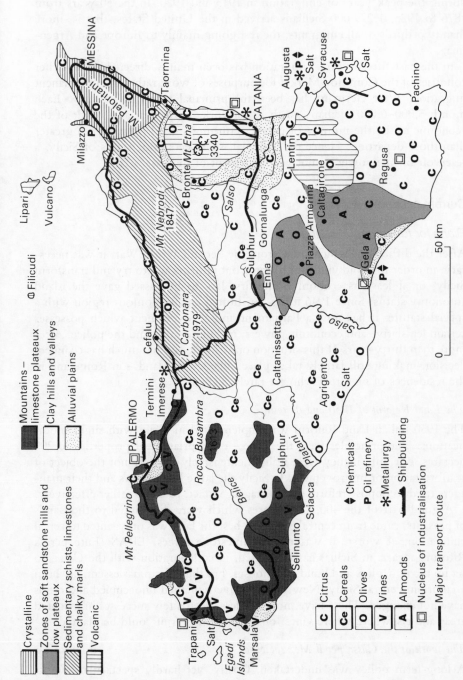

Mountains –
limestone plateaux

Zones of soft sandstone hills and
low plateaux

Sedimentary schists, limestones
and chalky marls

Alluvial plains

Crystalline

Zones of soft sandstone hills and
low plateaux

Sedimentary schists, limestones
and chalky marls

Volcanic

Lipari

Vulcano

Ⓞ Filicudi

C Citrus

Ce Cereals

O Olives

V Vines

A Almonds

◆ Chemicals

P Oil refinery

✳ Metallurgy

➤ Shipbuilding

▣ Nucleus of industrialisation

━━ Major transport route

MESSINA
Taormina
Milazzo
M. Peloritani
CATANIA
Bronte Mt Etna
3340
Augusta
Salt
P
Syracuse
Salt
Pachino
Salt
Lentini
Mt Nebrodi
1847
Salso
Gornalunga
Piazza Armerina
Caltagirone
Ragusa
Gela
P
Salt
Sulphur
Enna
A
O
Salso
P. Carbonara
1979
Cefalù
Caltanissetta
Agrigento
Salt
Termini
Imerese
PALERMO
Rocca Busambra
1613
Sulphur
Platani
Belice
Sciacca
Selinunto
Mt Pellegrino
Trapani
Salt
Marsala
Egadi
Islands

50 km

0

Fig. 8.1 Sicily: relief and economy

during the peak years of emigration in 1913 and 1920. In the 50 years from 1876 to 1925, 1,279,000 Sicilians arrived in the United States, that is, more than two-thirds of all emigrants, the rest going mainly to Europe and Argentina.

In the past fifteen years, emigration has been mainly directed at the richer countries of the Common Market for purposes of work rather than permanent migration. West Germany has been the principal receiving country. Each month 5,000–6,000 Sicilians go there to work. However, as a result of the economic crisis, the number of people returning since 1975 has been greater than those departing. Hence the 'colonial' socio-economic status of Sicily, a reservoir of manpower, is not yet an element of the past.

Current economic activities

Plans for fundamental change

After the difficulties which arose from the Second World War, it was necessary, in order to avoid violence, to carry out reforms and to try and transform Sicily, or at least its economy. The first law to be passed gave the island autonomy status. Since 1946 it has constituted an autonomous region with a special statute; it has now a Parliament and a government which possesses certain legislative and economic powers, including taxes and the police. After more than thirty years of this situation one cannot say that much has changed; decision-making still largely takes place outside the island – in Rome and in the residences of investors who are rarely Sicilian.

The Land Reform of 1950 and its results

The 1950 Italian Land Reform was implemented in Sicily with slight modifications. The principles were the same – expropriation of properties of 200 hectares, but only if they were utilised extensively or were not the object of reafforestation or improvement. In Sicily the large landowners and their managers tried to oppose reform and managed, in fact, to do so rather effectively.

A good part of the 400,000 hectares which were distributed to thousands of peasants, came from central Sicily. At best the land was only suited to cereal cultivation; at worst, it was useless limestone screes. ERAS (Ente per la Riforma agraria in Sicilia) has attempted, in collaboration with the *Cassa*, to set up the new plots and build new houses, but the reform has essentially been a failure in central Sicily. New villages have remained unoccupied and crops have not changed. There have, none the less, been a few successes in irrigated areas and elsewhere where vines, olives and citrus fruit could be planted.

The work of the Cassa per il Mezzogiorno

A long-term policy was undertaken. Costly, yet hardly spectacular, works aimed at reafforestation and soil conservation. Several barrage-reservoirs on the few rivers enabled flood control and the build-up of water resources; the largest are those on the Salso (150 million m³), on the Gornalunga near Catania (124 million m³), and on the Belice north of Mazara (over 100 million m³).

Eight 'areas' and 'nuclei' of industrial development were designated – Catania, Palermo, Syracuse, Caltagirone, Gela, Messina, Ragusa and Trapani. Since 1950 there have been 110 projects completed. These projects had cost by the end of 1977 the sum of 115,000 million lire (more than 11% of the Mezzogiorno total), of which 113,000 million lire were borne by the *Cassa*. This amount only relates to development projects strictly speaking. From 1951 to 1977 the fixed investments facilitated through the loans of the industrial credit institutes headed by the *Cassa* amounted to 3,357,000 million lire. The employment generated by the new industries and the expansion of existing ones was 68,000 and 56,000 jobs respectively.

Infrastructures after the Second World War were found to be archaic and inadequate, especially in terms of communications. At least one-third of villages were inaccessible by all-weather roads. Railways have been modernised by the construction of numerous double tracks. In particular, motorways have ensured a safe and speedy transport of persons and merchandise on the main axes. In 1978 Messina–Catania and Catania–Palermo via Enna were finished so that the latter, like Caltanissetta, is no longer isolated by the clays during winter rains. Palermo–Messina will shortly be completed, as will Palermo–Mazara–Marsala. Express routes – *superstrade* – will mean that one can go round the island by extending and linking up with existing motorways in the south: Syracuse, Ragusa and Gela.

The amount of port traffic is determined, as in Sardinia, by oil products. The largest port for freight is thus Augusta with 18.5 million tons annually (15.7 million tons imports), followed by Milazzo whose freight pattern, based on oil, is similar (9 million tons, of which 6.8 million are imports) and Gela 2.2 million tons. Catania and Palermo have a disappointing amount of international traffic with 350,000 and 180,000 tons respectively. In terms of national coastal shipping, Augusta heads the list with 9.9 million tons, of which 8.4 million (mostly oil products) are exports; Gela occupies the same relative position while Palermo acquires a greater standing with almost 2 million tons. Passengers still use boats a great deal. Thus the port of Palermo has 354,000 passengers passing through it, Trapani 270,000 and Milazzo, where one gets the boat for the volcanoes of Lipari, Vulcano and Stromboli, 400,000. However, competition with airlines is growing stronger so that in 1978 Palermo had more than 7,200 flights and 475,000 passengers moving in each direction, and Catania almost as many (6,200 flights and 445,000 passengers).

Sicilian agriculture: a rapid transformation

Archaic aspects

In much of the interior, in particular on the clays, wheat (90% of which is hard) remains the only crop planted. Cultivation occurs directly on crumbly rock or even on the moving earth of landslips, using old-fashioned methods which are, none the less, adapted to the particular qualities of this 'soil'. Fertilisers are not much used (besides would they be useful?) and yields are very low. Sicily is the region with the largest area of wheat – more than 610,000 hectares – but the yields for an average production of around 10 million quintals are only 16 quintals per hectare, compared to 44.3 in Emilia! This landscape of long, white hills hardly shows any signs of yellow stubble, but still shimmers in the summer sun as in Visconti's film *The Leopard*; the large villages still slumber on their hills; things seem to have the immutability of death and, in reality, little has progressed in the past thirty years.

The number of sheep, especially ewes, is the second largest of Italian regions with 871,000 head, and goats number 135,000. One needs to add a large number of beasts of burden, draught animals and horses and donkeys for riding. These reflect rural backwardness but also are adapted to a countryside lacking passable roads for cars and are linked to a rural tradition of multicoloured carts.

Vines, orchards and gardens in the fortunate part of Sicily

It is possible to contrast more or less sharply an 'immutable' Sicily of wheat and roaming herds and a 'fortunate' Sicily of fertile plantations and intensive, often irrigated cultivation.

Climatic conditions are almost everywhere suitable for the production of wine especially that with high alcoholic content. The vine area has continued to expand since the Second World War. This has been mainly due to individual decisions, since estates have not been publicly encouraged to plant vines due to European and Italian overproduction (only 2,086 hectares have been planted with the aid of *Cassa* finance). The only 'named' exports consist of wines for aperitifs or cooking, such as Marsala, grown near the town which gave it its name. Other important areas of viticulture are in the south-east (Pachino), near Catania and on the slopes of Mt Etna.

Olives are found mainly on hill and mountain slopes and produce 53,000 tons (second region after Apulia). Half of the Italian production of almonds (76,000 tons) are produced, as well as pistachio nuts.

Finally, the most profitable plantations are those with fruit trees, especially citrus trees which enjoy the favourable climate. In addition to the traditional zones of citrus cultivation – Conca d'Oro, the seaward slopes of Mt Etna and the *huertas* around towns – new zones have been added as a result of the construction of barrages and wells – the plains of Belice, Gela and especially Catania. In 1975 it was planned to provide irrigation for an additional 7,000 hectares.

Modern facilities for packaging and export have been set up and Sicily's undisputed advantage in this field is now really beginning to be exploited. In 1976 it produced more than 60 per cent of Italy's citrus production – 72,000 tons or two-thirds of Italian oranges, 126,000 tons or two-thirds of mandarins and one-third of the clementines.

Traditional fishing

Sicilians are much more sea faring than Sardinians, so that they have not left it to others to exploit the resources of the sea. The Arabs, instead of pushing Sicilians inland, left them their fishing traditions and some of their nautical expressions: for example, the head of the fishing fleet for tunny is called *rais*, the Arab word for 'chief'.

For tonnage of fish caught (53,200 tons per year) and shellfish harvested (7,000 tons), Sicily leads among Italian regions.

The development of modern activities

Sicilian industries

Industry has a solid base but no tradition, for, as in Sardinia, Sicilian capital was, with a few exceptions, not much interested in investing in industry.

Primary materials are firstly agricultural products and fish, construction materials (clay and limestone), rock salt and potassium. Sulphur production is in decline because it is increasingly in competition with petroleum deposits. Its production has fallen to 300,000 tons from 474,000 tons in 1974. Oil has been discovered at Ragusa and Gela – a production capacity of 1 million tons annually – and is mainly handled at the ports with refineries – Milazzo, Augusta, Ragusa and Gela. These installations export considerable quantities of refined products (about 10 million tons) and supply power stations which generated more than 10,000 million kWh in 1976.

What stands out most clearly in this picture of Sicilian industry is the lack of dynamism in most industries, compared with the modern technology and development of the large petrochemical plants. In effect, the refineries are all, except for that of Ragusa, much smaller in terms of employment than other modern industries. This is particularly the case for the industrial zone of Augusta where 15,000 people work in the manufacture of fertilisers, soda, plastics, cement and metal objects. Near Gela there is also a petrochemical plant and at Milazzo a Pirelli tyre factory. Of the older industrial nuclei only Catania can compete with the above although in a very different way. It specialises in small and medium-sized firms in all sectors, though concentrating on textiles, mechanical engineering and food. Industry is mainly located on the coast and, despite all that has been done, cannot provide sufficient employment for the local labour force. The choice of heavy industries dictated by the profit motive undoubtedly has much to do with this.

Skin-deep tourism

Sicily, being more accessible and better endowed than Sardinia, has had tourists for a long time. It still has better facilities and is visited more than its other southern Italian competitors. Visitors are attracted by the climate of the Sicilian rivieras and most of the coast, its numerous and varied beaches, the volcanoes of the Eolian islands (Stromboli, Lipari and Vulcano) and Mt Etna, its Greek edifices (of greater splendour even than those of Greece itself and including the monuments and ruins of Segesta, Selinunte and Agrigento, Syracuse and Taormina), and finally, the splendid monuments of the Arab–Norman period in Palermo. Its previous disadvantage of distance has lost much of its importance in an age of long holidays and relatively cheap transport.

New tourist facilities have been added. These new hotels and holiday clubs had 48,000 beds (43,000 in hotels) in 1976 and accounted for 5.3 million nights of accommodation in that same year.

An apparently balanced urban network: dynamic and stagnant towns

A deceptive urban network

From an initial examination of statistical information on population and spatial distribution, the towns would seem to be an asset for the development of the island. Four have a population of more than 100,000 inhabitants (Syracuse, Messina, Catania and Palermo), four have between 50,000 and 100,000 (Caltanissetta, Ragusa, Agrigento and Trapani), and more than 20 have over 10,000 inhabitants. Although the distribution favours the coast, there are towns inland.

While this view is in some ways correct, it is false on two points. Firstly, population size is not a very good criterion for urban development, for most of the nucleated settlements up to 10,000 inhabitants, and even 20,000, are no more than enormous villages. Secondly, the real towns have populations not in direct relationship to the importance of their activities.

Small and medium-sized towns

These are all alike. Set in defensive positions, their old buildings cling closely together along the streets that follow the slopes and around the massive central church; all have palaces with wrought-iron railings contrasting with the poor, rather rural style, housing with washing hanging out of windows. Where tourism exists, there is a newer area of apartments, detached houses and hotels that jars with the ancient core. The different sites and activities are a source of some variation. Enna, the *belvedere* of Sicily, is set high around its prison and is hardly developing (29,000 inhabitants); Caltanissetta (61,000) is a large agricultural centre in the process of industrialising; Ragusa (66,000), in a cramped position on the spur of a plateau that is cut off by deep valleys, is mainly an agricultural centre despite its small refinery; Trapani (72,000) is a fishing port and commercial centre; Agrigento (52,000) overlooks the valley of the Greek Temples which provides it with a good tourist industry.

The higher-order towns

Syracuse (120,000 inhabitants) lives mainly from tourism, thanks to its Greek monuments (theatre, Latomie quarries) and the charm of its ancient town located on the island where the Arethusa fountain still flows, sheltered by papyrus. It is also a provincial capital and, being near Augusta, serves as a tertiary centre for it.

Messina (271,000) is without ancient monuments and has streets that were strung out after the 1908 disaster. It is the main embarkation point for the peninsula; its activities are mainly commercial, related to the port, railway line and roads, although it also has administrative and university functions.

Catania (400,000) symbolises to some extent the modern Sicily, that which is changing. Also destroyed, by Mt Etna in the seventeenth century, it nevertheless stretches in a geometrical pattern of roads up the sides of the volcano, except for the lower slopes where the renovated ancient quarter, built around the Castel Ursino. is a reminder of the Hohenstauffen. The town has few tourist attractions and serves merely as a convenient point of departure for Etna. It is, however, the most active town in the island, for it is the centre of a highly prosperous old agricultural area, and has a small, yet active, port. It therefore remains a major commercial node and constitutes an administrative, intellectual (university) and artistic centre with an opera house where the memory of Bellini is still alive. The inhabitants of Catania are sometimes said to be the Milanese of the South and take an active role in modern development, as evidenced by the industrial zone south of the town.

Palermo (694,000) was termed a 'veritable geographical fraud' by Rochefort (1960), a view that is equally valid today. The activities of this large city, which one would not want to call a metropolis, have, in effect, hardly varied. Industrial development is still limited though it has profited from recent developments. The excessive tertiary sector due to the plethora of diverse administrative services and a large university is incapable of satisfying all the demand for employment. The supplementary, more or less declarable, resources of the small trades are not sufficient either, so that the number of unemployed and those without any designated occupation remains exceptionally high.

Given these conditions, it is not surprising that in certain districts and among the poorest sections of the population, life is squalid and poverty-stricken. It is in Palermo that the Mafia can most easily pursue its rewarding activities.

Palermo is a town of contrasts. Topographically it juxtaposes the irrigated plain of Conca d'Oro with the limestone mountains that hem it in – in the north, Mt Pellegrino, to the south-east, Mt Guggio backed by Monreale with its celebrated cloisters. The marvellous Arab–Norman buildings in the San Giovanni degli Eremiti basilica, the cathedral and Norman-period Kings' Palace contrast with the baroque palaces of noble families, banks and administrative buildings. In terms of the residential areas, the narrow streets of the poor quarter, south of the Law Courts and between the centre and the Kings' Palace, are as much part of the landscape as the modern, large blocks of flats that line the straight streets in the northern part of the city and the luxurious villas interspersed in the orchards of Conca d'Oro.

Sardinia

In all respects Sardinia is as much as Sicily a world apart. This is as true geo-morphologically, where it reveals more Hercynian than Mediterranean fea-tures, as it is in its history, its settlement patterns, its Latin-like dialects, or its economic activities where the ancient conflict between pastoralists and pea-sants has been replaced by coastal land-use competition between industry and tourism. In these ways it is quite distinctive.

Relief: massive and often contrasting landforms

Sardinia does not have the Alpine physiognomy of neighbouring Corsica. For a European, it evokes the monotonous horizons of the ancient landscapes of central Europe.

Morphological regions

Mountains and plateaux

These landforms constitute three-quarters of the island, although the land-scapes produced by the underlying structures are diverse.

In the south-west, the Iglesiente and Sulcis uplands are separated by a cor-ridor of plains along the rift valley of Cixerri. Their altitudes (1,236 and 1,017 m) are similar. The landforms have cut into metamorphic rocks, particularly Primary schists, a dissection which has carved out long, eroded ridges, sep-arated by deep, straight-sided valleys.

The whole of eastern Sardinia is formed of a block of highlands where litho-logical and tectonic variations have created a large number of morphologi-cally distinctive areas.

The granitic regions, Gallura in the north, and the Sette Fratelli in the south-east, constantly bring together two types of landforms: straight peaks, sharp-ened by erosion which has carved out fantastically shaped rocks (taffoni); and flat plateaux, especially marked in the tablelands around Bitti.

The region of limestone chains is mainly situated in the eastern part of the Nuorese. They form the karst plateaux of Sopramonte above Oliena and the high peaks of Mt Albo and the Dorgali mountains which tower above the less resistant granites.

The rolling, high plateau surfaces form the central part of the south, unfold-ing their flat landscapes in the Barbagia, Gerrei and Sarrabus regions. These planed surfaces are the result of Miocene erosion and are traversed by very deep valleys like that of the Flumendosa. The faults divide them into sections at different levels, the highest of which forms the massive Gennargentu ridge.

The north-west of Sardinia is at a lower altitude than this massive eastern ridge (Mt Ferru 1,050 m), though the differences are even more sharply accentuated in a mosaic of small morphological areas that can be briefly described in the following manner:

(a)   the long, limestone ridges of the eastern Nurra;
(b)   the Miocene chalky sandstones of the Sassarese which are easily cut into by deep, cliff-edged valleys;
(c)   Anglona which juxtaposes bumpy plateaux and pyramids of acidic lava (Osilo) which has cavities filled with soft Oligocene;
(d)   the Logudoro strewn with recent lava volcanoes (Santa Trinità di Saccargia) and ash cones (Mt Annaru);
(e)   the southern volcanic country formed of trachytic plateaux (Bosa) and the basalt shields of Macomer (Campeda and Planargia).

The plains

These are composed firstly of numerous small coastal plains in the western Nurra laid down by river alluvia and by the ancient sea-levels of the Würm period and, secondly, by the more important plains of the Campidano region.

The western Campidano from Oristano to Cagliari is still subsiding so that the balance between subsidence and sedimentation has not yet gone in the latter's favour. Marshes are still to be found at the extremities and in the centre of this extensive plain. The eastern Campidano, east of the Cagliari–Oristano road, has not been a tectonic trench since the end of the Miocene period. Higher, and in the process of being cleared, it combines hills eroded in sandstone and Miocene chalks (Trexenta and Marmilla) with valleys which are sometimes enlarged into small interior plains.

The coasts

These are generally straight or slightly curved as in the Gulf of Dorgali. These alignments gave the island its ancient name of Sandaliota, the Sandal. This is due to recent subsidence which has edged into the structural mass of the island.

Coastal landforms are varied and are largely determined by the nature of the countryside inland. The variety includes granite coasts broken up into coves and notched by promontories and reefs with rocks pierced by taffoni (Costa Smeralda), steep cliffs cut into by grottoes in the Nurra limestones (Capo Caccia) and in the Dorgali area (Bue Marino Grotto), and sandy spits that cut off lagoons (Oristano, Cagliari).

A highly degraded biogeographical milieu

A specific Mediterranean climate

The Mediterranean characteristics of the climate are the same as in Sicily: on the whole, mild temperatures, a pronounced summer aridity and considerable variations from one year to the next. However, extremes of autumnal rainfalls are accentuated by the relief, as evidenced by the 1,534 millimetres of rain which fell from 15 to 20 October 1954 on the Dorgali mountains. In particular, the nature of the winter rainfall is a little different – the wettest months, November and February, are interspersed by a period of dry sunny weather called the *secche di gennaio*. There are also other specifically Sardinian climatic features.

These general climatic elements are further modified by the position and physiognomy of Sardinia. The fairly high altitude (half the island is above 500 m) modifies the temperatures and the distribution and total amount of rainfall. High up, frosts are common in the four months from November to February and there is definitely a cooler summer climate in the mountains. These lower temperatures lead to snowfalls which, in the highest altitudes, can exceed several metres. This means, for example, that the Barbagia cannot retain its herds during the winter without supplies of hay. Despite their undramatic appearance, the higher slopes are part of a mountain system that supports transhumance. Herds came down to the lower pastures, as does the abundant flow of water resulting from orographic rainfall. The Gennargentu receives more than 1,200 millimetres and, in general, all the zones above 900 metres more than 1,000 millimetres.

A hydrographic system clearly influenced by the terrain and climate

The majority of Sardinian watercourses have an irregular flow for the long, dry season causes them to dry up.

Nevertheless, the presence of relatively well-watered mountains and wells in the limestone areas give rise to numerous proper rivers which have been controlled to provide irrigation. This is the case of the Cedrino fed by the large well of Su Cologone near Oliena, the Flumini Mannu south of Campidano, the Coghinas at the southern limit of the Gallura and especially the two large rivers, the Flumendosa and the Tirso.

Soils and vegetation degraded by man

The deterioration of the natural environment is very great in Sardinia because it has been occupied for a long time and land use is dominated by a pastoral system.

The natural vegetation cover has completely disappeared. The present forests, which have been greatly affected by the population, only cover a small area (estimates vary, according to the definition of forest, from 5 to 13.2%, compared to 20.6% for Italy), and are composed of cork-oaks in the north-west, holm-oaks in the east and north-east of the Gennargentu, pines on the coasts and on reafforested slopes.

The inheritors of a long history

At the end of 1979 Sardinia's population was estimated to be 1,601,000 people in an area slightly greater than 24,000 sq. kilometres, or a density of 66 inhabitants per sq. kilometre, which is considerably less than the Italian average. There may be physical reasons for this low density but it is basically due to the historical factors which have profoundly affected the island.

The effects of historical vicissitudes

Population distribution

The distribution is tied to the necessity, for more than a millenium, to struggle, or at least guard against, organised invaders from the sea and simpler pirate incursions. The island, therefore, became land-oriented; villages turned their back on the sea. In the Ogliastra around Lanusei it is impossible to see the old houses from the sea, so that they might escape from view and pillage. After the Roman domination, the coastal sites were totally abandoned in favour of the interior.

Sardinian isolation

Sardinians say quite openly that they are *isolani*, a play on words indicating that they are both islanders and isolated. In the past this was true, but the situation has been modified to a large extent by the recent social and economic evolution of the island. It should, however, be noted that Sardinia did not always exist in this isolated state which seems to be its destiny. Of course, Sardinia is far from Continental Europe and Africa, but in periods of security and when an integrated political system has arisen, the island is perfectly capable of playing its part in it. In Roman times, it certainly held a quietly prominent place in an Empire which set out to keep the peace. Isolation is, therefore, only the simple result of circumstances.

Tangible vestiges from the past

Besides the general factors of economic and social history, the past has left visible traces in the present and has partly influenced tourism. Sardinian monuments are not as famous as those of Sicily, but they offer a far from negligible cultural attraction – medieval churches (Porto Torres), black and white Pisan-style basilicas (Santa Trinità di Saccargia near Sassari), and the unique *nuraghi* or megalithic forts (Barumini, Sant' Antine).

  The isolation of the island and of its villages has preserved many traditions. These are expressed in a language which remains close to Latin (e.g. *domus* for *casa*); in songs, which are the heritage of an age-old tradition (the famous poet-singers of Bitti); and, in a visible form, by the varied and beautiful costumes.

A society for long self-contained, now in the process of disintegrating

Sardinia's ancient, closed society has a number of important features and constraints. One of them is manifested in the agglomerated settlement pattern. Isolated houses are rare, existing as places of work rather than residence (e.g. the *stazzi* of Gallura). In many cases village parishes are the centre of communal customs. On the plain, as in the Campidano, a two-year rotation cycle was the rule with considerable common grazing land – a system that only disappeared in the eighteenth century. Then there followed another constraint, that of the large landowners who reappropriated most of their land by means

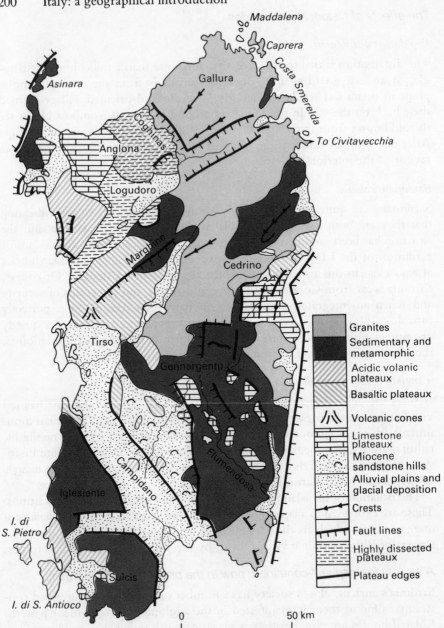

Fig. 8.2(a)   Morphological map of Sardinia

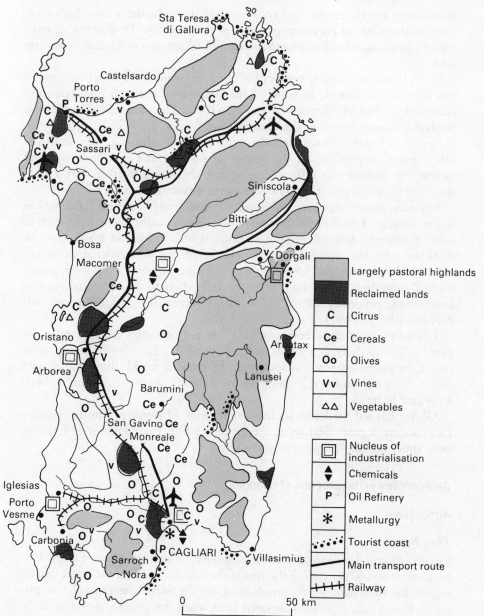

Fig. 8.2(b) Economic activities in Sardinia

of enclosure and the construction of stone walls isolating the *tancas* which gives much of the island its present appearance of a stone *bocage*. Despite the agrarian reform, large estates still exist and account for 60 per cent of Sardinia's grazing land.

Given these limitations, conflict has been the major traditional element of this society, an example of which is the classic feud between pastoralist and peasant described by Maurice Le Lannou (1941). The pastoralists, possessing herds that cannot be fed in the mountains in winter, are in competition with the peasants lower down. The balance turns to the advantage of one or the other group, depending on the degree of security and economic ups and downs. At present the difficulty in selling cheese made from ewe's milk (*pecorino*) seems to give the advantage to the peasants.

Sardinian society has been subjected to considerable external influences in recent decades. Initially, the Second World War brought about migration to other places and, later, development projects built roads and made communications with the mainland easier. The beginning of industrialisation has introduced new jobs and life-styles to a growing number of the population. Internal migration has brought many rural dwellers to the industrial centres. Emigration, originally slight, has suddenly increased – 153,000 people left between 1961 and 1971.

Television, now quite common (164 sets per thousand inhabitants, compared to 209 for Italy as a whole and 138 for Sicily), has played an important role in the opening up of this society to the modern world. Illiteracy, though clearly declining among the young, remains significant (8 per cent in Sardinia, 4 per cent in Italy).

All this has led Sardinian society to the brink of rupture. Family relations are changing a great deal, as is shown in the film *Padre Padrone* and, at the same time, economic ways are also altering.

An economy in the process of changing

Agriculture

The pastorizia

Pastoralists still dominate, if not the economy, at least the greatest areas. Pastoralism covers 60 per cent of the area of the island, including the entire eastern region, the mountains of the south-west and the north-western volcanic plateaux. It encroaches on the cultivated areas when it is able to, or wants to, in winter. Nowhere in Sardinia can one ignore the herds.

Much of the *pastorizia* is sheep grazing, that is ewes. In 1977 the island had 2,017,000 ewes out of 2,745,000 sheep (43 per cent of the Italian total of 6,314,000). The form this grazing takes is fairly standard: animals move around in specific paths in herd sizes of about forty to fifty watched by shepherds.

These circuits exist throughout the island, though they are lengthiest and most regular in the east-centre. Gennargentu and the Barbagia are full of herds in the summer; but the October transhumance takes them down to the east coast and Campidano, where they often have long-standing agreements with the farmers.

The products of grazing are varied. Milk remains the most important, with wool and meat secondary. Different types of sheep's cheese are made: *fiore* and *dolcesardo, ricotta* and, above all, the hard and salty *pecorino* which keeps well and is exported mainly to the United States where immigrants find again in its taste the 'smell' of their country.

All attempts to settle the shepherds permanently on small agricultural plots have, however, failed. The land reform parcels allocated to them in the Ottana region were too small and therefore abandoned. The 1971 law which fixed a ceiling on the price of leases for grazing lands was no more than a timid attempt at social justice and only restricted the rights of large landowners while hindering widows whose only source of income came from this.

Other types of grazing, for example, goats, are much less important even though Sardinia has, with 276,000 goats, the greatest number in Italy.

Aspects of agriculture

There are many different types of crops and products within the agricultural system. Unlike the *pastorizia* stuck in its own traditions, agriculture is changing under the pressure of external forces.

Agricultural systems are quite distinct. In the mountain areas farming is fairly poor and limited to the land near villages. Plots are small and fertilised by animal manure; techniques remain basic. Lower down, on the plains and hills, cereals are still the traditional crop, covering the non-irrigable areas, even on fairly steep slopes.

On the other hand, the zones near the valley bottoms and the alluvial plains have benefited from the improvements brought by modern methods. Hydraulic works together with hydroelectric installations have irrigated numerous regions. The main areas to be affected include the lower valleys of the Cedrino and Coghinas, the large irrigated areas in the Tirso valley supplied by the old dam (1923) which created Lago Omodeo, zones watered by the reservoir constructed on the Flumendosa (317 million m³ stored) in the river's lower valley and the Campidano, land along the Flumini Mannu to the north-west of Cagliari (331 million m³ in the Mulargia barrage) and, finally, the east coast opposite Sant'Antioco irrigated from small coastal rivers. The total irrigated area is now 60,000 hectares.

Reclamation is something totally different. The *Cassa per il Mezzogiorno* has financed irrigation works and aided the development of most of the plains, but has only undertaken one real reclamation project, that of the Nurra. This concerns the completion of an older project which led to the clearing and irrigation of a low, limestone plateau with fertile soils. The plots are now cultivated in tree crops and artichokes. This success story is the same as that of the old Fascist reclamation of Arborea south of the Oristano lagoon.

Cereals provide the main agricultural products – wheat (1.5 million tons of which 80 per cent is hard wheat), rice, a little corn, barley and oats. Broad beans (25,000 tons) are still rotated with wheat. Wines of high alcoholic content are produced (often more than 15°) and this permits them to be used in blending. There are also better-quality wines such as Anghelu Ruju (Alghero), Cannonau (Jerzu), Vernaccia (Campidano). In 1976, 1.5 million hectolitres were produced.

Tree plants include the olive which is, nevertheless, not all that widespread, and various fruit trees which are in the process of considerable development. Peaches, mandarins and pears are the main products of the orchards in the Sassari region and all the irrigated zones.

Vegetables are also expanding because of Sardinia's southerly position which permits the production of early vegetables. Artichokes are the oldest and most important crop in the Sassarese and in the irrigated zones of the Campidano and the lower Coghinas valley; with a production of over 1.1 million tons, Sardinia is the third region in Italy for this specialised crop.

Semi-industrial exploitation of forest and maritime resources

Cork-oaks

This is the only forest activity of any note. Cork is collected in the north, particularly in Gallura, and it constitutes three-quarters of Italian production.

Marine resources

The curse that for so long hung upon the coast is not yet forgotten, for the majority of fishermen are 'foreigners' who have been here for some time, but have forgotten neither their language nor customs – examples are the Catalans in Alghero and the descendants of Genoese at Sant'Antioco.

The number of boats is considerable (1,212 motorised craft), yet the catch is mediocre. In 1976 the catch was 700 tons of fish (compare 5,300 tons in Sicily), of which 15 tons were tunny and 105 tons anchovy. To this one can add a few lobsters (41 tons) and 9,500 tons of shellfish which are not worth a great deal.

Industrial development

Traditional industries

A list of these is quickly drawn up. With respect to mining, two companies with international connections, Monteponi and Montevecchio, have, for a long time, mined lead and zinc in the Primary rocks in the western Nurra (Argentiera) and, particularly Iglesiente, whose production forms 80 per cent of Italy's supply of these minerals.

Outside of agriculture the only plentiful resource is salt. The geographical conditions for extraction are very good, for the salt marshes of Cagliari are among the largest in Europe. Part of the production is exported to industrial centres and abroad.

Recent changes

The instruments of change have nearly all emanated from the policies of the *Cassa*. This has been an 'external' effort for, until now, Sardinian capital has invested very little in industry. The money that has been pumped in has led firstly to improvements in infrastructure. Because of old track and difficult terrain, little could be done for the railways which have been pruned, except for some quaint, narrow lines, to the main Cagliari–Olbia line with a branch link to Sassari and Porto Torres. On the other hand, the road network has been extended and much improved; only 10 per cent of roads were surfaced in 1950, but this now reaches 90 per cent.

Ports too have been improved: Porto Torres, Cagliari, Olbia and Tortoli-Arbatax can now handle large ships. A new industrial port is being built at Cagliari. In 1976 4.5 million passengers and 36 million tons of freight passed through Sardinian ports. For freight, Porto Foxi, west of Cagliari, had the most traffic with 8.6 million tons in 1976, but this is the port which feeds the oil refinery at Sarroch. Porto Torres follows closely (8.5 million tons) with oil and various sorts of freight, agricultural products for export, cork, etc. Finally, Cagliari handles 3.4 million tons; coastal shipping between Italian ports forms two-thirds of this, highlighting its important role as the port for the mainland.

Airports also have substantial traffic. Alghero has 270,000 passengers, mainly tourists in summer, Olbia 147,000 and Cagliari, clearly the largest, 720,000.

In addition to the resources provided by the *Cassa*, Sardinia also has the advantage of its position in the centre of the Mediterranean, an ideal factor for the coastal location of industry. What other justification could there be for the location of a paper mill at Arbatax in a region so devoid of wood?

The first new industries to be established in Sardinia were the two big oil refineries at Sarroch west of Cagliari (SARAS, an independent Italian company) and at Porto Torres (Gulf and SIR). Part of the refined product is exported but refining has also generated large petrochemical installations at Porto Torres (the SIR complex, together with its own desalinator) and at Macchiareddu near Cagliari (the smaller Rumianca plant).

Other coastally located industries have followed. An electrometallurgical concern has been set up at Porto Vesme and Sant'Antioco Ponte. A large paper mill (Scott Paper of Philadelphia) uses wood imported from the Soviet Union at Arbatax. There are also mechanical construction and metallurgy (General Cable) and aluminium (Montedison) at Cagliari itself.

To counteract this coastal concentration, textiles have been set up at Macomer with large chemical plants (ANIC) at Ottana in the very heart of the island.

A colonial-style tourism

In 1976 there were 486 hotels and almost 30,000 beds, as well as 40 holiday villages with 18,000 beds. The number of nights spent by tourists in Sardinia was 2,596,000, 710,000 of them by foreigners.

Tourism is essentially concentrated on the coast, for inland, despite the efforts of the *Ente Sarda per l'Industria Turistica* (ESIT), hotels are rare. Luxury hotels, often in isolated and very beautiful sites (Villasimius, Siniscola) are on the coast. While there is some concentration in the best locations, it is not terribly dense. The main coasts are those near to Sassari and Alghero and the Costa Smeralda north-east of Gallura. This last-named complex, together with those near the Maddelena archipelago, symbolise a certain type of Sardinian tourism – a highly successful integration with the natural setting, though charging very high prices, and isolated from the rest of the population in such an artificial setting that it could be on another planet.

A barely altered urban system

Inland towns

The two most notable examples here are the provincial capitals of Oristano (29,000 inhabitants), elevated to this administrative rank in 1962, and Nuoro (36,000), at the foot of Mt Ortobene and centre of the Sardinian mountain region. Only their size distinguishes them from smaller settlements such as Macomer, town of shepherds, or Lanusei, centre for the Ogliastra. The exception is Ottana, where the old core is adjoined by an industrial zone with modern housing for thousands of factory workers.

Sassari and Porto Torres

These two towns, 20 kilometres apart, form two poles which historically have been separate, but which today are being drawn closer together through their economic activities.

Until its virtual destruction by the Genoese in 1166, Porto Torres was the main settlement, Sassari being no more than a village. There is little evidence of its brilliant past other than the magnificent basilica of San Gavino, although the town now has some of its former activity as an industrial centre.

Although more recent, Sassari (115,900) is actually the more traditional. According to the inhabitants of Cagliari the Sassaresi are *tutti pastori*, all shepherds, to which the Sassaresi reply that the Cagliaritani are *tutti facchini*, all slaves! Sassari is built on a plateau cut by deep valleys, a good defensive site and far enough from the sea and its dangers, yet near enough to use it. It is surrounded by an *agro* which still basically supplies it, and it dominates the whole of the northern economy of Sardinia. As a university town and guardian of traditions, it has a demographic surplus absorbed by not very attractive suburbs that, none the less, do not alter the old-world charm of the ancient centre surrounded by nineteenth-century walls.

Cagliari

Cagliari has become the largest town through its port functions and in spite of its peripheral position. In its opening to the outside world, it has naturally been influenced by the former and has profited more than any other town from the new industrial Sardinia. Originally it was a port and defensive site, situated on a rocky spur crowned by a castle and cut off by lagoons and marshes. However, all this has been transformed by its new port facilities and urban growth. The still crowded old quarters around the cathedral and citadel descend in busy and picturesque streets towards the commercial port. Tourists, civil servants (capital of the autonomous region) and businessmen add life to the hotels and give the town a cosmopolitan air, quite unlike anywhere else in Sardinia. The high buildings of the suburbs stretch north and are like those of any other urban extension. The size of these suburbs, considerably larger than those of Sassari, the night-lights of the industrial zone, the city's football team (Italian champions several years ago), show that Cagliari is the only town in Sardinia to have fully embraced this century.

Crisis or transition?

It is not possible to come to any definite conclusions about Italian geography at the present time. The factors outlined in this book give an overall picture whose positive elements should not be underestimated. Of course, Italy remains now, as it was on the eve of the Second World War, hardly what could be called a world power. What we mean by this is that it is continuing to improve its economic position with respect to its partners, who have also managed to transform their production structures during the preceding period of favourable economic circumstances. At the very least, Italy has been able to follow this trend and hold its place among developed nations. Its rise as an industrial power is no mean achievement, given that it was accompanied by a significant reduction in international emigration.

Italians are also no less aware of the negative aspects, especially the heedless pressure on the environment, whether it results from increasing urban or other encroachment, air and water pollution, the growth of uncultivated land and various pressures on rural space. Even more serious is the deliberate sacrifice of the agricultural sector, which is still not the object of a national policy of restructuring and modernisation, as in other European countries. This *laissez-faire* policy, even if relative, is beginning to cost the Italian economy dearly. Yet more serious still seems to be the continuation of considerable differences between North and South. This should more precisely be stated as the difference between rich and poor provinces, for a good number of northern and central regions, such as Veneto and Liguria, display characteristics of the Mezzogiorno: underemployment, low productivity of investment, social inertia. The results of regional policy, though not negligible, are, none the less, disappointing to the extent that the development of the wealthier provinces is also accompanied by disequilibria which, in social terms, assume a worrying 'southern' aspect.

These imbalances, both regional and sectoral, are evidence of the gap between unequally developed phenomena: *avant-garde* urbanism and dilapidated slums, social legislation and child employment, state enterprises and illegal businesses. And no one doubts that these various differences are partly at the root of the present crisis besetting Italian society.

The existence of dual sectors, often represented as a characteristic of developing countries, can be observed almost everywhere in Italy. It seems to be inherent in any evolution but can be accentuated by the mode and pace of the change. It would appear that in Italy's case economic and social change occurred too rapidly to be totally integrated with each other. Thus the present crisis could be linked to a period of transition, the actual scale and length of which remains to be seen. One might also ask if a more unified society in a more integrated space is an eventual possibility.

Literature cited

Birot, P. and Gabert, P. (1964) *La Méditerranée Occidentale*. Paris: PUF.

Dalmasso, E. (1973) *Milan, Capitale Économique d'Italie*. Gap: Orphrys.

Demangeot, J. (1965) *Géomorphologie des Abruzzes Adriatiques*. Paris: Mémoires et Documents du CNRS.

Dematteis, G. (1973) L'influence de Turin sur les Alpes occidentales italiennes, *Revue de Géographie Alpine*, **61**(3), pp. 371–90.

Desplanques, H. (1969) *Les Campagnes Ombriennes*. Paris: Colin.

Gabert, P. (1964) *Turin, Ville Industrielle*. Paris: PUF.

Gottmann, J. (1961) *Megalopolis*. New York: Twentieth Century Fund.

Gribaudi, D. (1971) *L'Italie Géo-Économique*. Paris: Bordas.

King, R. L. (1973) *Land Reform: The Italian Experience*. London: Butterworths.

Le Lannou, M. (1941) *Pâtres et Paysans de la Sardaigne*. Tours: Arrault.

Mainardi, R. (1973) *Le Grandi Città Italiane*. Milan: Angeli.

Mori, A. and Cori, B. (1969) L'area di attrazione delle maggiori città italiane, *Rivista Geografica Italiana*,**76**(1), pp. 3–14.

Muscarà, C. (1978) *Megalopoli Mediterranea*. Milan: Angeli.

Neboit, R. (1975) *Plateaux et Collines de Lucanie Orientale et des Pouilles*. Paris: Champion.

Prost, B. (1973) *Le Frioul, Région d'Affrontements*. Gap: Orphrys.

Rochefort, R. (1960) *Le Travail en Sicile*. Paris: PUF.

Santos, M. (1979) *The Shared Space*. London: Methuen.

Sereni, E. (1962) *Storia del Paesaggio Agrario Italiano*. Bari: Laterza.

Sereni, E. (1968) *Il Capitalismo nelle Campagne 1860–1900*. Turin: Einaudi.

Sion, J. (1934) L'Italie, in *Géographie Universelle*. Paris: Colin, Vol. 7, Pt. 2, pp. 235–394.

Tagliacarne, G. (1971) *Il Reddito nelle Province Italiane 1963–1970*. Milan: Unione Italiana delle Camere di Commercio, Industria e Agricoltura, Quaderni di Sintesi Economica, No. 1.

Tagliacarne, G. (1975) *Il Reddito nelle Province Italiane nel 1973 e Confronti con gli Anni 1951, 1971 e 1972*. Milan: Unione Italiana delle Camere di Commercio, Industria e Agricoltura, Quaderni di Sintesi Economica, No. 4.

Tomasi di Lampedusa, G. (1963) *The Leopard*. London: Collins-Fontana.

English language bibliography

compiled by Russell King

In view of the large amount of material in English on various aspects of the geography of Italy, this bibliography cannot attempt to be encyclopaedic. In following the slant adopted by this book, which is basically a geographical interpretation of the social and economic crises afflicting present-day Italy, I have selected mostly recent material from the field of human geography. I hope, therefore, that the bibliographical notes which follow will help English language readers to explore the contemporary geography of one of Europe's most fascinating countries.

The basic texts on the general geography of Italy were all published in the 1960s and, in terms of source material and statistics, are about twenty years out of date. Nevertheless they still provide valuable reference material, particularly on historical and physical geography. These books are:

Cole, J. P. (1968) *Italy*. London: Chatto and Windus.

Kish, G. (1969) *Italy*. New York: Van Nostrand Reinhold.

Walker, D. S. (1967) *A Geography of Italy*. London: Methuen.

Excellent for the physical and rural landscape is:

Houston, J. M. (1964) *The Western Mediterranean World: An Introduction to its Regional Landscapes*. London: Longman, pp. 370–544, 623–36.

Italian geographers have not generally ventured outside their native tongue but two recent and very worth-while exceptions have been the volumes produced in connection with the 23rd and 24th International Geographical Congresses:

Pecora, A. and Pracchi, R. (eds) (1976) *Italian Contributions to the 23rd International Geographical Congress*. Rome: Consiglio Nazionale delle Ricerche.

Pinna, M. and Ruocco, D. (eds) (1980) *Italy: A Geographical Survey*. Pisa: Pacini.

The rest of this survey roughly follows the chapter sequence of the book. There has been little original research published in English on Italian physical geography; the best accounts are in Houston and Walker, quoted above, which in turn rely on mainly French and Italian sources.

There have been several studies on population and social geography, including a number of articles on settlement types. On the growth, distribution and problems of Italian population see:

Del Panta, L. (1979) Italy, in W. R. Lee (ed.) *European Demography and Economic Growth*. London: Croom Helm, pp. 196–235.

Dickinson, R. E. (1955) *The Population Problem of Southern Italy: An Essay in Social Geography*. Syracuse: Syracuse University Press.

Lenti, L. (1979) Population growth and employment in Italy, *Review of the Economic Conditions of Italy*. **33**(1), pp. 7–18.

Rodgers, A. (1978) Mediterranean Europe, in G. T. Trewartha (ed.) *The More Developed Realm: A Geography of its Population*. Oxford: Pergamon, pp. 79–97 (pp. 81–93 is on Italian population characteristics).

Wise, M. J. (1954) Population pressure and national resources: some observations on the Italian population problem, *Economic Geography*, **30**(2), pp. 144–56.

Several studies have picked on the distinctiveness of Italian rural settlements:

Blok, A. (1969) South Italian agro-towns, *Comparative Studies in Society and History*, **11**(2), pp. 121–35.

Dickinson, R. E. (1956) Dispersed settlement in Southern Italy, *Erdkunde*, **10**(3), pp. 282–97.

King, R. L. and Strachan, A. J. (1978) Sicilian agro-towns, *Erdkunde*, **32**(2), pp. 110–23.

Kish, G. (1953) The 'marine' of Calabria, *Geographical Review*, **43**(4), pp. 495–505.

Unger, L. (1953) Rural settlement in Campania, *Geographical Review*, **43**(4), pp. 505–24.

There has been little systematic treatment of urban issues except housing:

Angotti, T. (1977) *Housing in Italy: Urban Development and Political Change*. New York: Praeger.

Dandri, G. (1978) The evolution of the Italian housing situation from 1951 to 1978, *Review of the Economic Conditions of Italy*, **32**(2–3), pp. 137–52.

Sbragia, A. M. (1979) Milan and public housing policy: a case of municipal initiative, in M. C. Romanos (ed.) *Western European Cities in Crisis*. Lexington: Heath, pp. 135–51.

Tagliacarne, G. (1974) The state of housing in Italy, *Review of the Economic Conditions of Italy*, **28**(6), pp. 524–36.

Other urban studies have generally been on certain aspects of particular cities, such as the planning of Rome, the sinking of Venice, or historical development:

Coleman, A. (1958) The town of Lecco: urban structure and industrial location in an Alpine setting, *Geography*, **43**(4), pp. 243–52.

Fleure, H. J. (1924) Cities of the Po Basin, *Geographical Review*, **14**(3), pp. 345–61.

Fried, R. C. (1973) *Planning the Eternal City*. New Haven: Yale University Press.

Gribaudi, F. (1968) Functions and physiognomy of Turin, *Acta Geographica*, **20**, pp. 101–11.

Piasentin, U., Costa, P. and **Foot, D.** (1978) The Venice problem: an approach by urban modelling, *Regional Studies*, **2**(5), pp. 579–602.

Pacione, M. (1974) The Venetian problem: an overview, *Geography*, **59**(4), pp. 339–43.

Robinson, G. W. S. (1958) The resorts of the Italian Riviera, *Geographical Studies*, **5**(1), pp. 20–32.

Rodgers, A. (1958) The port of Genoa: external and internal relations, *Annals, Association of American Geographers*, **48**(4), pp. 319–51.

Migration – rural–urban, highland–lowland, South–North and Italy–abroad – has been one of the most dramatic aspects of Italy's social geography. This topic has been treated in a number of studies:

Alberoni, F. (1970) Aspects of internal migration related to other types of Italian migration, in C. J. Jansen (ed.) *Readings in the Sociology of Migration*. Oxford: Pergamon, pp. 285–316.

Barberis, C. (1968) The agricultural exodus in Italy, *Sociologia Ruralis*, **8**(2), pp. 179–88.

King, R. L. (1976) Long range migration patterns in the EEC: an Italian case study, in R. Lee and P. E. Ogden (eds) *Economy and Society in the EEC: Spatial Perspectives*. Westmead: Saxon House, pp. 108–25.

King, R. L. and **Strachan, A. J.** (1980) Spatial variations in Sicilian migration: a stepwise multiple regression analysis, *Mediterranean Studies*, **2**(1), pp. 60–87.

Lucrezio-Monticelli, G. (1967) Italian emigration: basic trends and characteristics with special reference to the last 20 years, *International Migration Review*, **1**(3), pp. 10–24.

Lutz, V. (1961) Some structural aspects of the southern problem: the complementarity of emigration and industrialisation, *Banca Nazionale del Lavoro Quarterly Review*, **59**, pp. 367–402.

Mottura, G. and **Pugliese, E.** (1972) Observations on some characteristics of Italian emigration in the last 15 years, *International Review of Community Development*, **27–28**, pp. 3–20.

Rodgers, A.(1970) Migration and industrial development: the Southern Italian experience, *Economic Geography*, **46**(2), pp. 11–136.

There are a number of good books by economists which also touch on Italy's economic geography. Vera Lutz's book remains the best of an earlier generation of economic surveys, while Allen and Stevenson is the most detailed recent treatment:

Allen, K. J. and **Stevenson, A. A.** (1974) *An Introduction to the Italian Economy*. London: Martin Robertson.

Brown, M., Di Palma, M. and **Ferrara, B.** (eds) (1978) *Regional–National Econometric Modelling: with an Application to the Italian Economy*. London: Pion.

Lutz, V. (1962) *Italy: A Study in Economic Development*. Oxford: Oxford University Press.

Podbielski, G. (1974) *Italy: Development and Crisis in the Post-War Economy*. Oxford: Clarendon.

On agriculture and agrarian structures, including land reform and land reclamation, see:

Dickinson, R. E. (1955) Geographic aspects of unemployment in Southern Italy, *Tijdschrift voor Economische en Sociale Geografie*, **46**(2), pp. 86–97.

Diem, A. (1963) An evaluation of land reform and reclamation in Sicily, *Canadian Geographer*, **7**(4), pp. 182–91.

King, R. L. (1970) Structural and geographical problems of South Italian agriculture, *Norsk Geografisk Tidsskrift*, **24**(2), pp. 83–95.

King, R. L. (1971) Development problems in a Mediterranean environment: history and evaluation of agricultural development schemes in Sardinia, *Tijdschrift voor Economische en Sociale Geografie,* **62**(3), pp. 171–9.

King, R. L. (1973) *Land Reform: the Italian Experience.* London: Butterworths.

Kish, G. (1956) The Pontine Marshes, *Canadian Geographical Journal,* **52**(2), pp. 118–25.

Longobardi, C. (1963) *Land Reclamation in Italy.* London: King.

Manella, S. (1978) Agricultural reality in Apulia, *Norsk Geografisk Tidsskrift,* **32**(4), pp. 173–8.

Medici, G. (1952) *Land Property and Land Tenure in Italy.* Bologna: Agricole.

Mottura, G. and **Pugliese, E.** (1980) Capitalism in agriculture and capitalistic agriculture: the Italian case, in F. H. Buttel and H. Newby (eds) *The Rural Sociology of Advanced Societies.* London: Croom Helm, pp. 171–99.

Patella, L. V. (1978) Changes in transhumance in the central Apennines, *Geographia Polonica,* **38**, pp. 215–22.

Robertson, C. J. (1938) Agricultural regions of the North Italian Plain, *Geographical Review,* **28**(4), pp. 573–96.

Robertson, C. J. (1957) Land utilisation in Calabria, *Geography,* **42**(4), pp. 256–8.

Sacchi-De Angelis, M. E. and **Patella, V.** (1978) Reduction of agricultural land in Umbria 1970–1975, *Geographia Polonica,* **38**, pp. 11–18.

Sermonti, E. (1968) Agriculture in areas of urban expansion: an Italian case, *Journal Town Planning Institute,* **54**(1), pp. 15–17.

Italy's chronic energy position is highlighted in two short articles by Pacione and in a number of studies published in the Banco di Roma's authoritative *Review of the Economic Conditions of Italy:*

Angelini, A. M. (1974) Electricity generation and distribution in Italy, *Review of the Economic Conditions of Italy,* **28**(1), pp. 14–27.

Fogagnolo, G. (1975) Contribution of the Italian nuclear industry to the solution of the energy crisis, *Review of the Economic Conditions of Italy,* **29**(3), pp. 205–33.

Ippolito, F. (1980) Italy's position in the current world energy scenario, *Review of the Economic Conditions of Italy,* **34**(1), pp. 9–40.

Pacione, M. (1976) Italy and the energy crisis, *Geography,* **61**(2), pp. 99–102.

Pacione, M. (1979) Natural gas in Italy, *Geography,* **64**(3), pp. 211–15.

On transport and other aspects of infrastructure see:

Apicella, V. (1978) The evolution of the Italian motorway system, *Review of the Economic Conditions of Italy,* **32**(5–6), pp. 330–46.

Kalla-Bishop, P. M. (1971) *Italian Railways.* Newton Abbot: David and Charles.

Pacione, M. (1974) Italian motorways, *Geography,* **59**(1), pp. 35–41.

Panunzio, V. (1978) Italian ports and their problems, *Review of the Economic Conditions of Italy,* **32**(1), pp. 27–40.

The Banco di Roma's bi-monthly *Review* is again the best source for up-to-date material on the progress of Italian industries. Among recent articles are:

Bracco, F. (1976) The Italian chemical industry: prospects and problems, *Review of the Economic Conditions of Italy,* **30**(2), pp. 109–18.

Girola, A. (1977) Machine tools: advanced technology for Italian industry, *Review of* *the Economic Conditions of Italy*, **31**(4–5), pp. 221–40.

Latis, M. (1976) The electrical engineering and electronic industries, *Review of the Economic Conditions of Italy*, **30**(6), pp. 499–516.

Moretti, G. (1973) The Italian plastic materials industry, *Review of the Economic Conditions of Italy*, **27**(3), pp. 162–77.

Picarelli, A. (1977) The Italian textile industry: problems and prospects, *Review of the Economic Conditions of Italy*, **31**(1–2), pp. 43–68.

Sicca, L. (1978) The food industry and its growth prospects in Italy, *Review of the Economic Conditions of Italy*, **32**(2–3), pp. 121–36.

The semi-public nature of much of Italian 'big industry' such as oil, steel, shipbuilding, etc. has been analysed in detail by:

Fraenkel, G. (1975) Italian industrial policy in the framework of economic planning, in J. Haywood and M. Watson (eds) *Planning, Politics and Public Policy*. Cambridge: Cambridge University Press, pp. 128–40.

Frankel, P. H. (1966) *Mattei: Oil and Power Politics*. London: Faber.

Holland, S. K. (ed.) (1972) *The State as Entrepreneur: the IRI State Shareholding Formula*. London: Weidenfeld and Nicolson.

Martinelli, A. (1980) The Italian experience: a historical perspective, in R. Vernon and Y. Aharoni (eds) *State-Owned Enterprise in the Western Economies*. London: Croom Helm, pp. 85–98.

Posner, M. V. and **Woolf, S. J.** (1967) *Italian Public Enterprise*. London: Duckworth.

Votaw, D. (1964) *The Six Legged Dog: Mattei and ENI – A Study in Power*. Berkeley: University of California Press.

The regional devolution issue has stimulated much interest and a good deal of speculation as to the likely outcome in terms of concrete policy and action:

Bastianini, A. and **Urbani, G.** (1975) Land use planning in Italy, in J. Haywood and M. Watson (eds) *Planning, Politics and Public Policy*. Cambridge: Cambridge University Press, pp. 358–77.

Compagna, F. and **Muscarà, C.** (1980) Regionalism and social change in Italy, in J. Gottmann (ed.) *Centre and Periphery: Spatial Variations in Politics*. London: Sage, pp. 101–9.

Evans, R. H. (1979) Regionalism and the Italian city, in M. C. Romanos (ed.) *Western European Cities in Crisis*. Lexington: Heath, pp. 215–31.

Scattoni, P. and **Williams, R.** (1978) Planning and regional devolution: the Italian case, *The Planner*, **64**(2), pp. 38–40.

Selan, V. and **Domnini, R.** (1975) Regional planning in Italy, in J. Haywood and M. Watson (eds) *Planning, Politics and Public Policy*. Cambridge: Cambridge University Press, pp. 269–84.

Much more important than devolution has been regional economic policy, especially that concerned with developing the Mezzogiorno. See:

Cao-Pinna, V. (1974) Regional policy in Italy, in N. M. Hansen (ed.) *Regional Policy and Regional Economic Development*. Cambridge: Ballinger, pp. 137–79.

Chapman, G. (1976) Development and underdevelopment in southern Italy, Reading: University of Reading Geographical Papers, 41.

Dickinson, R. E. (1966) Geographical aspects of economic development in Southern

Italy, *Heidelberger Geographische Arbeiten*, **15**, pp. 340–59.

Holland, S. K. (1971) Regional underdevelopment in a developed economy: the Italian case, *Regional Studies*, **5**(2), pp. 71–90.

King, R. L. (1971) The Questione Meridionale in Southern Italy. Durham: University of Durham Department of Geography, Research Paper 11.

King, R. L. (1977) Recent industrialisation in Sardinia: rebirth or neocolonialism? *Erdkunde*, **31**(2), pp. 87–102.

King, R. L. (1981) Italy, in H. D. Clout (ed.) *Regional Development in Western Europe*. London: Wiley, pp. 119–49.

Mountjoy, A. (1973) *The Mezzogiorno*. London: Oxford University Press.

Pacione, M. (1976) Development policy in Southern Italy: panacea or polemic? *Tijdschrift voor Economische en Sociale Geografie*, **67**(1), pp. 38–47.

Podbielski, G. (1978) *Twenty-Five Years of Special Action for the Development of Southern Italy*. Rome: SVIMEZ.

Rodgers, A. (1966) Naples: a case study of government subsidisation of industrial development in an underdeveloped region, *Tijdschrift voor Economische en Sociale Geografie*, **57**(1), pp. 20–32.

Rodgers, A. (1978) Southern Italy: a case study of regional inequalities of industrial growth within an underdeveloped region, in F. E. I. Hamilton (ed.) *Industrial Change*. London: Longman, pp. 99–119.

Rodgers, A. (1979) *Economic Development in Retrospect: the Italian Model and its Significance for Regional Planning in Market-Oriented Economies*. New York: Winston-Wiley.

Ronzani, S. (1980) Regional incentives in Italy, in D. Yuill, K. Allen and C. Hull (eds) *Regional Policy in the European Community*. London: Croom Helm, pp. 134–56.

Saville, L. (1968) *Regional Economic Development in Italy*. Edinburgh: Edinburgh University Press.

Tagliacarne, G. (1973) The regions twenty years later: socio-economic dynamics of the regions between 1951 and 1971, *Review of the Economic Conditions of Italy*, **27**(3), pp. 127–61.

Wade, R. (1977) Policies and politics of dualism: the Italian case, *Pacific Viewpoint*, **18**(2), pp. 187–200.

Wade, R. (1979) Fast growth and slow development in Southern Italy, in D. Seers, B. Schaffer and M.-L Kiljunen (eds) *Undeveloped Europe: Studies in Core-Periphery Relations*. Hassocks: Harvester Press, pp. 197–221.

On political and social issues as they affect Italian human geography and regional development see:

Acquaviva, S. S. and **Santuccio, M.** (1976) *Social Structure in Italy*. London: Martin Robertson.

Allum, P. (1973) *Italy: Republic without Government?* London: Weidenfeld and Nicolson.

Archibugi, F. (1978) Italian prospects: capitalist planning in question, in S. Holland (ed.) *Beyond Capitalist Planning*. Oxford: Blackwell, pp. 49–68.

Della Seta, P. (1978) Notes on urban struggles in Italy, *International Journal of Urban and Regional Research*, **2**(2), pp. 303–29.

Marcelloni, M. (1979) Urban movements and political struggles in Italy, *International Journal of Urban and Regional Research*, **3**(2), pp. 251–68.

Moss, D. and **Rogers, E.** (1980) Poverty and inequality in Italy, in V. George and R. Lawson (eds) *Poverty and Inequality in Common Market Countries*. London: Routledge and Kegan Paul, pp. 161–94.

Salvati, M. (1972) The impasses of Italian capitalism, *New Left Review*, **76**, pp. 3–33.

Zariski, R. (1972) *Italy: the Politics of Uneven Development*. Hinsdale: Dryden Press.

Finally there is a plethora of local or regionally focused material which does not fit very neatly into the framework used above. The following list includes some of the more recent of such studies.

Alexander, D. E. (1980) *I calanchi:* accelerated erosion in Italy, *Geography*, **65**(2) pp. 95–100.

Fuller, G. J. (1962) *The Sele Plain: Geographical Studies in Campania, Italy*. Nottingham: Geographical Field Group.

Humlum, J. (1974) The province of Salerno, the Sorrentine Peninsula and San Cataldo, *Kulturgeografi*, **25**(122), pp. 49–98.

King, R. L. (1973) *Sicily*. Newton Abbot: David and Charles.

King, R. L. (1975) *Sardinia*. Newton Abbot: David and Charles.

McManis, D. (1967) The core of Italy: the case for Lombardy–Piedmont, *Professional Geographer*, **19**(5), pp. 251–7.

Mihelić, D. (1969) The political element in the port geography of Trieste, Chicago: University of Chicago Department of Geography, Research Paper 120.

Rodgers, A. (1960) The industrial geography of the port of Genova, Chicago: University of Chicago Department of Geography, Research Paper 66.

Staffa, N. (1974) Regional and local planning in Calabria, *The Planner*, **60**(3), pp. 609–11.

Turton, B. J. (1970) The Western Po Basin in Italy: a study in industrial expansion and journey-to-work, *Town Planning Review*, **41**(4), pp. 357–71.

Short filmography

Cinema is one of the most representative means of expressing the reality of a nation in the images it reveals of a country and its economic and social structures. This is particularly true in Italy where, since 1943, following on from the realist tradition in literature, many directors have interpreted national reality through neo-realism.

The short list of films below seems to us especially interesting in what they show of Italian life and its evolution since the Second World War. Regional coverage has been very unequal, with Sicily, Sardinia and Rome gaining the most interest from directors.

Translator's note

(Only films currently available in Britain have been included. All films are 16 mm, except those indicated with an asterisk which are 35 mm.)

Recent history

R. Rossellini, *Paisa*, 1946. The liberation of Italy.

R. Rossellini, *Rome – Open City*, 1946–47. A blend of fiction and documentary about a resistance leader.

Politics and power

R. Rossellini, *Italy, Year One*, 1974. Biography of post-war leader Alcide De Gasperi, head of the Christian Democratic Party.

F. Rosi, *Hands Over the City*, 1963. Corruption and property speculation.

F. Rosi, *The Mattei Affair*, 1972. An investigation of the life and death of Enrico Mattei, president of ENI.

F. Rosi, *Lucky Luciano*, 1973. A film about the Mafia.

F. Rosi, *Illustrious Corpses*, 1976. About a rash of killings of High Court judges in an unnamed European country (probably Italy).

Northern Italy

M. Antonioni, *L'Avventura*, 1960.

M. Antonioni, *La Notte*, 1960.

M. Antonioni, *L'Eclisse*, 1962.

These three films reveal an alienated urban landscape and a cold architecture.

M. Antonioni, *The Red Desert*, 1964. Industrial pollution at Ravenna.

B. Bertolucci, *1900*, 1976, Parts I and II.

V. De Sica, *Miracle in Milan*, 1950.

E. Olmi, *Il Posto*, 1960. Youth's job in Milan.

★E. Olmi, *The Tree of the Wooden Clogs*, 1978. The Lombardy countryside east of Milan.

L. Visconti, *Rocco and His Brothers*, 1960. Migration to northern Italy.

General urban conditions

F. Fellini, *I Vitelloni*, 1953.

F. Fellini, *I1 Bidone*, 1955.

These deal with the demands of urban living.

Rome

V. De Sica, *Bicycle Thieves*, 1948. Unemployment and living conditions after the Second World War in a peripheral zone.

F. Fellini, *Roma*, 1972.

F. Fellini, *Amarcord*, 1973.

P. Pasolini, *Accatone*, 1961.

Naples

W. Schroeter, *The Reign of Naples*, 1978.

Sicily

F. Rosi, *Salvatore Giuliano*, 1961. An investigation into the death in 1950 of the folk hero/bandit.

★L. Visconti, *La Terra Trema*, 1948.

★L. Visconti, *The Leopard*, 1963.

Sardinia

V. and P. Taviani, *Padre Padrone*, 1976. Backwardness and conflict in a patriarchal society in Sardinia.

Short films and 'roving reports'

Italy – Pollution and Poison (11 mins), 1977. This reports on the explosion at Seveso, northern Italy, and effects on the local population.

Naples and Venice: Cities in Distress (24 min), 1977. This illustrates the threat to Naples by subsidence from underground fissures and volcanic activity, and the danger that Venice faces from the rising waters of the Adriatic and industrial pollution.

Naples: The Baby Killer, 1979. Report on the epidemic in Naples which resulted in the deaths of many infants.

Rome: The Fading Glory (12 min), 1979. Report on Rome's traffic problems and the threat they pose to the city's ancient monuments.

The Italian Way (30 min each 6 parts), 1976. Each part looks at a different community in Italy, its problems and customs.

Sardinia – A Meeting with Civilization (15 min), 1976. This examines places and objects of historical and archaeological interest in Sardinia.

World In Action: Living (26 mins), 1976. Reports on the explosion at Seveso and the effects of toxic gas (Granada Television).

Index